Cybercrime

⊞ Berkeley College

From the Library

of

Ex Machina: Law, Technology, and Society
General Editors: Jack M. Balkin *and* Beth Simone Noveck

The Digital Person: Technology and Privacy in the Information Age
Daniel J. Solove

The State of Play: Law, Games, and Virtual Worlds
Edited by Jack M. Balkin and Beth Simone Noveck

Cybercrime: Digital Cops in a Networked Environment
Edited by Jack M. Balkin, James Grimmelmann, Eddan Katz,
Nimrod Kozlovski, Shlomit Wagman, and Tal Zarsky

Cybercrime

Digital Cops in a Networked Environment

EDITED BY

*Jack M. Balkin, James Grimmelmann,
Eddan Katz, Nimrod Kozlovski,
Shlomit Wagman, and Tal Zarsky*

The Information Society Project at Yale Law School

New York University Press

NEW YORK AND LONDON

NEW YORK UNIVERSITY PRESS
New York and London
www.nyupress.org

Library of Congress Cataloging-in-Publication Data

Cybercrime : digital cops in a networked environment / edited by Jack M.
Balkin .. [et al.]
p. cm.
Includes bibliographical references and index.
ISBN-13: 978-0-8147-9970-3 (cloth : alk. paper)
ISBN-10: 0-8147-9970-1 (cloth : alk. paper)
ISBN-13: 978-0-8147-9983-3 (pbk. : alk. paper)
ISBN-10: 0-8147-9983-3 (pbk. : alk. paper)
1. Computer crimes—United States—Prevention. 2. Internet—Law
and legislation—United States. 3. Computer security—United
States—Evaluation. I. Balkin, J. M.

HV6773.2.C93   2006
364.16'80973—dc22   2006030943

New York University Press books are printed on acid-free paper,
and their binding materials are chosen for strength and durability.

Manufactured in the United States of America
c 10 9 8 7 6 5 4 3 2 1
p 10 9 8 7 6 5 4 3 2 1

For our families

Contents

Introduction

Jack M. Balkin and Nimrod Kozlovski

As more aspects of our life move to digital networks, crime comes with them. Our lives increasingly depend on the Internet and digital networks, but these create new vulnerabilities and new ways for criminals to exploit the digital environment. Not only can many existing crimes be replicated in online environments, but novel crimes that exploit specific features of digital networks have emerged as well. With new crimes come new forms of policing and new forms of surveillance, and with these come new dangers for civil liberties. These issues are the subject of the present book.

The shift to digital environments alters our understanding of crime in five different ways. First, it alters the scene or location where crimes occur. Second, it facilitates the commission of new types of crimes. Third, it produces significant changes in law enforcement methods, for example, a shift to prevention and to new forms of cooperation between public and private actors. Fourth, it gives law enforcement new tools of digital surveillance and new methods of sorting data and managing online risks. Fifth, it presents new challenges to the existing legal process and spurs the development of new forms of proof and procedure. We have arranged the essays in this book to correspond to these five key phenomena: the *new scenes* of crime, the *new forms* of crime, the *new methods* of law enforcement, the *new tools* of digital surveillance and crime prevention, and the *new procedures* that courts and legislatures will have to adopt to deal with threats to Internet security.

The essays in Part I describe the new crime scene—the digital networked environment. Online criminal behavior exploits the physical and social features of the Internet. Five key features of the online world create new security risks and shape the kinds of criminal behavior we find there.

The first is *digitization*—common standards for data transmission that enable manipulation and modification. The second is *anonymity*—the ability to act and spy on others without disclosing one's identity. The third is *interconnectivity*—the fact that everyone on the network is connected to everyone else. The fourth is *decentralization*—the lack of centralized control over digital networks. The fifth is *interdependence*—the shared vulnerabilities that inevitably exist between and among all the people who use digital networks.

Digitization, anonymity, interconnectivity, decentralization, and interdependence structure the online world as we currently know it. Hence they structure the opportunities for crime and the ways that people commit crimes and breach network security. However, the task of cybercrime policy is not simply to create new laws banning new practices. It also requires us to redesign digital architectures to reduce the risk of criminal conduct and security breaches in the first place; this requires policy makers and technologists to decide how we should shape the digital networked environment.

Dan Geer's essay, "The Physics of Digital Law," introduces some of the basic problems of cybersecurity. When addressing the dangers and risks inherent in the digital environment, he argues, our everyday intuitions are likely to fail us. The physics of the digital environment is quite different from the physics of the offline world. In cyberspace, events occur almost instantaneously across large distances, network boundaries do not align with physical and political boundaries, and everyone on the network is your neighbor. In the digital environment copying is costless, the cost of data acquisition approaches zero, and it is easier to retain information than to delete it selectively. Digital environments are subject to attacks from a wide range of locations, including machines of unsuspecting users that have been commandeered by attackers; and successful attacks can have systemwide repercussions. Geer argues that the new physics of the virtual environment will reshape legal concepts like jurisdiction and ownership; it will require us to rethink doctrines of tort liability and duties of care, and it will revolutionize the way we think about privacy.

Lee Tien points out that the design of software and hardware in networked systems—their "architecture"—is a central device for regulating network activity, one that also has enormous influence on the practical liberty and privacy that ordinary people enjoy. Because architecture is such a powerful method for regulating activity on digital networks, governments will attempt to employ it for their own ends. Nevertheless, Tien argues, government regulation of digital architecture—for example, by requiring a back door to facilitate government eavesdropping—poses serious problems of transparency, because most people will not be aware of the design or who required it. They will tend to accept the architectural constraints as normal and natural and thus fail to properly contest them as they would laws that restrict their freedom. "Architectural regulation," Tien points out, "is less visible as law, not only because it can be surreptitiously embedded into settings or equipment but also because its enforcement is less public."

Tien argues that architectural regulation creates an additional and even more worrisome problem of transparency, particularly where privacy is concerned. Our notions of reasonable expectations of privacy are determined by social norms, which in turn are shaped by our interactions with the technology we see around us. For example, our experience with doors and locks helps us determine when it is reasonable to believe that we will not and should not be disturbed or spied on. Tien worries that if government is given free rein to regulate software architectures in secret it will undermine our experience with the resources necessary to develop privacy norms for the digital age. Because people will not know when and under what conditions they lack privacy, they will not be able to develop the relevant social norms to protect themselves. This is doubly problematic because constitutional rights to privacy depend on these social norms and expectations.

Just as the technical design of security systems has political ramifications, political visions shape technical design, Helen Nissenbaum argues in her essay. She contrasts two current approaches to technological design that flow from two different visions of the problem of cybercrime. The technical community of computer designers and programmers gravitates toward what Nissenbaum calls a model of "technical computer security." It focuses on protecting computer systems and their users from attacks (and threats of attacks) "that render systems, information, and networks unavailable to users," "that threaten the integrity of information or of systems and networks by corrupting data, destroying files or disrupting code," and "that threaten the confidentiality of information and communications." For the technical community, computer security is about safeguarding systems and creating mechanisms of trust and assurance so that users can use the information they want more or less as they like.

The national security community, by contrast, has a very different vision, which Nissenbaum calls the model of "cybersecurity." The goal here is to meet imminent and existential threats to the social order. Officials see the world as rife with conditions that pose immediate and dire threats to the community's very existence and that must be dealt with by whatever means necessary, a way of characterizing the world that Nissenbaum calls "securitization." Because the "cybersecurity" approach sees digital networks as creating potential conditions of catastrophe, it leads to far more extreme responses, and it tends to legitimate special and extraordinary measures that bend the rules and restrictions of normal governance. As applied to computer security, the cybersecurity model calls for centralization of control, technical barricades that prevent access, a shift toward full identification of users, and greater monitoring of traffic. Nissenbaum argues that the choice between these two design visions will be crucial for the digital environment we inhabit in the future, and the rights and liberties we enjoy in that environment. She points out that while securitization might make digital networks marginally safer, the model might succeed at the expense of the Internet's core purpose of providing a relatively uninhibited realm of public discourse.

Part II explores new crimes in the digital networked environment. Anonymity, interconnectedness, and accessibility to vast amounts of information facilitate older crimes and set the stage for new ones, including pure information crimes. Among the activities that governments now seek to prevent are third-party misappropriation of trade secrets over the Internet, economic espionage, unauthorized access to encrypted virtual spaces, computer fraud, and dissemination of circumvention programs. And because the Internet demands ever new forms of authentication to conduct business, new forms of identity theft have emerged. The central questions now are whether extending traditional criminal remedies to new crimes is the right solution; whether civil remedies or technological solutions might be more effective; whether pure information crimes need to be dealt with differently than other kinds of crime; and whether legislative expansion of crimes and the growing criminalization of online activity will do more harm than good.

Beryl Howell describes some of the key legal problems through a series of case studies. Her stories show that the law is not always clear about whether specific conduct is a crime, or which tools investigators may legally employ to collect evidence. For example, in regulating computer hacking, the law faces the task of settling upon a definition that can differentiate legitimate from illegitimate access to data. Developments like peer-to-peer (P2P) technology have made it increasingly difficult to define illegal possession of material such as child pornography. The new information crimes have proved to be a challenge for a criminal law that demands clear lines between the legal and the illegal. Howell contends that many current laws are written far too broadly, with the result that they hamper legitimate attempts at self-help to identify perpetrators of harmful online crimes. She argues that we need more specific prohibitions that clarify the boundaries of illegal conduct and guide law enforcement officials about how to conduct investigations with appropriate respect for civil liberties and privacy. "It would be ironic, indeed," Howell concludes, "if the concern over harmful online activity results in over-regulation of the use of certain technologies with the effect of hamstringing victims and investigators from using those or similar tools to stop or prevent the harmful conduct."

Part III describes new methods of law enforcement for the digital networked environment. The Internet puts into question long-established notions about how to investigate crime and enforce criminal law. It has led to an increasing emphasis on decentralization of intelligence gathering, privatization of enforcement, and delegation of powers to nongovernmental entities. To address the problems of cybersecurity, technologists, businesspeople, and government officials have experimented with public-private collaborations, self-help measures, automated enforcement, community vigilance, and collective sanctions, leading to what may well become a new system of law enforcement. But this new model is not without its own problems. How can we protect civil liberties and constitutional rights when intelligence gathering is decentralized, when prevention and self-help are strategies of first resort, and the criminal law is increasingly enforced by private parties? How will incentives change when sanctions are invisible, decentralized, and privatized? What is the proper role of the community in sanctioning bad behavior and how can we design technology to strengthen appropriate collective enforcement and discourage inappropriate methods? What are the long-term consequences of replacing human judgment and prosecutorial discretion with automated sanctions?

Nimrod Kozlovski believes that we are in the midst of a paradigm shift in law enforcement. The technological and social conditions of criminal activity have changed and the conventional law enforcement response to crime is ill-equipped to address these changing conditions. Law enforcement offline is mainly a reactive system, relatively centralized, publicly managed, and rooted in human discretion. The emerging system of online law enforcement, by contrast, is largely preventive, strongly decentralized, involves a hybrid of public and private enforcement, and is highly automated. This new model, Kozlovski argues, is influenced by information security strategies. Far more pervasive than traditional offline law enforcement by state actors, it tries to achieve ubiquitous policing of online activities to monitor, control, deter, deflect, detect, prevent, or preempt risky and potentially malicious activities. Kozlovski warns, moreover, that this new system of policing is emerging without a clear legal structure and with few restraints other than the limits on the ingenuity of the persons involved.

The legal, institutional, and technological settings of conventional law enforcement have been based on the conditions of physical crime scenes; they do not translate well to online law enforcement, and so are ill-suited to restrain overreaching and limit illegitimate uses. In a democratic society, Kozlovski insists, those invested with policing power—whether public or private—must be accountable for their activities. This means that they must have a legal responsibility to account for actions taken and actions not taken, and to explain or justify them; in short, there must be an obligation to expose one's policing decisions to review and to the possibility of sanctions for improper behavior. In the online world, Kozlovski argues, civil liberties will best be protected by creating new accountability mechanisms that will deter public and private police from abusing their power, and at the same time promote efficiency and democratic dialogue about how power is exercised. The time to develop such accountability mechanisms is now, when the technology for the new policing model is still being developed.

One of the key features of the new model is self-help, and this is the subject of Curtis Karnow's essay. Karnow argues that the traditional legal system is increasingly incapable of policing online illegal behavior or enforcing its laws. Given the growing threats posed by computer malware and the relative ineffectiveness of the legal and technological responses to them, it is no surprise that people have turned to defensive technologies; and when these have proved unavailing in an increasingly complex networked environment, they have turned to self-help.

Self-help mechanisms try to identify an attack on the network, trace back the source and shut down, or partially disable, the attacking machines. The goal is to minimize the attack and secure the environment. While promising in theory, Karnow argues that there are many practical difficulties. Using current Internet routing protocols, it is often quite difficult to pinpoint the perpetrator of an attack, causing the risk of disabling or damaging the wrong machine or the wrong piece of code. In addition, some counterstrikes turn out to be far too broad, creating a cure worse than the disease.

Even if these technical problems are surmounted, important legal concerns remain. Many cybercrime statutes make it illegal to attack or disable computers. Although Karnow notes that self-defense may be available in some cases, one would need to establish both good faith and reasonable belief that there were no adequate alternatives to a self-help counterstrike. This burden of proof is likely to deter self-help. A better approach, Karnow argues, is to invoke the common law right to abate nuisances. Internet-mediated attacks, such as viruses and worms, Karnow believes, fit comfortably within the definition of nuisance; moreover, the doctrine permits the defendant to impose a reasonable amount of collateral damage in order to abate the nuisance.

Part IV considers the new tools available to public and private actors to detect, investigate, and prevent criminal behavior. Law enforcement agencies now have at their disposal sophisticated means for surveillance and ever more powerful ways to analyze vast amounts of information. These technological tools can deter illegal activity, investigate crime, collate personal information, and track criminals with increasing efficiency. In addition, advanced analysis software and data mining tools can preempt crimes by identifying suspicious patterns of behavior, allowing private and public actors to neutralize threats before they are realized. At the same time, these new tools create threats to civil liberties, particularly personal privacy. Moreover, new technologies attempt to predict and prevent crime before it occurs. But these technologies raise the obvious question of whether it is wise to delegate social control to automated systems with little possibility of an appeal to human judgment. No computer model is perfect, and the cost of predictive systems may be constraints on individual liberty and sanctions against the innocent.

Kim Taipale argues that the trade-off between privacy and security is largely illusory; the real issue is how to design technologies so that we can enjoy both values. New information technologies hold the promise of analyzing vast amounts of information to identify potential terrorists and to preempt terrorist acts. Nevertheless, Taipale argues that the public anxiety about electronic privacy is out of proportion to the actual privacy risk; moreover, such fears obscure the very real threat posed by our failure to improve security. Privacy, Taipale contends, is less about preserving secrecy than protecting autonomy, and he suggests how we might design identification systems and data collection techniques to achieve that goal. In particular, Taipale argues that we protect privacy by separating observation of behavior from knowledge of identity. Much data analysis, including list and pattern matching, can be accomplished with anonymized or pseudonymized data. This data can be collected and analyzed to improve security, but kept in a form that does not identify specific individuals and compromise their privacy interests. Legal rules, in turn, can provide procedures to determine when law enforcement officials are permitted to connect particular behavior to a particular person or persons.

Emily Hancock is concerned that the demand for new law enforcement tools can stifle innovation. Her specific focus is the Communications Assistance for Law Enforcement Act (CALEA), which requires telecommunications carriers (including telephone companies) to make it possible for law enforcement officials to intercept communications when they are legally authorized to do so. CALEA was directed at standard telephone service when it was originally passed in 1994. Since then telecommunications technologies have changed rapidly, and now include a wide panoply of services, including VoIP (Voice over Internet Protocol) technologies that use the Internet to make phone calls. Hancock warns that expanding CALEA's reach to include these new technologies carries risks not only for individual privacy but also for innovation. She notes that all technological change affects law enforcement, sometimes rendering existing methods less effective or irrelevant. Nevertheless, she argues, dictating the design of new technologies to facilitate law enforcement has its own costs, and may even be self-defeating; for example, telecommunications innovation will simply move overseas.

Part V considers the new legal procedures and legal sanctions that digital networked environments require and make possible. Inevitably, rules of procedure and evidence will have to adjust to changes in the nature of crime and the nature of law enforcement. For example, cybercrime, like much Internet activity, respects no boundaries, leading to complicated problems of international law enforcement. Geographical rules of jurisdiction do not always follow the geography of information flows. Evidence introduced in court in digital form may lack the necessary authenticity because it is susceptible to manipulation. Conversely, new kinds of sanctions can be invisibly and automatically imposed without human discretion, bypassing the normal criminal procedural protections of the Bill of Rights. These and other changes in the nature of crime and law enforcement will require governments to adapt—and in some cases reconstruct—criminal procedure to meet the challenges posed by digital networks.

Susan Brenner focuses on some of the international aspects of computer crime through an examination of the Council of Europe's Convention on Cybercrime. The Cybercrime Convention arose to deal with recurring legal problems: Unlike real-world crime, which requires proximity between the perpetrator and the victim, cybercrime tends to operate remotely and to transcend national borders; hence, national laws have often proved inadequate to deal with it. Investigation and prosecution of cybercrime also requires much more robust mechanisms to facilitate cooperation between different countries with different laws and different rules of criminal procedure. Finally, cybercrime investigations are often based on digital evidence that tends to be fragile, volatile, and easily deleted or manipulated.

Although the Cybercrime Convention was drafted to address these challenges, Brenner argues that in many ways it does not go far enough. It continues the tradition of the localized, decentralized system of law enforcement we employ for real-world crime. The convention requires countries to outlaw certain behaviors and to help in international investigations, but it still employs antiquated structures of nationally based law enforcement that are unsuitable for nonterritorially based crime. Brenner concludes that global investigative and law enforcement authorities, or what she calls "a sort of super-Interpol," may ultimately become necessary to deal with the problems of global crime.

Finally, Orin Kerr predicts the development of a special subfield of criminal procedure devoted to cybercrime. Existing rules of criminal procedure, he argues, were naturally tailored to investigations of traditional crimes using physical evidence and eyewitness testimony; they are poorly equipped to handle prosecutions involving primarily digital evidence. Collecting evidence for cybercrimes is so different, in fact, that the older rules of criminal procedure sometimes make little sense. Extraordinarily invasive exercises of governmental power are completely unregulated while comparatively minor privacy concerns can stifle legitimate investigations.

Courts have begun to take tentative steps to create special rules for computer crime cases, but their powers to make new rules are limited, often exercised too late to do much good, and, moreover, are still rooted in a Fourth Amendment jurisprudence designed for physical crimes. Legislatures and executive officials, Kerr believes, are best suited to design new methods of handling digital evidence and new rules of criminal procedure for computer crimes.

The essays in this book show how the traditional concerns of criminal justice are merging with newer questions of cybersecurity. Many of the key questions of cyberlaw apply here as well: how government officials can regulate a medium that does not respect national borders, the extent to which law enforcement goals are best served by hardware and software solutions, and the unintended consequences of relying on hardware and software architectures rather than legal norms to structure and control social life.

This book presents a snapshot of a rapidly growing and changing field in the first decade of the twenty-first century. Our working assumptions in preparing this volume—that we must recognize new scenes of crime, new kinds of crimes, new methods and goals for law enforcement, and new tools of surveillance and crime prevention—will surely be tested in the years ahead. We can only wonder at how similar the issues will appear a generation hence, and whether the trends we have identified will have become even more pronounced or will have been displaced by still newer and more pressing concerns.

Part I

The New Crime Scene
The Digital Networked Environment

The Physics of Digital Law
Searching for Counterintuitive Analogies

Daniel E. Geer, Jr.

"Digital law" is and must be counterintuitive—an intuitive understanding of sticks and stones does not translate to digital worlds. Because our intuition about the digital sphere can so easily be wrong we need to substitute solid facts for faulty intuition. It is said that the practice of law is a search for analogies, so law is most susceptible to mistakes when the digital reality differs from our commonsense intuitions about the physical world. In this chapter, I use the neologism—"digital physics"—to describe the important features of digital spaces and the parameters they set on computer security. Some of the principles of digital physics are directly related to concepts of physics like space and time. Others have no physical world analogy, but rather describe a fundamental truth about the digital world in the same way that the laws of physics describe fundamental truths about the physical world. Just as these laws of physics dictate what is and is not possible in the physical world, the laws of digital physics dictate what is and is not possible in the digital world, which will prove crucial for making policy choices.

In this chapter, I offer a guided tour of some of the important problems of computer security, including risk management and the interaction between trust and identity. These examples not only show how our intuitions about the physical world can be misleading in the digital world, but they also provide a good model for approaching the other issues addressed in this book.

I. Risk and Risk Management

Risk is not an enemy of good policy per se, but unmanaged risk can be. Sometimes, risk is easy to recognize—for example, climbing a high-tension transmission tower in a thunderstorm. When it comes to computer security, however, risk is harder to understand, harder to apportion, harder to manage, and harder to clean up after. One reason why digital risk is hard to manage is the lack of warning time before an attack. In the physical world, the bigger the attack the longer the warning time—for example, you can see an invading army coming from a long way off. Our intuition about time in the physical world might lead us to believe that we will be able to see a cyberattack coming and have time to defend against it. But a principle of digital physics challenges this intuition: information travels faster over the network than humans can react to. Thus, in the digital world the warning interval between detection and attack decreases toward zero. And after that brief interval between detection and attack, further attacks often materialize with no warning at all.

Not surprisingly, infections become more effective over time. For example, the infection rate of the infamous Slammer worm doubled every 8.5 seconds.[1] The Witty attack on various ISS firewall-related products offered only two days' warning between announcement of the vulnerability and the appearance of an exploit of it in the wild. Any further contraction of warning interval is operationally irrelevant.[2,3] As this was written, the Sober.P virus has gone from first detection to 77 percent of all inbound virus payloads in email—in a matter of sixty hours. It is delusional to believe that we will have sufficient reaction time to prevent cyberattacks.

These are examples of "cascade failures"—security failures where the infection converts prey to new predators. The only way to control them is to limit the rate at which the failure spreads. Much like a dangerous crown fire moving quickly upward on steep terrain, spread rates for digital infections are too fast for reaction on a human time scale. As a result, the only way to protect the Internet commons is, as with forest fires, to block further spread by precut "firebreaks."[4]

In the network world, preventing the outbound spread of toxic digital traffic is called "egress filtering," while preventing toxic digital traffic from flowing inbound is called "ingress filtering." Should the law require egress filtering as a sort of digital firebreak, or should it instead try to block incoming toxic content? Many enterprises, like universities, which have strong free speech traditions, have policies against blocking suspect inbound communications, while other enterprises are simply too poorly managed for effective ingress filtering. Thus, egress filtering may be the Internet's last line of defense. It is helpful to make an analogy with public health law: While it is not criminal to get a disease, it may be criminal to break quarantine and pass the disease on.

Thus the law might make enterprises pick from a menu of options, including ingress filtering, egress filtering, and immunizing its computers with regular security patches. To be effective, enterprises will be forced to choose at least two.[5] But of these options, egress filtering may be the most important. A bank will certainly want to protect its internal systems from incoming attacks but it may be even more important for the law to require that the bank's computers not be the source of an attack on others.

A machine that has already been penetrated by a successful attack (hacker slang is "owned") may exhibit no outward symptoms. This defies our physical world intuition that as long as a machine is doing what it is supposed to do, it is probably not broken. Digital physics teaches us, however, that the outward appearance of a "working" machine will not tell us whether the machine is doing *more* than what it is supposed to do. Hence the user might never have any reason to detect that the machine is under an attacker's remote control; in this way the culprit can stockpile owned machines.

There are technical measures to detect owned machines. Even so, we must decide who will be responsible for the scanning required to detect infection. Should the responsibility fall on the owner of the machine, or should it fall on the owner of the transmission capacity—for example, the Internet Service Provider (ISP)—that an infected machine uses when it tries to attack other sites? Should we require ISPs to scan their customers' computers? ISPs are certainly capable of doing so, but scanning a host machine for vulnerabilities will itself trigger warnings on the scanned host. If the ISP learns that Machine 12345 is infected, should the ISP then be obligated to notify, to terminate service, to report to other authorities, or to put that host under increased surveillance?

These questions might focus on the wrong level of concern. Perhaps the proper analogy is public health: It was public hygiene and not individual medical treatment that solved London's cholera epidemics in the nineteenth century.[6] Today, in the United States, the Centers for Disease Control play a global role, which has become ever more essential as the world has grown smaller. The CDC regulations include mandatory reporting, forced treatment and/or quarantine of the ill, publication of an authoritative Morbidity and Mortality Weekly Report, formal predictive work to aid officials who seek to anticipate epidemics, and public identification of locales with an excess of incidence or prevalence of any particular pathogen.

In a 2002 paper, Stuart Staniford and his collaborators proposed a CDC for the Internet[7] and in the fall of 2004 the NSF funded this as the Center for Internet Epidemiology.[8] How closely should the CIE parallel the CDC? A close parallel would require extraordinary things—mandatory reporting of security incidents, forced quarantine of sources of electronic infection, publication of definitive analysis of infection sources and vectors, and the kind of longitudinal expertise that identifies countermeasures before crises occur. No corporate counsel will happily accept mandatory reporting. Suppose such reporting requires entities to turn over logs from their Internet-facing networks. These logs may contain evidence of an attack the entity failed to notice, and as such, the logs may provide evidence of the entity's negligence. On the other hand, if an entity does not share its network logs, it is impossible to determine if it is a specific *target* of attack, or if it was just opportunistically attacked along with many other random targets. Despite the long-term benefits of sharing logs, most corporate counsel, who are paid to be risk adverse, will resist both voluntary sharing and regulatory measures that mandate sharing.

The few attempts at voluntary sharing of information have had very limited success. The Information Sharing and Analysis Centers (ISACs), created by President Clinton in 1998,[9] are "sector-specific," meaning that information gathered by entities in the financial services industry are not necessarily shared with information gathered by the telecommunications or information technology industries. In an attempt to assuage the fears of corporate counsel the data collected by the ISACs is exempt from the Freedom of Information Act and from antitrust laws. These exemptions, however, have not yet been tested in the courts, and because those exemptions are untested, information sharing has been modest at best. All this may change, however, if the Department of Homeland Security's Infrastructure Analysis and Protection Authority succeeds in its bid to take over the ISACs.

A central issue is whether and how the private sector of the U.S. economy, which owns over 90 percent of the nation's critical infrastructure, can ensure that infrastructure's protection from shared risks. The government's interests and industry's interests align when stated abstractly but less so at the levels where details matter. In some cases federal regulation may be necessary while at other times self-regulation works just as well. Generally, lawyers are paid to be risk averse and to act in the particular interests of their clients. In the digital world, however, private tragedy can produce a public debacle. Self-regulatory solutions require incentives for private parties to share information, and this may require immunizing companies from liability. Government regulation, on the other hand, must balance protection against privacy. Neither solution is an easy task.

Thus far we have been discussing the risk of cascade failure, which begins with a single computer or a small number of computers. There are, however, many risks on a national scale: the collapse of an essential component of the public Internet, the discovery of infiltration across many firms, the leak of an attack method against which there is no current defense, and a loss of public confidence in the banking system as a whole after a security failure.

How do we assess the risk of one of these failures occurring? If there has been no overt catastrophe to date, can we conclude that the risk is low? Once again our intuitions about the physical world fail us. It does not follow that the absence of a history of loss means that the risk is low. The key question is whether the events that produce loss arrive more or less independently, or whether they tend to come in bunches. If the risks are small and spread out at random you would expect to see some events over any sustained period of observation; if you do not, then that means that the risk is quite low. If, however, the small events come in bunches, then it may merely be that their time has not yet come.[10] If attacks in the digital world are mostly independent of each other, then recent history does have some (limited) predictive power; but if the attacks are calculated, rather than opportunistic, then a history free from a large-scale attack is not particularly meaningful.

The question for the law is what we should require of the owners of digital assets, especially those assets that are part of the critical information infrastructure. Do we require that these owners plan for disaster in order to mitigate it when it comes? Do we require them to share their plans with coordinating agencies? If not, how do we ensure their preparedness?

The problem is that each attack always requires two responses: First, we must regain operational recovery; second, we must preserve evidence of the crime. Without an effective plan for handling incidents, these goals tend to diverge—you can have prompt operational recovery at the cost of losing forensic evidence, or you can cleanly recover forensic evidence but at the cost of delaying operational recovery. Should we impose reliability standards for digital assets in the way we already do for electricity generation and clearance of banking transactions? Or would it be better to require incident reports whenever intentional damage cannot be ruled out? Either way, we must alter our physical world intuitions about the relationship between private and public risk. The idea that "It's my computer and I'll protect it if I want to" makes no sense in a digital world; every important cyberattack has involved the recruitment—or, more correctly, the hijacking—of the computers of unsuspecting users. Digital physics teaches that your failure to protect yourself is not just a risk to you; it is also a risk to me.

We assume that the government's job is to protect us from those things that we cannot protect ourselves from. But if private tragedies in the digital world threaten public security, we cannot separate purely private risks from national ones. If so, is there a risk management strategy at the national level that can protect against national tragedies? Digital physics can assist us by delimiting the possible classes of security failure. Only two classes of failures qualify as threats on a national scale: (1) inherently single points of failure; and (2) cascade failure.

A "single point of failure" is a part of a system which, if it fails, interrupts the entire system. Inherently single points of failure are those which by necessity or design must be so. An example is the fabled Red Telephone that the President uses to communicate with key foreign leaders; nine Red Telephones in the President's office would be worse than one.

In the digital world, the assignment of network addresses is a single point of failure because without a unique authoritative source of network information there would be chaos. If instead of a single Domain Name Service (DNS) there were multiple sources of network information, different users could receive different answers to their requests to be directed to a particular URL. However, the Domain Name Service must not only be a single authoritative source; it must also be reliable. In reality, responses to queries may come from any of thirteen primary service providers which provide identical answers. Disabling them all simultaneously is hard; we know that because it has been tried before. This sort of redundancy is essential for an inherently single point of failure, and it is yet another example of where our physical world intuitions do not work well in the digital world. In the physical world we do not expect that a single authority—say, the King of England—is a position that could be held simultaneously by thirteen different individuals each of whom is guaranteed to make the same decision regardless of which one is asked—and you won't be able to tell which one is answering anyhow.

The classic method for protecting a single point of failure is "defense in depth"—that is, using rings of protection, where each ring of protection exists to catch the failure of the ring outside it. No single ring of defense need be a technical masterpiece nor is any particular ring—considered in isolation—difficult to get through. Rather, it is the sum of the rings that secures the protected object. Medieval castles relied on defense in depth, as do modern prisons (though in this case the rings serve to keep the prisoners in).

Defense in depth works in the digital world as well. For example, the root servers that operate the Domain Name System are protected by (1) redundancy (so that an attack on any of the thirteen servers does not affect the other twelve), (2) caching (creating a short-term memory on individual computers which makes them less dependent on the root servers), and (3) diversity in design (none of the root servers are designed the same way, so that a successful attack on one server does not increase the risk of a successful attack on the other twelve).

If we wanted to, we could add more root servers or require ISPs to put upper bounds on how many nameservice requests they could forward per second. In other words, we could add more levels of defense. In this sense, defense in depth is not a technical problem, but rather a matter of how much money we want to put into the project.

Our real attention, then, should be on the second class of failure at the national scale: cascade failure. In a cascade each part that fails increases the probability that the next part will fail too. A row of dominoes or a multicar pileup are familiar examples. Infectious diseases are also cascade failures. Because of international air travel, a breakout of the flu in Hong Kong increases your chance of getting the flu in New York; any place where people congregate in large numbers, such as airports, increases the transmission rate.

Digital viruses are cascade failures, and the main contributor to the problem they pose is digital monoculture—the fact that most people use the same operating system or other key software components. The term "monoculture" reminds us that all healthy ecosystems are diverse. Unlike the defense of singular points of failure, there are no easy solutions to protecting against cascade failures. Defending a singular point of failure assumes that there are insiders and outsiders. A good system of defense in depth prevents outsiders from getting in, leaving only the more difficult problem of preventing insider attacks. But in a software monoculture, no one is an "outsider"—to the contrary, everyone is an "insider." When everyone uses the same software, an effective attack against one computer can be an effective attack against all. And if that attack can be automated, then only network bandwidth constrains the spread rate.

Again, this defies our intuitions about the physical world and the spread of infectious disease. You cannot kiss me or sneeze on me from an arbitrary location anywhere in the world, and you cannot do so without revealing that it is you; but you can do both things in the digital world. Distance, as a concept of digital physics, is radically different from distance in the physical world. In the digital world, every computer is essentially equally distant and equally close to every other computer; this makes the risk of monoculture far more frightening than our intuitions about the physical world suggest. To understand this, one need only look at the spread-rate videos of computer viruses that the Cooperative Association for Internet Data Analysis (CAIDA) puts out; what we see is a simultaneous worldwide crescendo, not ripples in a pond spreading neatly from the point the rock entered the water.[11]

What should the law do about the shared risk to the national economy directly traceable to our common digital vulnerabilities? We refuse children admittance to public schools unless their parents agree to immunize them against common biological vulnerabilities. We grant special status to public utilities because they are natural monopolies but regulate the quality of their services because that monopoly creates a common vulnerability. In the digital economy, however, we have yet to face the shared vulnerability produced by our digital monoculture; indeed, even the Department of Homeland Security acknowledged on the floor of the U.S. House of Representatives that it is internally a computing monoculture and that this practice creates risk.[12]

II. Identity and Trust

In addition to the overarching issue of risk and risk management, we must deal with questions of identity and trust. The two issues are conjoined, and in the digital world our intuition and the digital reality tend to diverge.

In a digital economy, information is the coin of the realm. Electronic commerce requires amassing useful information and putting it to productive use; the challenge is keeping that information valid and available only where it should be. Getting the most use out of the business's information while not losing control of it is the core of a successful electronic business. For example, the information on Lexis/Nexis would be useless if people could not search for and find it, but equally useless if people could not trust its integrity. Security policies draw the fine line between having the most information in play and having too much. Composite services like travel websites must pass data around between multiple corporate entities; they must do it seamlessly, and they must do it safely. The customer's identity must be handed around yet not be subject to confusion, alteration, unauthorized exposure, or other mischief.

Passing around information to coordinate multiparty transactions, while necessary, is a source of risk. Sharing financial details necessary to organize a multiparty transaction can easily undo any number of good practices in-house. But not sharing information creates inefficiency. Consider, for example, a user visiting a travel website. She is probably interacting with several websites, and her personal information is being passed around and shared with each of these. This is efficient and convenient for users but this efficiency and convenience requires trust. Trust is efficient because having to prove trustworthiness in each case is so inefficient.

But trust can be dangerous as well. The problem is finding a balance between the inefficiency of not trusting enough and the danger of trusting too much. In the physical world, we attempt to strike this balance by tolerating a certain degree of transitive trust—"Any friend of Bill's is a friend of mine." Such transitive relationships are usually quite open; that is why they work so well. Transitive trust occurs in the digital world as well, but it is often implicit and generally quite difficult to detect.

Consider the travel website again. If you provide your credit number to the travel site, you may not even question whom the site gives that information to, and even if you do, you will not be able to independently evaluate the trustworthiness of these partners. You trust the travel site to use your credit card number carefully and to only pass that number on to other trustworthy sites. What happens, though, if that trust is broken? Who do we blame and where do we place liability? Placing liability on the deepest pockets won't do in the digital world. When a credit card association like MasterCard allows acquiring banks to obtain credit card financial information in full it exposes itself to security failures at that third-party processor—and if that processor fails to protect the data, whose fault is it? MasterCard deals with that uncertainty by imposing its own private body of regulation on its third-party processors. Because it cannot easily measure how secure it is, MasterCard tries to eliminate all known faults.

To the extent that trust is built on identity, assertions of identity must be testable across functional and corporate boundaries. Each party to a transaction undertaken in the name of an individual needs to know the individual's name and to be able to test that it is authentic and authorized.[13] This task must be carefully managed. One industry strategy has been to patronize data aggregators such as credit bureaus. They make good checkers because they know so much more than you, so they can give you a trust rating.[14] Aggregating data improves the inferences that can be made from it while at the same time creating the risk that the aggregated data is itself subject to theft or modification.

For data aggregation to be most useful, the infrastructure of its use must itself be shared. Yet if any one member of a shared infrastructure does a particularly good job at risk reduction then that member's residual risk due to shared infrastructure will be dominated by risks caused by the other parties. Is there a moral hazard here? Is there some as yet undesigned underwriting process that can adequately take into account counterparty risk? These are hard questions. In the physical world, contracts supplement norms of human trust; the value of contracts is apparent precisely when things go wrong. In the digital world, however, it is not obvious when we should rely on trust mechanisms and when we should rely on enforceable contracts; our intuitions about the physical world are not a reliable guide.

III. Recording and Records

In a free society, it is impossible to enumerate all the things that one is permitted to do. Instead we attempt to define what is impermissible. This system creates fuzziness; there is a zone of uncertainty between the obviously allowed and the obviously disallowed. Lest this gray area be exploited, we temper the freedom it offers with a strong notion of accountability. That is, unless the law is so unclear that it offers no guide to the well-intentioned citizen, we leave it to individual citizens to ensure that they are on the right side of the law; if they move too far into the gray we may even place the burden of proof on them to demonstrate that their actions are legal. A good example is the IRS auditing authority. Even if a taxpayer's deductions might ultimately be considered legal the fear of an audit keeps many citizens far within the zone of the permissible.

Because much cybercrime takes place in the gray area between what is clearly permitted and what is clearly forbidden, accountability must play an increasing role in preventing it and ensuring safety in general. What records must we keep to enable meaningful accountability, and to determine which entity is responsible for which problems? After we have determined what kind of records we need, how do we gather them? This is by no means an easy task; digital services and hence digital crimes may be located simultaneously within the facilities of many different owners and, consequently, many different jurisdictions. Adding a third layer of difficulty is the multijurisdictional nature of the Internet. Even if we know what records we need and even if we are able to assemble and complete these records, they are rendered useless if they are not shared across jurisdictional lines. Susan Brenner has looked long and hard at the problem of sharing and accessing records. Her solution is to create interjurisdictional search warrants endowed with the full faith and credit of the issuer in the server's jurisdiction.[15] This solution recognizes the degree to which crimes involving computers and networks tend to have none of the locality or physicality of traditional crimes.

A second issue concerns how long records should be retained. Again, the answer to these questions may be counterintuitive. Paper records take up space, and space is a precious resource in the physical world. But not so in the digital world. Available electronic storage space has increased astronomically to the point that neither volume (of data) nor cost (of storage) are inhibiting factors. Simultaneously, in the digital world it is much easier to create records; thus the sheer volume of information has increased dramatically. The combination of these two has made it cheaper to keep everything; the labor involved in sorting through information and making individualized choices about what to save and what to delete soon becomes greater than the cost of keeping everything or nothing.

Keeping everything might not seem like such a bad thing, but corporate firms are understandably hesitant to do so because of the many new liabilities imposed on corporate governance. Consequently, many firms have an internal policy of destroying all records whose preservation is not mandated by law. Other firms, noting the Morgan Stanley case,[16] conclude the

opposite and keep everything so as not to have to defend routine destruction as some kind of conspiratorial activity. In either case, digital physics
redirects our policy inquiry. Space is no longer an issue in the digital
world. Thus the question is not what *can* we keep, but what *should* we
keep?

IV. The Use of Data versus Its Existence

Zero-cost data acquisition challenges our notions of reasonable expectations of privacy. Much public discussion about privacy focuses on limiting
the collection of certain data. In response, the law has a rich history of dictating what data must be, or must not be, collected.[17] But what is reasonable for a person to expect when digital physics is counterintuitive? What
is a reasonable expectation of privacy for a general population that does
not understand how technologically feasible it is to gather, aggregate, and
disseminate information? Society does not need laws that forbid impossible actions. Hence there are no rules against data collections that are, or
rather were, impossible. But in the digital world the technically "impossible" rapidly becomes technically possible, meaning that the ability to act
will always precede any political motivation to regulate that action. Lawmakers are thus inevitably faced with a need to make policy decisions
about data collections after such collections are already well established.

Therefore, policy discussions must be centered not on the existence of
collectible and observable data but on the *use* of that data. If the price of
collection, storage, retrieval, and analysis of data is effectively free, these
practices will occur and cannot effectively be outlawed. Hence legislatures
can act only on what people do with the results of the process. For example, it is unlikely that legislatures will ever attempt to criminalize taking a
photograph in a public street. Nevertheless, by continuously taking pho-
tographs in the public street one could conclude that one's neighbors are
never home on Tuesday nights. In like fashion, one could collect the make
and license numbers of undercover police cars from information observable by anyone in the public street. Sean Gorman, a Ph.D. student at
George Mason University, assembled all available maps on the Internet
into one map, leading several people to label his work a serious security
threat.[18] The key question for policy makers is not whether data should be
collected but what limits we can (constitutionally) place on its publication
and use.

V. Network Boundaries Have Zero Alignment with Political Boundaries

As everyone knows, on the Internet network boundaries are not political boundaries (indeed, for this very reason China has tried to control information flows in and out of the country).[19] Hence it is equally logical to say that the Internet is outside all jurisdictions (hence no one's laws apply) and to say that the Internet is inside all jurisdictions (hence everyone's laws apply). The former assumption appears in Barlow's "Declaration of the Independence of Cyberspace"[20] and Hughes's "A Cypherpunk's Manifesto."[21] The latter assumption will seem familiar to any global business, especially financial institutions, who regularly find that by having no real location they must conform to the laws of every country.

If we decide that no one's jurisdiction applies, then the Internet will resemble the high seas before 1930. While certain pockets of the Internet remain secure, it is still dangerous to travel between those good neighborhoods when bad neighborhoods lie in between. At the very least, without the equivalent of the Conventions on the Law of the High Seas, there will be no effective or binding control over spam, host-hijacking, or pornography. On the other hand, if we assert that the Internet is within all jurisdictions, we invite the problem of conflicting laws. The League against Racism and Anti-Semitism's suit against Yahoo in France,[22] and the WTO's finding that American prohibitions against Internet gambling violate the rights of Antigua and Barbuda,[23] illustrate the point.

Assuming that we want some jurisdiction's laws to apply, the next question is how to define the boundaries of the relevant jurisdictions. There are two possibilities. Either the boundaries of the physical network—for example, the ends of the wires, the locations of satellite uplinks, and the physical locations of servers—define the jurisdictions or the jurisdictions define the boundaries. If we choose the former approach, we might pick, for example, all the property of Verizon or all the computers with names in the *.edu domain to be the boundary. If we choose the latter, then we might declare that citizens of France are bound by French Internet Law regardless of where they live in the world or how it is they get online. Here in the United States, skirmishes over who has the right to tax interstate transactions made on the Internet illustrate how the boundary and the jurisdiction are in considerable tension.

One could imagine a solution to this choice of law problem where every website includes a consent form or a disclaimer that reads, for example, "By choosing to visit this website you agree to be bound by Brazilian law." But this, of course, raises a different question: Why shouldn't a country be allowed to protect its citizens from the actions of foreign websites? Another solution, although one fraught with unintended consequences, might be to create a single, international jurisdiction for the Internet, governed by some international body such as the United Nations. This type of solution is being hotly debated in at least one area: control of the Internet Corporation for Assigned Names and Numbers (ICANN). The Internet's structure assumes that users rely on names to find the underlying network numbers. Thus control over the translation of names to numbers is a point of leverage that would control everything else. Is there an international body ready to handle such responsibility? Or, as I believe, is international political control of the root nameservers a recipe for disaster?

VI. So, Where to Put Policy?

As we noted in our discussion of risk and risk management, every location on the Internet is equidistant from every other. This turns our understanding of the physical world, with its separation between good neighborhoods and bad ones, on its head. In real estate location is everything because good neighborhoods are worth paying for. But given the law of equidistance in the digital world, there is no way to fence off the good areas from the bad. The National Academies of Sciences, for example, recently published *Youth, Pornography, and the Internet,* a book that explores the difficult policy choices that we face when trying to protect children from adult material on the Internet. The authors offer two important insights. First, technical change will perpetually outpace our notions of justice and accountability. That is, the technology will allow us to do many things long before we can decide whether or not we *should* do those things. Second, the interests of adults will perpetually trump the needs of children. My own view is that we should deny adults some privileges when they cannot be limited to adults and will prove harmful to children. But the courts, with a few recent exceptions, have often concluded otherwise.[24]

The question for lawmakers is whether we should rely on the market to produce a solution or whether we should intervene by creating criminal or civil sanctions. If we choose the latter approach we can either impose regulation and sanctions in the network itself (for example, at the level of the ISPs), or at the end-nodes (that is, at the level of users' computers or network routers). The Internet and its many standard protocols are designed to be "end-to-end."[25] This means that the network between two end-points serves as a delivery mechanism and only as a delivery mechanism; this leaves the nature of any communication between end-points to the end-points to negotiate as they see fit. The freedom this structure created is precisely what enabled the Internet to grow and evolve as it has. Had it not been this way, every design change would have had to go through review by governments, ISPs, or some other party whose interests might well have been contrary to those who were innovating.

Forcing the network to implement policy is a seductive idea.[26] It is particularly attractive to regulators because the number of entities one has to regulate are the few (backbone providers) and not the many (individual computer owners). The Internet's end-to-end nature has been the key to its success; regulating networks is a bad idea because it will harm innovation. If the state deputizes networks to regulate on-net behavior, one can be assured that the many unfortunate features of telephone monopolies will be visited on the Internet. Attaching devices to phone lines was strictly forbidden until the early 1970s and even then allowed only if one rented bulky and expensive equipment from the phone company. Only after that monopoly control was broken did fax machines become feasible. If one had to register one's fax machines with the phone company one could well imagine that fax adoption would have been delayed a decade. A more current and contentious example concerns whether network providers should be responsible for file sharing across their infrastructures. Clearly (and in line with the Betamax decision),[27] file sharing has substantial noninfringing uses even if adoption rates are driven by parties partial to infringement.

Nevertheless, protecting the end-to-end design principle presumes competent end-nodes or users. That is, it assumes that users want to make and are capable of making effective decisions about self-protection. If the users are unwilling to make such decisions we may need stronger regulation to provide them with the motivation they lack. And if they are not capable of making such decisions, then it is not only futile to hold them accountable for their actions, but also unfair.

Thus, before deciding to place policy at the level of end-users, we should closely examine our assumptions about the desires and capabilities of those users. Though the growth in Internet users shows signs of slow-ing, it still occurs at an impressive rate. If the number of persons with access to the Internet doubles every six months worldwide then at any given time only one-tenth of 1 percent of all users have more than five years' experience with the Internet. Even if we assume that every user with substantial experience with the Internet will make informed decisions about self-protection, the sheer volume of inexperienced users should make us hesitate to place a large degree of confidence in the group of users as a whole.

I am no fan of protecting people from themselves, but I recognize that often people democratically demand to be taken care of. Physical world examples include the treatment of diseases that are themselves pure products of unhealthy lifestyles, or the mandates for passive restraint systems in automobiles that followed when it became clear that a majority of motorists would not use active restraint systems. It would thus seem likely that people will demand to be taken care of in the digital world.

Unwanted email (spam) is the majority of all email and, of that, a majority is relayed through unsuspecting end-nodes. Many of these end-nodes demonstrate that they are incompetent, for example, by refusing to scan for hijacking viruses or by clicking on links that are falsified. Calling this behavior incompetence is not a normative judgment; rather it is to say, as a descriptive matter, that these users are ignorant of the danger their own computers create. As noted earlier, it is natural for users to feel that if their computer is doing what they want it to do then everything is fine. The ignorant user, of course, is unaware that the computer may be doing much more than that. Of course, the average user would prefer that the computer not be doing these things, but the problem is that the user does not even know to check for this hidden undesirable behavior.

If users are incompetent, even blamelessly so, it seems useless to regulate them. But if we do not regulate the users, should we then regulate the ISPs? For example, should we require ISPs to read users' email content before deciding whether to forward it? Should we require ISPs to take responsibility for the security problem of their incompetent users by scanning users' computers for virus infections and taking them off the Internet if they are infected? Should we require ISPs to impose traffic limits on end-nodes that would prevent both file-sharing and email relays (used by spammers)? Answering yes to any of these questions, of course, raises the same chilling effects on innovation discussed above, not to mention dangers to civil liberties.

But if regulating end-users is useless because they are incompetent, and regulating the ISPs is too chilling to either innovation, civil liberties, or both, then what is left? Perhaps the focus should be on how to create competent users or at least prevent incompetent persons from becoming users. That is, we might require Internet users to demonstrate their competence, to prove they know something before they get to have what would amount to an Internet Drivers' License. Yet, in a borderless world, who would be the issuing authority and, given the technical rates of change, how often would a retest be required? If, as I suspect, access to the Internet is becoming a practical necessity for citizens of modern societies, such a license would probably have to be a "shall issue" license. That is, one would not have to prove competence to have the license issued, but some demonstration of malfeasance or incompetence might be grounds for revoking it.

Adam Smith's "invisible guiding hand" will not push the Internet toward order and security, because the players are in a classic prisoner's dilemma: the self-interest of each player leads to a result that is bad for the common good. Consider, for example, the problem of record keeping we discussed above. Each corporation would benefit if every corporation shared logs of attempted external attacks, yet the self-interest of each individual corporation is to keep its logs secret because they might contain evidence exposing the corporation to liability. Leaving the Internet to its own devices will thus not ensure any sort of order or safety, and given the rapid growth rate of Internet users, we can no longer rely on a conception of the Internet as solely the province of a well-behaved scientific and military elite. Considering that in the laboratory we double the price-performance value of CPUs every eighteen months, of storage media every twelve, and of bandwidth every nine, it is inevitable that our future is one of ever greater volumes of data in ever faster motion. Is data security or at least data regulation therefore the thing we should concentrate on? Is it time to say that the real question is not *should* we regulate, but *where* do we regulate?

VII. Problems Eventually Converge

The wonderful thing about electronic information is that it costs zero to reproduce. This is also the terrible thing. In the physical world, objects have unique identities and take up unique locations in space and time. If an object is located in one place, it cannot be simultaneously located in another. Similarly, if I possess your car, you cannot simultaneously possess it. But space and locality are vastly different in the digital world. Digital physics allows the same object to exist simultaneously in a multitude of different locations and, consequently, it allows the same object to be possessed simultaneously by a multitude of users. This principle of digital physics fundamentally changes the nature of business in the digital world.

Another important principle of digital physics is that bits are bits, whether they are an MP3 tune, your mother's date of birth, or a picture of you holding the front page of today's newspaper. Very different types of objects (e.g., a song, versus a fact, versus a photograph) are indistinguishable at the atomic level—they are each just a collection of bits. Thus, unlike in the physical world, we do not need to know the type of object we are dealing with in order to protect it. To borrow an engineering phrase, the "problem statement" is the same for any piece of digital information: How do we control that information when we cannot be present to protect that information either in space (because a user can be located anywhere on the network) or in time (because a user can access the digital information or re-create it at any time)?

This statement of the problem produces a remarkable convergence: Either we get both digital rights management and privacy, or we get neither. Digital rights management attempts to prevent one copy of an audio recording from becoming many copies even when the originator of the recording has lost all physical access upon commercial release. Privacy management attempts to prevent one copy of personal information from becoming many copies even when the originator of the information has lost all control of it once he or she has entrusted it to another. These are the same solutions at the level of the bits even though at the philosophical level it would appear that most of those who hate DRM love privacy and most of those who love DRM do not find privacy a matter of high concern.

How should we negotiate this tension? Should we grant an ownership right to a (U.S.) social security number? Should we encourage digital works of art and science to be rented in a pervasive, always-on networking environment rather than being owned as copies? That would permit enforceable contracts, but is that what we want? Or, in the least attractive formulation, do we want to build in digital rights management protections into our hardware itself? Congress keeps returning to this approach as if it were the only solution: The V-Chip, the Broadcast Flag, and many other examples come to mind. Nothing can be as harmful to innovation and ultimately self-defeating as such requirements even if, as the example of region coding in DVDs illustrates, some of them do make it to the light of day.

In each of the above examples, we face the principles of digital physics and how those principles affect where we direct public policy. Maybe the only way to implement policy is hardware design; maybe we should simply acknowledge that in a free world there is always risk; and maybe we should stop assuming that every hard problem calls for a technology solution and not a behavioral one. Let us explore this last possibility.

VIII. Designing for Failure and Creating Accountability

Digital/information goods and services tend to fail suddenly rather than wearing out the way a pair of shoes might. Hence, losses caused by those failures will be sharp and sudden. Once you crack a code—as DeCSS cracked the protection measures that prevented DVDs from being copied[28]—the whole protection program is rendered useless.

Perhaps the greatest question before the law with respect to digital goods is who bears the costs for the risk of failure in digital goods and mechanisms and, in consequence, who owns the liability. The digital arena is increasingly essential to everyday life; yet it contains security faults that produce customer losses with neither warning nor any ability by the end-user to prevent them. Should liability for cybercrimes be placed on those who manage digital goods? That is, should we adopt the strict liability rules that courts and legislatures apply to manufacturers of physical consumer goods? Or should the risk of loss (or liability) be placed on the customer? And if we place either or both risks on the consumer, should negligence be the appropriate standard? For example, if the customer is fully up to date with all patches officially released by the vendor, then should this constitute due care and absolve the consumer of either risk of harm or liability?

During the 1990s the commercial world largely caught up with the military world in the use of cryptography. The replacement of the Data Encryption Standard (DES) with the Advanced Encryption Standard (AES) is a case in point; the AES was chosen after an open public competition between commercial and academic contestants from the entire global technical community and was won by a group of software designers from Belgium.[29] The current decade will see the commercial world overtake the military world in the skills of traffic analysis—the study of who said what to whom and with what frequency. Traffic analysis will quickly become a commercial reality as invisible and as widespread as surveillance cameras. Traffic analysis is extremely powerful, far more so than nonspecialists tend to realize. It is the core of what surveillance is about in the digital age. It is no longer necessary to know what a communication *contains*; traffic analysis allows us to figure this out just by observing the *pattern* of communication. Indeed, traffic analysis and not code breaking is the (U.S.) National Security Agency's true specialty. Code breaking is too expensive unless you are reasonably sure that the message in question is worth breaking, and that question—is this message worth breaking?—can be answered through traffic analysis.

Traffic analysis poses genuine problems for policy makers. On one hand, traffic analysis could make it much easier to hold Internet users accountable for their behavior. Every router could, in principle, record the traffic going through it, making it easier to identify, and thus investigate, suspicious activity. Traffic analysis would be also useful in reconstructing both cybercrimes and negligent acts that cause damage. On the other hand, traffic analysis presents many dangers. One can misuse traffic data just as much as any other sort of data.[30] As mentioned above, the cost of data acquisition is effectively zero, and the process of data aggregation is automatable and thus also increasingly inexpensive. Thus to safeguard against misuse and to protect privacy rights we must decide whether we want to regulate the data acquisition, the data aggregation, or the use of the data once it has been aggregated. If we try to regulate data acquisition we face the problem of knowing when data acquisition is occurring. Is it better to require specific lifetimes for data and order its subsequent destruction (as the FTC has apparently decided to do)?[31] Or should we rather assume that acquisition and aggregation are occurring (because we cannot tell when either or both is happening) and thus require notice? In effect, the law would say (akin to the European Union's Data Privacy Directive), "You can collect, you can aggregate, and you can use but not without my knowledge."

IX. Conclusion

Our brief survey has illustrated a key point: The digital world is not the physical world. Relying on intuitions derived from the physical world to make policy choices will get us into trouble every time. Digital law is and must be counterintuitive. Because our intuition about the digital sphere can so easily be wrong, it is enormously helpful whenever possible to base our policy choices on solid facts.

This is the last time we will have as much hybrid vigor among the leadership of the security field and it is the last time we will have as clean a slate to work with. Although the law is a valuable resource for security, more important is the diversity of talent and energy we have now, a diversity we must mine while we can.

NOTES

1. D. Moore, V. Paxson, S. Savage, C. Shannon, S. Staniford, and N. Weaver, "Inside the Slammer Worm," IEEE Security and Privacy, v1 n4 p33–39, July–August 2003; *see* http://csdl.computer.org/comp/mags/sp/2003/04/j4033abs.htm.

2. S. Berinato, "Why Wasn't the Witty Worm Widely Worrisome?" CSO Magazine, 14 January 2005; *see* http://www.csoonline.com/alarmed/01142005.html.

3. C. Shannon & D. Moore, "The Spread of the Witty Worm," Cooperative Association for Internet Data Analysis (CAIDA), 27 April 2004; *see* http://www.caida.org/analysis/security/witty/.

4. Firebreaks in forests are optimal when they take advantage of natural terrain breaks and can be serviced.

5. Some major technical universities do no inbound filtering, delegate security management to individual laboratories, and do egress filtering both for the campus at large as well as on a building by building basis. Most cable operators today block outbound email connections except to the message transfer agents they themselves control so as to prevent high-volume, high-speed spread of spam from within their networks to the outside world.

6. Written up extensively, e.g., the historical record of Doctor John Snow at the UCLA School of Public Health; *see* http://www.ph.ucla.edu/epi/snow.html.

7. S. Staniford, V. Paxson, & N. Weaver, "How to Own the Internet in Your Spare Time," Proceedings of the 11th USENIX Security Symposium, San Francisco, August 2002; *see* http://www.usenix.org/events/sec02/full_papers/staniford/staniford.pdf.

8. Center for Internet Epidemiology, NSF Cybertrust Award, Stefan Savage, Principal Investigator, University of California, San Diego, 24 September 2004; *see* http://www.jacobsschool.ucsd.edu/news_events/releases/release.sfe?id=293.

9. Presidential Decision Directive #63, "Policy on Critical Infrastructure Protection," 22 May 1998, since superseded by Homeland Security Presidential Directive #7, "Critical Infrastructure Identification, Prioritization, and Protection," 17

December 2003; *see* http://www.usdoj.gov/criminal/cybercrime/factsh.htm and http://www.whitehouse.gov/news/releases/2003/12/20031217-5.html, respectively.

10. A statistician calls this independent "memoryless" arrival a Poisson distribution. The reader encounters these every day; just because the roulette ball has landed on red five times in a row has no bearing on whether it will land on red the next spin. Just because you were not hit by a meteor yesterday does not change your chance of being hit by one today.

11. For example, animations of the spread of the Witty worm, as found *at* http://www.caida.org/analysis/security/witty/#Animations.

12. Steve Cooper, CIO of DHS, as grilled by Rep. Adam Putnam, R/Florida, 10 October 2001.

13. Some cryptographers believe you can have trust without knowing the identity of the person/company you are trusting; for perhaps the best example, see the work of David Chaum and, within that, perhaps his invention of the "blind signature" in 1982 (D. Chaum, "Blind Signatures for Untraceable Payments," Advances in Cryptology—Crypto '82, Springer-Verlag, pp. 199–203). For an explanation, *see* http://www.rsasecurity.com/rsalabs/node.asp?id=2339.

14. This is, of course, a risk management trade-off, inasmuch as the data aggregator can put too much information into play. *See* Bob Barr's FindLaw commentary on the ChoicePoint matter at http://writ.news.findlaw.com/commentary/20050415_barr.html.

15. S.W. Brenner, "Full Faith and Credit for State Search Warrants Subpoenas and Other Court Orders," Working Group on Law & Policy, National Institute of Justice, Electronic Crime Partnership Initiative, 26 August 2002; *see* http://ecpi-us.org/FullFaithnCredit.html.

16. "Age of Discovery: How Morgan Stanley Botched a Big Case by Fumbling Emails," Wall Street Journal, p. 1, 16 May 2005; *see* http://online.wsj.com/article_print/SB111620910505034309.html.

17. Olmstead v. U.S., 277 U.S. 438 (1928), which found no equivalent to trespass in interception of telephone calls (hence such interception did not require a search warrant), was eventually reversed by Alderman v. U.S., 394 U.S. 165, 175 & nn. 8, 9 (1969), which found that the expectation of privacy with respect to telephone calls did exist (and hence a warrant was required for their interception). Now that telephone service is moving away from regulated utilities with defined circuits to the simple "peer to peer" connections of two parties over the Internet, Congress has responded with "CALEA," the Communications Assistance for Law Enforcement Act of 1994, Pub. L. No. 103-414, 108 Stat. 4279, defining the existing statutory obligation of telecommunications carriers to assist law enforcement in executing electronic surveillance pursuant to court order or other lawful authorization and requiring carriers to design or modify their systems to ensure that lawfully authorized electronic surveillance can be performed. At the same time, cellular telephone service providers are required to provide the geolocation of the

user of a cellular telephone to within a hundred yards at all times, thus begging the question of whether "Where am I?" is somehow not subject to the expectation of privacy that "What am I saying?" has.

18. Gorman almost had his dissertation seized. No less a person than Richard Clarke, cyberterrorism czar for both Clinton and Bush, said that his work should be burned and the Washington Post declined to print it, though they did do a story about not printing it; *see* http://www.washingtonpost.com/ac2/wp-dyn/A23689-2003Jul7.

19. J. Zittrain & B. Edelman, "Empirical Analysis of Internet Filtering in China," Harvard Law School, Public Law Working Paper No. 62, IEEE Internet Computing, v70 March/April 2003; *see* http://cyber.law.harvard.edu/filtering/china/.

20. J.P. Barlow, "A Declaration of the Independence of Cyberspace"; *see* http://homes.eff.org/~barlow/Declaration-Final.html.

21. E. Hughes, "A Cypherpunk's Manifesto"; *see* http://www.activism.net/cypherpunk/manifesto.html.

22. San Jose District Court, C00-21275. But in the spirit of this chapter, *see* the discussion in M.K. Bratt & N.F. Kugele, "Who's in Charge?" Michigan Bar Journal, v80 n7, July 2001; *see* http://www.michbar.org/journal/article.cfm?articleID=305&volumeID=20.

23. Difficult to get in full, but if interested in reading the WTO decision, begin at this URL: http://docsonline.wto.org/ and search for the "Document Symbol" WT/DS285/R.

24. To go further, look at court cases as to whether pornographic websites available in publicly funded facilities represent a hostile workplace under Title VII of the Civil Rights Act, the various attempts to mandate filtering and the challenges thereto, the record of zero federal obscenity prosecutions during the whole of the Clinton administration, the many attempts to do something about pornographic spam email, and the Ninth Circuit's decision that an image on a web page should be assumed to be fabricated until proven real—notably that a depiction of a child engaged in sexual acts is not a child unless the child can be provably identified by name.

25. J.H. Saltzer, D.P. Reed, & D.D. Clark, "End-to-End Arguments in System Design," ACM Transactions on Computer Systems, pp. 277–288, 1984.

26. H. Kruse, W. Yurcik, & L. Lessig, "The InterNAT: Policy Implications of the Internet Architecture Debate," Telecommunications Policy Research Conference (TPRC), September 2000; *see* http://www.tprc.org/abstracts00/internatpap.pdf.

27. Sony v. Universal Studios, 464 U.S. 417 (1984) states that "the sale of copying equipment, like the sale of other articles of commerce, does not constitute contributory infringement if the product is widely used for legitimate, unobjectionable purposes. Indeed, it need merely be capable of substantial non-infringing uses."

28. CSS stands for Content Scrambling System, so DeCSS stands for converting the otherwise scrambled content into viewable content, and that is the name of a somewhat notorious program for breaking DVD protections. The matter began on January 20, 2000, when U.S. District Judge Lewis A. Kaplan of the Southern District of New York issued a preliminary injunction in Universal City Studios et al. v. Reimerdes et al., in an action under 17 USC 1201(a)(2), also known as section 1201(a)(2) of the Digital Millenium Copyright Act. For a discussion that compares programs to text, *see* http://www.cs.cmu.edu/~dst/DeCSS/Gallery/.

29. Sponsored by the National Institute for Standards and Technology, the ultimate selection was the Rijndael algorithm from the University of Leujeuven; *see* http://csrc.nist.gov/CryptoToolkit/aes/rijndael/ and/or http://www.esat.kuleuven.ac.be/~rijmen/rijndael/.

30. A likely apocryphal tale is that the reason certain telephone companies, e.g., the French PTT, do not send an itemized bill is that an itemized bill allows one spouse to know whom the other spouse is calling even if the call itself was unrecorded. (Use your imagination.)

31. Disposal of Consumer Report Information and Records, Federal Trade Commission, 16 CFR Part 682, effective 1 June 2005; *see* http://www.ftc.gov/os/2004/11/041118disposalfrn.pdf.

Architectural Regulation and the Evolution of Social Norms

Lee Tien

We normally think of law in terms of textual rules. The ubiquity and malleability of computer software, however, has led scholars to coin and popularize another concept, that of architectural regulation.[1] Scholars like Joel Reidenberg and Larry Lessig argue that software, or computer "code," regulates human action as do codes of law, especially in network environments.[2] As Lessig puts it, software "constrain[s] some behavior (for example, electronic eavesdropping) by making other behavior possible (encryption)."[3]

Code and law regulate behavior in different ways, however. While law typically regulates behavior after the fact, code or architecture regulates "more directly," as "present constraints."[4] Furthermore, code-as-law—and, more generally, architectural regulation—poses transparency problems. Because government regulation in the architectural mode can "hide its pedigree,"[5] Lessig contends that "[w]hat a code regulation does should be at least as [apparent] as what a legal regulation does."[6]

While Lessig is right that architectural regulation poses a serious transparency problem,[7] especially where privacy and "high-tech" architectures are concerned, I suggest that architectural regulation has deeper transparency problems. Lessig's concern that architectural regulation can hide its pedigree is significant, but it is not that different from the transparency problem posed by many ordinary legal rules. Much law in the modern administrative state, such as agricultural subsidies or tax breaks, is also invisible to the average person.

This essay, therefore, directs attention toward a more significant aspect of architecture's transparency problem: that because architectural regulation regulates settings or equipment in order to regulate behavior, it changes the nature of rule presentation and rule enforcement in ways that are likely to decrease law's publicity or visibility. This might be acceptable if all we care about is the effectiveness of social control, but not if we care about law as a public process.

Furthermore, as the old saying "freedom of the press belongs to those who own the presses" suggests, our rights often depend on resources. Architectural regulation can shape or foreclose social experience with resources used to exercise or protect rights, thus distorting the evolution of both social norms and the rights tied to those norms. For example, a proposal to "outlaw encryption methods that law enforcement cannot decipher"[8] could deprive society of experience with a privacy-enhancing technology.[9]

We should therefore be extremely careful about the use of architectural regulation. Stripped of its high-tech trappings, architectural regulation is simply government action directed at the real-world conditions of human activity, tangible or intangible, which in turn affects what people can or are likely to do.

Beyond software and computers, architectural regulation thus highlights the relationship between resources, rights, and norms. In the short run, government action directed at resources can affect the concrete exercise of rights. In the long run, such government action can affect or distort the evolution of the social norms that give life to those rights.

I. Comparing Legal Rules and Architectural Regulation

In this section, I argue that architectural regulation, provisionally defined as regulation intended to influence acts by shaping, structuring, or reconfiguring the practical conditions or preconditions of acts, challenges the traditional view of law as rules.

Architecture inhabits the realm of context, not text: it is embedded in settings or equipment, and can affect us directly without our being aware of what it does. As a result, architectural regulation exploits asymmetries in the social distribution of knowledge. Its effects are normatively significant because we often are not aware that architecture is deliberately being used to constrain our action. And even if we are aware of it, we might not understand how we are being constrained.

A. Differentiating Legal Rules and Architectural Regulation

We generally think of law in terms of rules and of "the law" as a system of rules.[10] Law as social control is often described in terms of rules[11] that state primary norms of conduct. We apply sanctions to those who breach these norms[12] in the hope of inducing compliance.[13] As sociologist Howard Becker puts it, "[a]ll social groups make rules and attempt, at some times and under some circumstances, to enforce them. Social rules define situations and the kind of behavior appropriate to them, specifying some actions as 'right' and forbidding others as 'wrong.'"[14]

One difference between legal and other social rules or norms lies in the administration of sanctions, that is, how rules are enforced.[15] Social norms are informally enforced through sanctions like social disapproval and motivated by the desire for esteem or to be perceived as a good potential transaction partner; legal rules are formally enforced.[16] On this view, both legal rules and social norms are backed by independently applied sanctions.

In short, legal rules and social norms are both typically backed by sanctions and aimed at an actor's decision to act. For economists and utilitarians, sanction-backed rules influence behavior by changing the behavior's "price," that is, by decreasing its expected value to the potential wrongdoer. For those who emphasize law's expressive function, legal rules also signify our belief in, and commitment to, particular norms of conduct.[17] Either way, the point is to shape the actor's preferences among available options.

Architectural regulation does not work this way. Consider the following situation: in a drug-infested neighborhood, dealers use public coin telephones so that their calls cannot be traced to their home phones. The coin phones are then removed to stop such calls. Such regulation is not fully captured by the model of sanction-backed or duty-declaring rules. Neither sanctions nor duties are imposed upon the drug dealers by such action. They remain "free" to act, but their conditions of action have been changed through the elimination of a resource (phones) with a design feature that facilitated drug dealing (untraceability).[18]

While both architectural and legal regulation are intended to affect people's actions, the typical sanction-backed rule targets the actor's decision whether to act. The legal rule is an attempt to alter preferences. The implicit vision of the actor here is as one who chooses. Architectural regulation, by contrast, structures the conditions of action, for example, social settings and/or the resources available in those settings.[19] It thus regulates the behavior that occurs in those settings or that utilizes those resources. In my pay phone example, the option of making anonymous phone calls was simply removed. Choices, not preferences, were targeted. The implicit vision of the actor here is as one who can be manipulated.

Note, by the way, that human beings can be resources: one of Lessig's best examples of regulatory concealment is a law requiring doctors at federally funded clinics to say that abortion is "not . . . an appropriate method of family planning," thus exploiting the fact that patients are "unlikely to hear the doctor's statement as political broadcast from the government."[20]

Architectural regulation is also enforced differently than sanction-backed rules. It creates a present constraint on action: no human being or social institution need impose a cost after the fact. As Lessig puts it: "Think of the constraints blocking your access to the air-conditioned home of a neighbor who is gone for the weekend. Law constrains you—if you break in, you will be trespassing. Norms constrain you as well—it is unneighborly to break into your neighbor's house. Both of these constraints, however, would be imposed on you *after* you broke into the house. They are the prices you might have to pay later. The architectural constraint is the lock on the door—it blocks you *as you are trying to enter* the house."[21]

In addition, the regulatory target need not be aware that there has been a decision to constrain his or her actions.[22] While the deterrent effect of a sanction-backed rule generally requires some knowledge about the rule and may be enhanced by the target's awareness, architectural regulation may be more effective when it is not perceived as a deliberate constraint. Most parents know that an effective way to keep a small child from playing with a noisy toy is to secretly remove it.

Given the importance of social settings, resources, and equipment to people's everyday behavior, it is clear that architectural regulation as I have defined it can take many forms. My pay phone example illustrates one of the simplest forms: changing the availability or distribution of resources in social settings. Changing the design of resources is another architectural technique. The coin pay phones could have been reconfigured as credit-card phones, creating traceability.

The criminal justice literature has long considered these possibilities under the rubrics of "situational crime prevention" and "crime prevention through environmental design."[23] For instance, the Washington, D.C. Metro subway system uses a variety of architectural techniques to control crime.[24] "Target hardening" was achieved by constructing seats, windows, and other fixtures from materials that resist vandalism.[25] The risk of pick-pocketing was lowered by placing escalators at each end of the subway platform, distributing passengers along the platform rather than crowding them in the middle, and providing clear signage to reduce tourist rider confusion and jostling among passengers.[26] Metro's planners deliberately did not provide public restrooms or many chairs and benches to discourage potential offenders from loitering and evaluating victims.[27]

Facilitation of surveillance or information gathering within a social setting or via equipment is another key technique of architectural regulation. Not only is the Metro system equipped with many conspicuous surveillance cameras, but the system was deliberately structured to ensure "a high level of natural surveillance."[28] Platforms are long; there are few supporting columns behind which offenders can hide; a high, vaulted ceiling arches over the tracks.[29] "Metro's planners deliberately avoided long, winding corridors and corners," which "create shadows that could hide criminals and serve as nooks" for panhandlers.[30] Indeed, Metro's walls were indented in order to reflect more light.

More subtle forms of architectural regulation can be imagined. If the government encourages equipment with a preferred design feature and discourages those without it, more behavior is regulated. Instead of requiring the elimination of coin pay phones, or their replacement by credit-card phones, the government could change the incentives faced by private telephone companies. Credit-card phones themselves, or the removal of coin pay phones, could be subsidized. Such techniques were used to attempt to control encryption. A national study of encryption policy explained that government officials hoped that "law-enforcement-friendly" encryption would become "a de facto standard for use in the private sector," perhaps eventually depriving consumers of a "genuine choice."[31]

B. Comparing the Careers of Legal Rules and Architectural Regulation

I have described, from a relatively static perspective, how architectural regulation is not like sanction-backed legal rules, and why this should matter. In this section I use a more dynamic perspective in order to emphasize the transparency issues associated with architectural regulation.

1. LEGAL RULES HAVE CAREERS

From a sociological perspective, legal rules and the norms they promote are often objects of social conflict. Becker observes that legal rules and the norms they embody have careers.[32] A rule's career begins with its promulgation or creation, and then continues in its enforcement (or lack of it).

For the most part, legal rules are publicly created and presented. We should not overstate the degree to which the process of rule creation really is public, of course. Much legislative activity takes place behind closed doors in the realm of lobbying, arm twisting, and influence peddling. Administrative regulation in federal agencies is also public—but again with a significant back-room component. Nevertheless, the ultimate output—the rules themselves—is generally published and available, theoretically, to everyone.

Rules, moreover, need some minimal level of enforcement to be meaningful. Enforcement of rules is normally a complex, enterprising human activity. Rule breaking must be detected; someone must bring that detected breach to the attention of the appropriate agency; that agency must decide to address the breach in some way, ranging from ignoring it to taking it to court. The human actors who perform these tasks generally possess discretion and exercise judgment about when, and under what circumstances, to act. Enforcement activities require resources, and many take place in public arenas that permit social contestation over the meaning and legitimacy of the rule itself. Resource allocation in public agencies is part of the more-or-less-public budgetary process; prosecuting offenders requires public accusations.

That these choices exist is integral to the social organization of law as we know it, because public processes like resource allocation and punishment tell us about the consequences of our rules. Rules perceived to be unjust may lead to a social outcry, an amendment, or even repeal. To some extent, rule enforcement operates as a social feedback mechanism.

2. ARCHITECTURAL REGULATIONS HAVE DIFFERENT CAREERS

We should expect the careers of architectural regulations to be quite different. It is not clear, for instance, how the removal of pay phones in my example would be "enacted." It might have been the decision of either the phone company or the government; the ordinary phone user is unlikely to know. Indeed, we may not even perceive that a decision intended to regulate our actions was made. Often, we simply have no clue as to who made the key design decisions regarding our settings or equipment.

Enforcement often occurs simply as a consequence of finding oneself in the architected setting or using the architected equipment or system. The role of human beings in enforcement is greatly reduced. Once the pay phones are removed, drug dealers simply cannot make untraceable coin pay phone calls.

The nature of noncompliance also changes. Drug dealers can continue to ply their illicit trade if they go to a neighborhood with coin pay phones. Or they might use cheap, disposable cell phones. Disobedience of architectural regulation, in other words, involves either exit from the architected system or circumvention of the architected constraint.

Architectural regulation can be quite a blunt enforcement instrument, lacking a mitigating feedback loop. Removing the pay phones affects everyone, not just the drug dealers. But if the pay phone removal is not perceived as regulation in the first place, no one will complain that the government acted unwisely. The constraint will simply persist. Changed conditions could lead to new pay phones being installed, of course, but the government's hand might still remain invisible.

From the enforcement perspective, then, architectural regulation bypasses many of the possibilities for human actors to modulate the effects or meaning of a rule in the enforcement process. Enforcement is instead delegated to equipment or social settings, lessening the possibility of social contest over the rule. The ordinarily public process of social conflict over rules may be short-circuited simply because we do not see what is happening.

C. Architectural Regulation and Its Vicissitudes

The metaphor of "architecture" suggests that architectural regulation possesses a structural nature, that is, it is built into or embedded in the practical conditions of everyday life. Two obvious candidates for architecting are the things we use—equipment—as well as social settings, most of which contain equipment. This metaphor also suggests the important role of architects: those actors or groups, or successions of actors, who designed or shaped equipment and social settings.

The metaphor suggests that third, beyond architecture and architecting, there is something distinctive about how we perceive architecture. Walter Benjamin says, "Architecture has always represented the prototype of a work of art the reception of which is consummated by a collectivity in a state of distraction."[33] Unlike a painting, which announces itself as art and before which one may concentrate, "Buildings are appropriated in a twofold manner: by use and by perception."[34] We experience architecture "not so much by attention as by habit. . . . [E]ven optical reception . . .

occurs much less through rapt attention than by noticing the object in incidental fashion."[35]

1. LAW AS LAW: ISSUES OF VISIBILITY OR RECOGNITION

We should pay close attention to "law as architecture" because part of what distinguishes law from social control is that it is perceived *as* law. Law at some level appeals to legitimacy: our vision of law as rules is linked to notions of public processes of competing readings, and appeals to metaphors of textuality, authorship, and audience reception.

By contrast, an architected setting or piece of equipment often appears to us as a *fait accompli*. We often take the architecture of our physical and social worlds for granted. A good architect or urban planner designs spaces and throughways to regulate flow; drivers and pedestrians need not be aware of his intent.

A danger of architectural regulation, then, is that we may perceive it, as Benjamin suggests, only "in incidental fashion." Architectural regulations are at the extreme perceived more as conditions than as rules to be followed or disobeyed consciously. Unlike ordinary sanction-backed rules, architecture achieves compliance by default rather than through active enforcement. To the extent that legitimacy and public deliberation are integral to our notion of law, the surreptitious enactment and enforcement of norms via architecture should give us pause.

2. NORMS AND SOCIAL PRACTICES

The danger of architectural regulation runs even deeper, I suggest. Even without a good theory of how social norms evolve, it should be uncontroversial to assert that law's normative grounding is a function of social experience, the environment in which social norms are born, live, and evolve, or die. Social experience and norms, in turn, are often reference points for law. Government action aimed at shaping equipment or organizing social settings directly alters the conditions of social experience.

Studies of disputes, for instance, suggest that a threshold factor in believing that one has a legal claim is the perception of an event as injurious.[36] If norms are architected into settings or equipment, however, they may seem like mere design features. As a result, we may not perceive architecture normatively, as something intended to control us, but rather as experienced background conditions that just happen to exist.

Much law acts on background conditions. Seat belt and air bag regulations, for instance, clearly architect automobiles in order to preclude social experience with unsafe cars. But the potential "distortion" of social experience is especially problematic when constitutional rights are at issue. Constitutional rights are supposed to constrain or limit government. But government power over the design and distribution of resources can influence the exercise of rights.

The First Amendment, for example, protects the right to speak anonymously,[37] but our ability to exercise that right depends on our having equipment, like coin pay phones, that does not "log" who we are. A common software program, like the Apache Web server, offers a different example. This program, by default, records those who visit a website and post information;[38] architectural regulation aimed at preventing a nonlogging configuration would make anonymous browsing harder.

It seems uncontroversial to think that the practical exercise of rights is important to sustaining them as rights. When social norms have a constitutional dimension—when they breathe content into constitutional law—architectural regulation of social settings in which these norms evolve,[39] possibly constraining the exercise or practice of rights, may weaken constitutional protections.

This issue is particularly important with respect to Fourth Amendment privacy. Our legal "reasonable expectation of privacy" supposedly turns on social conventions, norms, or "understandings"[40] that "are in large part reflections of laws that translate into rules the customs and values of the past and present."[41] And because the Fourth Amendment is meant to check government discretion,[42] the government ought not be free to strategically manipulate our privacy customs or practices.[43] Indeed, the Supreme Court has warned that if the government sought to manipulate our actual privacy expectations by announcing on national television that all homes are subject to warrantless entry, those expectations "could play no meaningful role" in determining the scope of Fourth Amendment protection.[44]

Architectural regulation, however, can manipulate the very resources we use to create or protect privacy. Our privacy is often a function of the design of social settings. The most familiar examples are physical: one who works in an office can create some privacy by closing a door; one who works in an open cubicle cannot. And of course, someone made decisions about whether to build cubicles, and someone else makes decisions about who sits in them. Extended settings, like the phone system and the Internet, also have architecture that structures information flows. At one time, for instance, the phone system had a default of caller anonymity—called parties did not see the phone number of the caller. The introduction of caller-identification technology changed that default, causing considerable public consternation over a shift that concerned a single fact.[45]

The general point here for privacy is that the organization or architecture of a setting regulates the distribution and flow of information about the persons present.[46] In particular, a setting's design affects informational exposure: our vulnerability to being monitored, and our capacity in a given setting to monitor our surroundings—including the possibility that we are being monitored.[47] Given our social knowledge of social settings, we rely heavily on what we believe to be normal for a setting, which often include expectations of privacy. For example, Goffman asserted that one normally assumes "that one's surround will be 'dead,' that is, contain no recording and transmission devices."[48] Whether or not we still make this assumption, our expectations and behavior are different when we know we are being recorded.

Conversely, our social expectations of privacy are often meaningless without boundaries of some sort. We create privacy when we can, by doing things like closing doors. An act like closing the door not only produces some physical privacy by limiting physical and sensory access, but it also invokes a common privacy norm—every well-socialized person understands that closing a door signals a desire for privacy. It is no accident that when the Supreme Court found that telephone calls from phone booths were entitled to legal privacy protection, it appealed to the fact that the defendant closed the phone booth door behind him.[49]

What if there had been no door to close? When a person makes a telephone call from an unenclosed public telephone, he or she has no privacy expectation against a nearby police officer listening in.[50] If the government facilitated surveillance by inducing telephone companies to remove phone booth doors, or had never permitted phone booth doors in the first place, would the Fourth Amendment apply? Government proposals to restrict the availability, strength, or use of privacy-enhancing technology like encryption present a similar possibility: we are prevented from exercising our right to privacy and we are deprived of social experience with that right.

The design and deployment of equipment reflects a normative vision of social activity.[51] The differences between law as sanction-backed rules and law as architecture—most of which revolve around lack of transparency— produce normative effects that are especially obvious when equipment is involved.

II. How High Technology Exacerbates
Architectural Regulation's Problems

So far, I have argued that architectural regulation risks distorting the "normal" social processes of norm formation for two major reasons. On the one hand, architectural regulation is likely to be less perceptible to the general public as law than legal rules. On the other hand, architectural regulation can affect social practices in a more direct way: it can put some practices in play and take others off the field entirely (or at least marginalize them).

Although architectural regulation is not inherently associated with technological change, these issues are raised most clearly in that context. In this section I explain in more detail how architectural regulation is less perceptible than sanction-backed legal rules and argue that these problems are more serious in the high-technology context.

A. Enactment, Authorship, and the Content of Architectural Norms

Lessig has framed the transparency problem mainly in terms of the government's attempt to "hide the pedigree" of regulation:[52] the public may be misled as to the fact that government sought to architect the situation. He is right, but the problems are more serious.

First, it may not be obvious to the ordinary person that anyone, much less the government, sought to architect the situation, that is, that equipment or a social setting was deliberately designed to regulate behavior. Second, the "content" of the architectural regulation, what it actually does and why, may not be obvious either.

1. SYSTEMS AND TIME

Although architectural regulation is not inherently associated with technological change, these issues are raised most clearly in that context. First, embedding regulation in equipment or settings affects how rules are presented to us. Equipment like e-mail and Web browser software embodies various default settings that affect users' privacy, but they are buried in the program's code. For instance, when you click on a hyperlink to go to a new web page, your browser by default automatically sends the URL of the page you came from to the next site. If you used a search engine to find a site, the entire query, including the search terms you used, is usually passed along to the sites you then clicked on.[53] How many people know that this happens?

These default settings may seem "normal" because the equipment is common, or have become "legitimate" as people have grown accustomed to the situation presented by the equipment.[54] This problem is especially significant for privacy rights, because privacy is already easily violated in secret. The general point here, however, is that defaults prestructure equipment-based activity by requiring us to take affirmative steps to change them, assuming we recognize the default and know how to make the change. Thus, equipment can coercively embody a set of conventions, and because there are often sunk costs associated with equipment, the conventions they embody may persist.[55]

Second, the perceptibility of architectural regulation (either at all or as an architected rather than "natural" constraint) can depend on apprehending the setting and the system to which it belongs. But as we do not experience the entire system of social settings all at once, the meaning of the overall design may be obscure. Small or gradual changes might go unnoticed. Not only might we be unable to "see" the entire setting or system at one time, but we might not understand what we see without extra knowledge as mundane as how a setting had previously been organized.

After the original pay phones had disappeared from the drug-infested neighborhood, people might not even realize that the setting had been deliberately architected at all. A visitor frustrated by being unable to find a pay phone might perceive no act of social control, simply an annoying circumstance.

These effects are greater with new technologies precisely because we have had less experience with them. We may notice pay phones that cannot receive calls because traditional pay phones did receive calls, but most of us have no basis for evaluating changes in the default settings of newer systems like the Internet. Thus, architectural regulation of new technological settings is more likely to be perceived as a "normal" part of social practice than a rule expressly declared to apply to that setting.

Finally, we cannot easily exit large-scale sociotechnical systems like telecommunications. The ordinary person who wants to make telephone calls or send electronic mail will be subject to the architecture of the public telephone network and the Internet.

2. INTERMEDIARIES AND THE MULTIPLE-ACTOR PROBLEM

Intermediated settings present additional problems. As a general matter, it's hard to make a phone call without using a telephone company, or to use the Internet without an ISP. Intermediaries are therefore useful pressure points for regulation; banks, for example, are required to keep records of their customers' transactions.[56] When there are multiple actors, it may be difficult to link an architectural change to the responsible party. Most of us know that speed bumps are the product of government action because we know that the government regulates public streets. But if a social setting is private, or has both private and public aspects, it may be difficult to say whether any state action has occurred. In my hypothetical example, the telephone company might have removed the neighborhood pay phones out of its own private concern about bad public relations about drug dealing, or the local government might have induced it to do so. It is plausible that the government's role might not be apparent to the public; the government might even seek to hide its role.[57]

B. Technical Ignorance

These effects are enhanced by the public's lack of technical knowledge about computers, software, and the Internet. Most people know little about what such equipment does. They may be unaware that a setting has changed in an important way or that their expectations about the setting are false. For example, a typical web page with banner advertisements looks like a single web page, but two banner ads on the same page can come from two different companies.[58] Also, we interface with only small parts of extended systems like the telephone system or the Internet. Such systems involve many intermediaries and much equipment that we cannot access; partly as a result, we know little about and have little control over what is going on inside the system.

This ignorance has normative implications. To say that a system is wrongly designed, or that it should have been designed differently, requires knowledge about design options and tradeoffs. If information about alternative design options does not reach the public, a basis for such normative judgments vanishes. But even if the public did perceive *bad* design, it might not perceive it as *wrong* design without knowledge that there was a decision to design it that way. Where equipment affects privacy, lack of knowledge is especially important because it is often difficult to detect privacy invasions.

Moreover, even if people did understand that a system had been wrongly designed, their lack of technical knowledge might prevent them from doing anything about it. One who realizes that web browsing leaves electronic traces by default and wants to avoid doing so might not know how to get access to or use web proxies or other technologies for anonymous browsing.[59]

C. Opportunities for Government Manipulation

The government often plays an important role in funding or shaping the infrastructure of these large, dispersed systems by endorsing standards for their deployment and design. Equipment usually becomes standardized around some design feature or feature set. Not only are there economies associated with standards, but many types of equipment must work together, requiring standard protocols.

Many standards are purely technical and may have no impact on constitutional rights, but some do directly affect our privacy or civil liberties. One example is the law enforcement-friendly Escrowed Encryption Standard (EES), which was promulgated as a Federal Information Processing Standard Publication (FIPS).[60] FIPSs (which are commonly used by federal agencies in their procurement specifications) "can have enormous significance to the private sector" even though private actors are not required to adopt them. In this case:

> [t]he government hoped that the adoption of the EES to ensure secure communications within the federal government and for communication of other parties with the federal government would lead to a significant demand for EES-compliant devices, thus making possible production in larger quantities and thereby driving unit costs down and making EES-compliant devices more attractive to other users.[61]

A current example is the Communications Assistance for Law Enforcement Act of 1994 (CALEA).[62] CALEA responded to the FBI's complaint that advanced telephone technologies would hinder law enforcement attempts to intercept communications. CALEA requires telephone companies to be able to provide law enforcement with the entire contents of a wiretapping target's communications. It also requires that they be able to provide "call setup information," that is, information about who is calling, who is being called, and other information not directly related to the content of the phone conversation.

CALEA in effect mandates that telephone systems be designed to facilitate government surveillance. Absent government interference, technological and economic change might have led some telecommunications service providers (TSPs) to offer encrypted telephone calls and other privacy enhancements that would safeguard call content and call-identifying information. These possibilities were largely foreclosed by CALEA for ordinary phone calls. Today, the FBI and other law enforcement agencies are seeking to extend CALEA to apply to certain Internet services such as broadband Internet access and the "Voice over Internet Protocol."

CALEA exemplifies how the state can make law with equipment, causing rules to be built into social practices. The design feature of "tappability" is embedded into the telephone system, and we have no choice about using TSPs if we are to make phone calls. We cannot exit the system. CALEA also shows how the opacity of architectural regulation tends to reduce barriers to governmental overreaching. During the CALEA debate, the law enforcement community assured Congress and privacy advocates that the FBI only wished to preserve its existing ability to surveil telephone calls. CALEA implementation, however, involved considerable private negotiation between law enforcement and the telecommunications industry, during which the FBI demanded and ultimately received significantly expanded surveillance powers. For instance, the FBI insisted that even when a wiretap target has left a conference call, it must be able to listen to the remaining call participants; as one commentator put it, "the FBI has insisted that the entire communications infrastructure of the United States must be redesigned to guarantee that it can always listen to those people after the crook disconnects from the call."[63]

In essence, the government is acting as a "norm entrepreneur": it has embedded a norm of tappability into the phone system, and seeks to embed that norm into other communications systems. Doing so may distort social processes of norm formation; even worse, courts may find that these equipment-defined parameters reflect a social consensus.[64] In my view, the government ought not act as a norm entrepreneur when the norms at issue concern constitutional rights.

D. Norms and Uncommon Knowledge

Obviously, a major theme in my discussion has been the role of knowledge—knowledge of equipment and social settings. But from the perspective of social norms, other kinds of knowledge are also important: knowledge about what other people think and do, and why.

For instance, privacy conventions or norms should be expected to arise from privacy practices—patterns of action that emerge over time, like our closing doors to protect our privacy, or our treating eavesdropping at keyholes as being improper.[65] When two people converse quietly in a park away from bystanders, they expect not to be approached or attended to by strangers, because a well-socialized person would recognize that they are speaking privately. If someone approaches or appears to eavesdrop, they adjust: stare silently, move away, or change the subject. The key relation here is between precautions and risks; precautions are geared to perceived likely risks, and vice versa.

Privacy behavior is thus interdependent: people "respond . . . to an environment that consists of other people responding to their environment, which consists of people responding to an environment of people's responses."[66] How privacy norms evolve remains unclear, but theorists suggest that behavior in repeated interactions can over time coordinate toward a norm, much as a well-trodden footpath visibly displays its popularity.[67] It is not implausible to hypothesize a "critical mass" model in which expectations "depend . . . on how many are behaving a particular way, or how much they are behaving that way."[68]

But the evolution of a convention or social expectation depends not only on the amount or frequency of behavior, but on our "common knowledge" of it.[69] Although we all may treat like situations alike, our actions are not "normal" without the second-order knowledge that others do and think the same as well, that we know they know, and so on.

In general, the coordination that leads to the emergence of norms requires common knowledge or at least publicity.[70] But a problem with privacy is that privacy risks and privacy behavior (for example, taking precautions) are often invisible. You might know that email is easily viewed by your Internet Service Provider (ISP), or that surfing the Internet exposes your browsing activity to your ISP, but you might not know whether others are also aware. Similarly, the precautions you take to protect your email or browsing, such as encrypting your email or browsing via an anonymizing service, tend to be private and are not visible to others as precautions.

Notions like critical mass and common knowledge help explain why public concern about privacy often has a "crisis" character. Many people are concerned about their privacy, but privacy breaches often happen in the background. And even when people are victims and know about the problem, they may think that theirs are isolated cases. But when at some point a privacy issue like identity theft becomes a mass media subject, the victims' private knowledge may become common knowledge that can support a normative judgment that something is wrong.[71]

III. Conclusion

We have come to accept that the law must adjust to the rapid pace of technological change. However, we should be alert to the possibility that government adjustments will also affect constitutional rights and norms. Government action that architects social settings and equipment can regulate our behavior as effectively as can sanction-backed rules.

In two respects, however, "law as architecture" is more dangerous to the concept of law than ordinary sanction-backed legal rules. Architectural regulation is less visible as law, not only because it can be surreptitiously embedded in settings or equipment but also because its enforcement is less public. Furthermore, it can be used to foreclose possibilities of social experience. It thus has a more secret social career than law as sanction-backed rules, and these effects are magnified with each new technology. Architectural regulation thus raises two important issues for law: the relationship between resources and rights, and the relationship between resources and social norms that translate content into constitutional law.

NOTES

1. *See, e.g.*, Joel Reidenberg, *Lex Informatica: The Formulation of Information Policy Rules through Technology*, 76 Tex. L. Rev. 553 (1998); Lawrence Lessig, Code and Other Laws of Cyberspace (1999) [hereinafter "Code"].

2. Reidenberg, *supra* note 1, at 554–555.

3. Lawrence Lessig, *The Law of the Horse: What Cyberlaw Might Teach*, 113 Harv. L. Rev. 501, 510 (1999).

4. Code, *supra* note 1, at 237.

5. *Id.*, at 98.

6. *Id.*, at 224.

7. Neal Katyal, on the other hand, argues that the transparency problem is overstated and recommends more government use of architectural regulation. See Neal Katyal, *Criminal Law in Cyberspace*, 149 U. Pa. L. Rev. 1003, 1105–1106 (2001); *id.*, at 1104 ("It is at least debatable as to whether government regulation of software and hardware would be less transparent than these realspace regulations.")

(noting lack of transparency associated with "informants, undercover cops, and many secret law enforcement techniques").

8. *Id.*, at 1049 (citation omitted).

9. *See generally* NATIONAL RESEARCH COUNCIL, COMPUTER SCIENCE AND TELECOMMUNICATIONS BOARD, CRYPTOGRAPHY'S ROLE IN SECURING THE INFORMATION SOCIETY 167–215, 265–273 (1996) (discussing government efforts to promote "law-enforcement-friendly" encryption) [hereinafter "CRISIS Report"].

10. *See, e.g.*, H. L. A. Hart, *Definition and Theory in Jurisprudence*, 70 LAW Q. REV. 37, 42–49 (1954) (using as a metaphor the rules of a game).

11. ROBERT ELLICKSON, ORDER WITHOUT LAW: HOW NEIGHBORS SETTLE DISPUTES 124 (1991) (describing social control in terms of different orders of rules and sanctions).

12. Ellickson uses the existence of "nonhierarchical systems of social control" to argue that social order often arises "spontaneously." *Id.*, at 4. But his notion of spontaneous social order is directed primarily against legal centralism, the presumption that the law is the center of social order. His characterization of social control remains grounded in "*rules* of normatively appropriate human behavior" that are "enforced through *sanctions*." *Id.*, at 124.

13. ELLICKSON, *supra* note 11, at 124. (Alternatively, a rule that carries no penalty for its breach may not really be a rule at all, at least not a legal rule.)

14. HOWARD BECKER, OUTSIDERS: STUDIES IN THE SOCIOLOGY OF DEVIANCE 1 (1997 ed.); *id.*, at 129–134 (using legislation as a model to analyze the career of both formal and informal rules).

15. ELLICKSON, *supra* note 11, at 130–131 (typing sanctions); *see also* ERVING GOFFMAN, RELATIONS IN PUBLIC 95 (1971) ("[a] social norm is that kind of guide for action which is supported by sanctions") (classifying sanctions as organized/formal or diffuse/informal).

16. *See, e.g.*, Richard McAdams, *The Origin, Development, and Regulation of Norms*, 96 MICH. L. REV. 338 (1997) (developing esteem theory); Daniel Gilman, *Of Fruitcakes and Patriot Games*, 90 GEO. L. J. 2387 (2002) (reviewing ERIC POSNER, LAW AND SOCIAL NORMS (2002) (arguing that compliance with social norms signals that one is a good cooperative partner)).

17. *See* Ted Sampsell-Jones, *Culture and Contempt: The Limitations of Expressive Criminal Law*, 27 SEATTLE U. L. REV. 133, 136–137 (2003) (showing how drug control laws have been championed as a way of expressing society's disapproval of drug use).

18. For an extended discussion of architectural crime-control techniques, *see* Neal Katyal, *Architecture as Crime Control*, 111 YALE L. J. 1039 (2002).

19. Because this focus on settings is probably the most important difference between legal and architectural regulation in my argument, it's worth thinking about settings for a moment. Some settings are spatially defined, like public streets; others are not, like the Internet or where we are when we're on the tele-

phone. Either way, settings are organized, usually by equipment. Curbs, traffic barriers, lane markers, stop signs, lights, and so on organize flows of cars and pedestrians on public streets.

Social settings are malleable; they can be organized in various ways. An intersection can be controlled by either signs or lights, and the initial decision between them will likely persist for some time. The equipment or resources in a setting can themselves be malleable; for example, lights along an arterial can be timed to promote flow at a certain speed, or lane dividers can be moved to accommodate traffic flow during commute hours. As the last example suggests, settings often are part of a larger system that may, depending on the system's need for coherence or compatibility, constrain what can be done in a particular setting.

It's important to distinguish internal and external constraints here. We might think of the public street setting in terms of a transportation frame of reference, but the First Amendment's "public forum" doctrine also frames public streets as areas for public expression. We might think of telephones and the Internet as a telecommunications system, but law enforcement thinks of it as a surveillance system. See text at nn.62–63 (discussing CALEA).

20. CODE, *supra* note 1, at 96–97.

21. *Id.*, at 237.

22. Katyal, *supra* note 18, at 1072 (noting that "crime-control strategies based on legal sanctions or public norms . . . generally work best when a potential offender has knowledge of them.").

23. *See generally* Nancy G. La Vigne, *Safe Transport: Security by Design on the Washington Metro, in* SITUATIONAL CRIME PREVENTION: SUCCESSFUL CASE STUDIES (R. V. Clarke ed., 1997).

24. Nancy LaVigne, *Visibility and Vigilance: Metro's Situational Approach to Preventing Subway Crime, in* NATIONAL INSTITUTE OF JUSTICE: RESEARCH IN BRIEF (Jeremy Travis, dir., Nov. 1997) (noting that situational crime prevention "aims to reduce criminal opportunities"), *available at* http://www.ncjrs.org/pdffiles/166372.pdf (last accessed Nov. 8, 2004).

25. *Id.*, at 2.

26. *Id.*

27. *Id.*

28. *Id.*, at 5. But see LaVigne, *supra* note 23, at 12 (surveillance cameras "mainly serve a psychological purpose because they are read out at the station manager's kiosk, and often no one is there.") (citation omitted).

29. *Id.*

30. *Id.*

31. CRISIS Report, *supra* note 9, at 187–188.

32. BECKER, *supra* note 14, at 129; *see also* Edna Ullmann-Margalit, *Revision of Norms,* 100 ETHICS 756 (1990) ("Norms, as social institutions, have careers. They emerge, endure, pass away.").

33. WALTER BENJAMIN, ILLUMINATIONS 239 (Hannah Arendt ed., Harry Zohn trans., 1988).

34. *Id.*, at 240.

35. *Id.*; *see also* Katyal, *supra* note 18, at 1072 (quoting an architecture dean as saying "you live in architecture, and it affects you whether you're even conscious of it.") (citation omitted).

36. William L. F. Felstiner et al., *The Emergence and Transformation of Disputes: Naming, Blaming, and Claiming*, 15 L. & SOC'Y REV. 631 (1981) (noting the role of "perceived injurious event"). Such perceptions can change over time; for many years, the vast majority of Americans likely conceived of curbs as lacking wheelchair ramps, which thus restricted the mobility of disabled persons. Those confined to wheelchairs probably thought of curbs differently.

37. *E.g.*, McIntyre v. Ohio Elec. Comm'n, 514 U.S. 334 (1995).

38. *See, e.g.*, Russell Dyer, *Apache Logs*, UNIX REVIEW, July 2004, *at* http//www.unixreview.com/documents/s=8989/ur0407i/.

39. Current legal scholarship views norms as evolving under competition. *See, e.g.*, Randal Picker, *Simple Games in a Complex World: A Generative Approach to the Adoption of Norms*, 64 U. CHI. L. REV. 1225 (1997); Symposium, *Law, Economics, & Norms*, 144 U. PA. L. REV. 1643 (1996).

40. Rakas v. Illinois, 439 U.S. 128, 143 n.12 (1978) (noting that the Fourth Amendment turns on social "understandings," and that "legitimation of expectations of privacy by law must have a source outside of the Fourth Amendment").

41. United States v. White, 401 U.S. 745, 786 (1971) (Harlan, J., dissenting); *cf. Rakas*, 439 U.S. at 143 n.12 (noting that it is "merely tautological" to base legitimate expectations "primarily on cases deciding exclusionary-rule issues in criminal cases").

42. United States v. U.S. District Court, 407 U.S. 297, 317 (1972) (the Fourth Amendment embodies "historical judgment," under which "unreviewed executive discretion" may endanger privacy and speech).

43. Cass Sunstein, *Social Norms and Social Roles*, 96 COLUM. L. REV. 903, 966 (1996) ("efforts to change norms . . . should not be allowed to invade rights").

44. Smith v. Maryland, 442 U.S. 735, 740 n.5 (1979) ("when an individual's subjective expectations had been 'conditioned' by influences alien to well-recognized Fourth Amendment freedoms, those subjective expectations obviously could play no meaningful role in ascertaining the scope of Fourth Amendment protection. . . . a normative inquiry would be proper.").

45. *See generally* Glenn Chatmas Smith, *We've Got Your Number! (Is It Constitutional to Give It Out?): Caller IdentiWcation Technology and the Right to Informational Privacy*, 37 U.C.L.A. Rev. 145 (1989).

46. *See generally* John Archea, *The Place of Architectural Factors in Behavioral Theories of Privacy*, 33 J. SOC. ISS. 116 (1977).

47. Goffman, *supra* note 15, at 294 (discussing "lurk lines").

48. *Id.*, at 286.

49. Katz v. United States, 389 U.S. 347, 352 (1967). The holding in *Katz* may illustrate Robert Sugden's point that conventions can spread by analogy. Robert Sugden, *Spontaneous Order*, 3 J. Econ. Persp. 85, 93–94 (1989).

50. United States v. Muckenthaler, 548 F.2d 240, 245 (8th Cir. 1978).

51. Sociologists of technology argue that when engineers design equipment, they make assumptions or hypothesize about the world into which the equipment will be inserted: a vision of the world is inscribed into the equipment, defining a framework of action along with the actions and the social space in which actors are supposed to act. *See* Madeleine Akrich, *The De Scription of Technical Objects*, in Wiebe E. Bijker and John Law (eds.), Shaping Technology/Building Society: Studies in Sociotechnical Change 208 (1992) (using example of African hoe designed to be used by two people); *see also* Helen Nissenbaum, How Computer Systems Embody Values, Computer 118 (March 2001) (arguing that scientists and engineers should design information technologies in light of social, ethical, and political values), *available at* http://www.nyu.edu/projects/nissenbaum/papers/embodyvalues.pdf.

52. Code, *supra* note 1, at 98.

53. Junkbusters Corporation, Junkbusters Alert on Web Privacy, *at* http://www.junkbusters.com/cgi-bin/privacy (last visited Nov. 10, 2004).

54. *See* Cass Sunstein, *Switching the Default Rule*, 77 NYU L. Rev. 106 (2002) (discussing the power of defaults, especially in the employment context).

55. *See* Howard Becker, Art Worlds 58 (1984).

56. *See* California Bankers Ass'n v. Shultz, 416 U.S. 21 (1974) (upholding Bank Secrecy Act record keeping and reporting requirements against constitutional challenge).

57. The FBI's 2004 petition to the Federal Communications Commission, which seeks to clarify telecommunications carriers' duties under the Communications Assistance to Law Enforcement Act of 1994, argues that "a carrier would not be permitted to describe any end-user surcharge applied by the carrier to recover its CALEA implementation and compliance costs as mandated by the Commission or the federal government (*e.g.*, the FBI)." U.S. Department of Justice, Federal Bureau of Investigation, and Drug Enforcement Agency, Joint Petition for Expedited Rulemaking to Resolve Various Outstanding Issues Concerning the Implementation of the Communications Assistance for Law Enforcement Act, RM-10865, at 67 n.13 (Mar. 10, 2004). The FCC initiated rule making on this subject in August 2004. *See* Communications Assistance for Law Enforcement Act and Broadband Access and Services, Notice of Proposed Rulemaking and Declaratory Ruling, FCC 04-187, 19 FCC Rcd 15676 (rel. Aug. 9, 2004).

58. Junkbusters Corporation, *supra* note 53.

59. For example, the Anonymizer http://www.anonymizer.com is a commercial service for privacy-enhanced web browsing; Tor is software that can help people browse and publish relatively anonymously. *See generally* http://tor.eff.org.

60. NATIONAL INSTITUTE OF STANDARDS AND TECHNOLOGY, U.S. COMMERCE DEP'T'S TECHNOLOGY ADMINISTRATION, FEDERAL INFORMATION PROCESSING STANDARD PUB. 185, ESCROWED ENCRYPTION STANDARD (1994).

61. CRISIS Report, *supra* note 9, at 222–225.

62. *See* PUB. L. No. 103-414, 108 Stat. 4279 (codified at 47 U.S.C. §§ 1001–1010 and various sections of Title 18 and Title 47 of the U.S. Code).

63. Stewart Baker, *Regulating Technology for Law Enforcement*, 4 Tex. Rev. L. & Pol. 53, 57 (1999).

64. Thus, in *Katz* the Supreme Court found that given phone booths with doors, closing the door clearly constituted a privacy precaution, while in *Smith* making phone calls, given that the telephone company logged one's calling records, negated any possible privacy claim.

65. *See* EDNA ULLMAN-MARGOLIT, THE EMERGENCE OF NORMS 8 (1977) (norms are "the resultant of complex patterns of behavior of a large number of people over a protracted period of time").

66. THOMAS SCHELLING, MICROMOTIVES AND MACROBEHAVIOR 14 (1978).

67. "Everyone conforms, everyone expects others to conform, and everyone has good reason to conform because conforming is in each person's best interest when everyone else plans to conform." H. Peyton Young, *The Economics of Convention*, 10 J. ECON. PERSP. 105 (1996).

68. SCHELLING, *supra* note 66, at 94.

69. "A proposition is 'common knowledge' among a group of individuals if all know the proposition to be true, all know that the others know the proposition to be true, all know that all others know the proposition to be true, and so on." Paul Mahoney and Chris Sanchirico, *Norms, Repeated Games, and the Role of Law*, 91 CAL. L. REV. 1281, 1301 n.42 (2003); *see* Michael Chwe, *Culture, Circles, and Commercials: Publicity, Common Knowledge, and Social Coordination*, 10 RATIONALITY & SOC'Y 47, 49–50 (1998).

70. *See, e.g.*, McAdams, *supra* note 16, at 388, 400–405 (discussing role of publicity and visible consensus to norm formation).

71. *Cf.* Chwe, *supra* note 69, at 59 (noting that network TV is "best mass common knowledge generator").

4

Where Computer Security Meets National Security

Helen Nissenbaum

Over the course of the past decade, the mandate of computer security has grown in complexity and seriousness as information technologies have saturated society and, simultaneously, the threats have multiplied in number and sophistication.[1] Although widely publicized attacks such as denials-of-service, viruses, worms, and unauthorized break-ins create the impression that the work of computer security specialists is clear-cut, this chapter holds that the broad purpose of computer security, in fact, is ambiguous. At least two prominent conceptions of security vie for the attention and resources of experts, policy makers, and public opinion. One, focusing on individual systems and networks, has its roots in computer science and engineering communities. The other, a more recent concern, focuses on collective and institutional systems, reflecting the influence of political and national security actors. Currently, these two conceptions exist side by side. But their inherent differences spell tensions in future social, political, and technical decision making.

The purpose of this chapter is to elaborate the sources and implications of these tensions so as to help guide choices. Although a full account would address outcomes in social, political, and technical arenas, this chapter focuses mainly on the technical, asking, for this arena, how the two conceptions of security are likely to play out and what reasons we might have for favoring one conception over the other. The decision to focus on implications for technical choices is not arbitrary but comes from one of the key motivating interests of this chapter, namely, how values, generally, are embodied in technical systems and devices (henceforth "technologies"), both in their design and regulation. Before picking up the chapter's main thread, we take a brief detour on the subject of values in design of technologies, showing how they have shaped our questions about security.

Values in Technical Design

A significant body of work in the humanistic and social study of technology advances an understanding of technology not merely as an independent material form which acts on people and societies but as political to its very core. That technical systems and devices can serve as venues for political struggle has found expression in a range of scholarly works, from Langdon Winner's famous assertion that artifacts "have politics"[2] to lesser-known claims such as Bryan Pfaffenberger's that STS (Science and Technology Studies) be conceived as "the political philosophy of our time."[3] While a large and excellent body of scholarship in STS and philosophy of technology has produced theories and case analyses that convincingly argue in favor of this fundamental claim, recent initiatives, spearheaded in the context of computer and information technologies, focus on the practical question of how to bring these ideas to bear on the design of the information and communications systems that increasingly shape the opportunities and daily experiences of people living in technologically advanced societies. The rationale behind this pragmatic turn is this: if values shape technical systems, then responsible creators and regulators should trust neither serendipity nor possibly illegitimate agency to produce the best outcomes. Ethical and political values ought to be added to traditional considerations and constraints guiding the design and regulation of these systems, such as functionality, efficiency, elegance, safety, and, more recently, usability.

Although we are still at the early stages of formulating appropriate methodological principles, this much is clear: implementing values in the design and regulation of information and communications technologies requires not only technical (engineering and scientific) adeptness and a firm empirical grounding in how people perceive and are affected by them (as may be learned from usability studies, surveys, and the like), but also an adequate grasp of key conceptual definitions as well as normative theories in which these are embedded. It is laudable for well-meaning designers and developers to seek,[4] for example, to preserve privacy, or provide accessibility to the disabled, or promote sociality and cooperation. However, unless such interventions are guided by sound concepts of privacy, equity, welfare, and cooperation, respectively, and well-reasoned, theoretically grounded justifications for choices and trade-offs, their efforts could easily miss the mark. For this reason, it is of far more than "academic" interest to ponder the meaning of security in computer security, given that the choices of designers and regulators could have a significant effect on outcomes for the users of computers and networked information systems. This chapter aims to sketch some of the alternatives that are likely to follow our two interpretations of security.

Security deserves a place alongside privacy, intellectual property, equity, and other values that have been vigorously debated in light of developments in and application of digital electronic information technologies. So far, security has been treated primarily as a technical problem, despite its being a rich, complex, and contested concept with variable shadings of specialized and general meanings. Like the values mentioned above, security has been stretched and challenged by radical alterations in information and communications environments generated by computing and networks. It is important to understand what precisely it is that is being sought and sometimes achieved in the technologies and regulations aspiring to produce a state of security. If we can unambiguously describe the valued outcome that is the goal of computer (and network) security, then, at the very least, we will be better qualified to judge whether the vast and loosely connected community of scientists and engineers working in academia, in governmental and corporate research institutions, and in the back rooms of enumerable private and public organizations and businesses is achieving its mission. Finally, an explicit expression of the goal, or goals, of security efforts will make an evaluation of these goals possible: are the goals morally grounded, are they worth pursuing, and, if so, at what cost?

Two Conceptions of Computer Security

Taking note of what has been said, over the past few years, about the mission of computer security, two conceptions seem dominant. One, here labeled "technical computer security," has roots in the scientific and technical field of the same name and has been developed and articulated by the field's leaders, in such venues as professional conferences, scholarly and research journals, and committee reports of the National Research Council.[5] The other, here labeled "cybersecurity" and a more recent entry to the public sphere, is typically articulated by government authorities, corporate heads, and leaders of other nongovernmental sectors. It links computer security to traditional notions of national security. At present, these two conceptions exist side by side, each one angling for the attention of key social actors including government agencies, technical experts and institutions, corporations, policy experts, pundits, the general public, and, importantly, the media (popular as well as specialized).

The two conceptions, while not strictly incompatible on all points, emphasize different issues and, as a result, pull in different directions. In order to understand why these differences are significant, we need to flesh them out a little more.

Technical Computer Security

Within the technical community, the core mission of computer (and network) security, traditionally, has been defined by three goals: availability; integrity, and confidentiality. In other words, the work of technical experts in the field of computer security has generally focused on protecting computer systems and their users against attacks, and threats of attack, in three general categories:

- Attacks that render systems, information, and networks unavailable to users, including for example, denial-of-service attacks, and malware, such as viruses, worms, and so on, that disable systems or parts of them.
- Attacks that threaten the integrity of information or of systems and networks by corrupting data, destroying files or disrupting code, and the like.
- Attacks that threaten the confidentiality of information and communications, such as interception of emails, unauthorized access to systems and data, spyware that enables third parties to learn about system configuration or web browsing habits.

Although instantiations of these types of attacks have evolved over time, the categories have remained surprisingly robust. This is not to say that the field has remained static, as each new form of even the same type of attack requires novel defenses. Those who undertake to provide security understand that their actions may not lead to total and permanent invulnerability, but at best a temporary advantage against wily adversaries who themselves are engaged in a race in continually evolving tools for penetrating these defenses. Further, the boundaries of what is included in technical security continue to expand to meet new applications. For example, as electronic commerce has become more common, security experts have sought technical means to authenticate identities and prevent repudiation of financial commitment. Some have argued for extending the mission of technical security even further to the broader concept of "trustworthiness," which includes features such as survivability and dependability not only in the face of deliberate attack but also accidental failures. (See for example the CSTB report on Trust in Cyberspace and DIRC project definition.)[6] For purposes of the discussion here, we will assume the narrower conception of computer security focusing on protection against deliberate attack.

Cybersecurity

In the conception that I will call cybersecurity, the issues of greatest danger fall roughly into three categories:

1. Threats posed by the use of networked computers as a medium, or staging ground for antisocial, disruptive, or dangerous organizations and communications. These include, for example, the websites of various racial and ethnic hate groups, sites that coordinate the planning and perpetration of crimes (especially fraud), websites and other mechanisms that deliver of child pornography, and—perhaps of most urgent concern as of the writing of this chapter—use of the Internet for inducing terrorist actions and for the operational planning of terrorist attacks.[7]
2. Threats of attack on critical societal infrastructures, including utilities, banking, government administration, education, health care, manufacturing, and communications media. Here, the argument is that because critical systems are increasingly dependent on networked information systems, they are vulnerable to network attacks. Potential attackers include rogue U.S. nationals, international terrorist organizations, or hostile nations engaging in "cyberwar."
3. Threats to the networked information system itself, ranging from disablement of various kinds and degrees to—in the worst case—complete debility.[8]

The central claim of this chapter is that two conceptions of security seem to drive efforts in computer (and network) security and that their differences are significant for regulation and design. A difference that is most immediately obvious is scope: cybersecurity overlaps with technical security but encompasses more. Scope, as I argue below, is not all that separates the two. Other differences will become evident as we develop the two conceptions through a series of questions, beginning with the most rudimentary: why security? In other words, why are the issues raised by the two conceptions matters of security? Closely connected with this is a second basic question: what contributes to the moral force of computer security, so conceived?

Security and Its Moral Force

A foundational assumption of both conceptions is that the material concerns they raise are rightly construed as security concerns. Although this apparently self-evident proposition may prove unproblematic, it is worth taking a moment to draw the connection explicitly, starting with a general or ordinary account of security as safety, freedom from the unwanted effects of another's actions,[9] the condition of being protected from danger, injury, attack (physical and nonphysical), and other harms, and protection against threats of all kinds. From here, the question to ask is why the activities cited by various accounts of computer security warrant the label of "threat of harm," against which people deserve to be secured.

With technical computer security, the promise is protection against attacks by adversaries whose actions deprive victims of access to or use of systems and networks (availability); damaging, spoiling, or altering their systems or data (integrity); and revealing or diverting information to inappropriate recipients (confidentiality). These are security concerns to the extent that we agree that the attacks in question, in the context of computing, information flow, digital electronic communication, and so on, constitute what we commonly agree is harm. This is key and not as obvious as it might at first appear. It is important because the quest for computer security has moral force only to the extent that it promotes the common value of freedom from harm. In other words, the issue is not merely why these are classifiable as security concerns but why people *deserve*, or have a right, to be thus secured.

Antithetical to this picture is a more cynical view of the goals of technical computer security as a quest for increasingly effective ways to protect individuals and institutions against actions that threaten the fulfillment of desires and subjective preferences, irrespective of their moral standing. Ross Anderson, a computer scientist who also comments on policy implications of technology, presents such a turn in computer security—driven more by what customers want than by a mission to provide protection against objectively (or intersubjectively) construed harm. Illustrative cases are moves by corporate entities to secure their assets and market standing, including, for example, Microsoft creating so-called "trusted computing" which would restrict individuals in the way they use their computers, particularly in relation to proprietary information. Anderson cites Hewlett-Packard as another example, applying cryptographic techniques to prevent consumers from installing third-party printer cartridges in HP printers. Cases like these portray computer security as an amoral practice and security engineers as guns for hire working to promote vested interests (securing parochial benefits) rather than as agents of the public good.[10]

If technical computer security were directed *only* to the task of securing the private interests of stakeholders who could afford such protection, it could not sustain the compelling claim on *public* attention, approbation, and financial investment that it currently holds. Our point of departure, therefore, is that the focus is broader in two ways. First, the implicit beneficiaries of computer security are all those who use, own, or possibly even are affected by computers and networks, including ordinary persons as well as individual institutional agents of any size. Second, still to be shown, is that the promised benefits are generally valued by the relevant surrounding communities. By implication, computer security is a value, and the activities of technical security experts are of moral import, if the stated end toward which they are directed result in protection from (conditions generally thought to be) harms.

More specifically, it is not surprising that a society that values the institution of private property and understands computer systems and information as possible forms of property would value integrity, given that assaults on system integrity can easily be construed as a form of property damage. Further, since confidentiality is typically a valued aspect of privacy, intrusions into systems or communications are readily conceived as instances of harm. The case of system and data availability is slightly more complex as one could argue for its protection on grounds of traditional property rights (both "use and enjoyment") and the owners' entitlement to alienate the property in question from others. But denying a user availability also constitutes a violation of autonomy as it interferes with an increasingly important means of identity formation as well as pursuit of self-determined ends in a world where so many important actions and transactions are mediated through networked computers. Because system availability, integrity, and confidentiality are also instrumental to achieving other ends, such as safe commercial transactions, productivity, robust communication, and more, threats to them may be harmful in many ways beyond those listed above.

When the two foundational questions are asked of cybersecurity, namely, why are the issues it raises matters of security and what are the sources of its moral weight? the answers are different. I argue that here, the meaning of security is drawn not from ordinary usage but from usage developed in the specialized arena of national security. The difference, therefore, is not merely one of scope but of meaning, and what follows from this difference is of practical significance. The argument is inspired by insights and a vocabulary developed within the Copenhagen School of thought in the area of international security studies.

Securitization: The Copenhagen School

In the field of international security studies, traditional approaches frequently called "realist" have been challenged by those taking more general and "discursive" ones. As depicted by these challengers, realist theories adopt an overly narrow view of national security, focusing on the protection of physical borders and strategic assets against military attacks by foreign states. The broader view includes not only terrorist attacks occurring within national borders but threats other than military ones. Also resisting the realists' treatment of threats as objectively conceived and characterized, some of the challengers opt for so-called constructivist or discursive accounts of national and international security. One such approach, offered by the Copenhagen School,[11] whose key proponents are Barry Buzan and Ole Waever, provides a useful framework for articulating differences between conceptions of security in cybersecurity and technical computer security. Any further discussion of differences between realist and discursive approaches to security studies, however, lie beyond the scope of this chapter.

In proposing a constructivist framework, Buzan and Waever are less concerned with providing an objective characterization of threats, vulnerabilities, and modes of defense, and more with providing a systematic account of the ways specific conditions, states of affairs, or events are posed by significant social actors as threats to security and come to be widely accepted as such. They call this rendering of a security threat "securitization," which becomes the fundamental explanatory construct of their framework. Before using the notion of securitization to highlight differences between the two conceptions of security in computer security, a few more features of the framework need to be specified.

The concept of securitization generalizes certain elements of traditional approaches to national security in which the typical landscape includes a threat of military attack, the nation-state under threat, and the specific steps leaders take to ensure the state's continued security (through such means as defensive action, shoring up vulnerabilities, and so forth). The Copenhagen School moves from this landscape to one in which the threat need not be military and the referent object need not be the state. Further, its assertions are not about actual threats, referent objects, and defensive maneuvers but about the successful portrayal of threats as security threats and what this means. Accordingly, the questions that concern Buzan, Waever, and their colleagues are about the typical threats, agents, and referent objects that characterize conditions in which securitization of a threat is attempted and also those in which securitization of that threat succeeds. We briefly summarize some of their answers.

From the traditional conception of security in national security, this account moves away from the paradigmatic military threat to a more general notion. What it retains as a key feature of threats capable of being securitized is that they be presented not merely as harmful but as dire, imminent, and existential. A threat must be presented to an audience and accepted by that audience as fatal to a referent object's very existence. These are life-and-death threats, existential threats to a group, a valued entity, a way of life, or ideology. In the case of the state, a securitized harm is one that threatens national sovereignty and political autonomy, of subjugation by a foreign will. Presenting something as a threat to a society, culture, or religion involves claiming it as a critical challenge to social, religious, or cultural identity, to a historical way of life, to hallowed traditions.

A similar extension occurs in what can count as the referent object— not only the state but other entities as well. The field is not entirely open, as Buzan and Waever argue that only general collectives or collective values count as such. Only entities that an audience believes *have* to survive are likely to rouse the necessary degree of salience and concern. The nation-state, at least in the present era, is an obvious contender but also such valued entities as the environment, religion, culture, economy, and so on. Obviously the range of threats will vary in relation to entities. Thus, pollution may be a dire threat for the environment, depression a dire threat to an economy, assimilation for a religion, and so on. Referent objects highly unlikely to be securitized include specific individuals, or what Buzan and Waever call midlevel, limited collectives like firms, institutions, or clubs, even if the threats in question are existential. An exception might occur if a clear link can be drawn between the survival of the midlevel entity and the greater collective.[12] The threat of Japanese automakers, for example, to the profitability of the Ford automobile company, or even to its continued existence, is unlikely to be securitized unless proponents are able to launch a convincing argument that Ford's demise will lead to a crash in the entire economy. In general, to securitize an activity or state of affairs is to present it as an urgent, imminent, extensive, and existential threat to a significant collective.

A third important aspect of the framework is agency. One half of the story is who has the capacity or power to securitize, to be a securitizing actor. These typically will include high-ranking government officials— elected or appointed, members of cabinet, high-ranking military personnel, the president (or prime minister). It is possible, however, that others in a society might have achieved sufficient salience and persuasive capacity to construct the conception of threat necessary for securitization. One could imagine that trusted media sources, high-ranking jurists, and possibly corporate personalities might accumulate this degree of salience. It is also possible that highly visible lobbyists, pressure groups, and the public media might have the capacity indirectly to move government officials toward securitizing given threats. The other half of the story is whether securitizing moves are accepted. Here, we must settle for something like a preponderance of views in the larger social or national context. Most importantly, however, in order for securitization of a threat to have succeeded we need both securitizing moves by relevant actors as well as acceptance by the surrounding communities.

Application to Cybersecurity

Examining in greater detail ways in which the three categories of threats to cybersecurity have been presented by prominent voices in government, the private sector, and media, we can detect clear moves to securitize.

These moves invest cybersecurity with the specialized meanings of securitization, in contrast with what I earlier called the general or ordinary meaning. In these moves, the dangers in question are posed as imminent, urgent, and dire for the United States and the rest of the free world.

The first threat category stems from the far-reaching power of the "new medium" to serve as a highly effective tool for one-to-one and many-to-many interactive communication, as well as one-to-many broadcast communication. Even prior to the attacks of September 11, 2001, the media played up government worries over the dangerous potential of the Net. In February 2001, for example, *USA Today* published a widely cited article claiming that government officials feared Al-Qaeda was using steganography, a cryptographic method for concealing secret information within another message or digital image, to convey instructions for terrorist attacks and for posting blueprints of targets on websites, such as sports chat rooms and pornographic bulletin boards.[13] Ralf Bendrath cites Leslie G. Wiser Jr.'s testimony before the House of Representatives in August 2001, asserting that terrorist groups are using the Internet to "formulate plans, raise funds, spread propaganda, and to communicate securely."[14]

In the period following the attacks, these themes cropped up regularly in the public media, as, for example, in this news report:

> Today bin Laden is believed to school his soldiers in high-tech tools of communication. E-mail, online dead drops, satellite phones, cell phones, encryption and digital camouflage called steganography . . . are all tools of Al Qaeda, bin Laden's terrorist network. Those high-tech tools enable members of Al Qaeda to communicate with terrorist cells (or groups) hidden around the world.[15]

Another article reported about Al-Qaeda communication strategy as described by one of its members, captured by the United States:

> The Qaeda communications system that Mr. Khan used and helped operate relied on websites and e-mail addresses in Turkey, Nigeria and the northwestern tribal areas of Pakistan, according to the information provided by a Pakistani intelligence official.
>
> The official said Mr. Khan had told investigators that couriers carried handwritten messages or computer disks from senior Qaeda leaders hiding in isolated border areas to hard-line religious schools in Pakistan's Northwest Frontier Province. Other couriers then ferried them to Mr. Khan on

the other side of the country in the eastern city of Lahore, and the computer expert then posted the messages in code on Web sites or relayed them electronically, the Pakistani official said.

Mr. Khan had told investigators that most of Al Qaeda's communications were now done through the Internet, the official said.[16]

The second and third threat categories, presented as catastrophic cyberattacks and debilitating attacks on critical infrastructure, have been aired in dramatic terms. In the following lengthy quotation from a January 7, 2000, White House press briefing, moves to securitize are evident as Chief of Staff John Podesta, Secretary of Commerce Bill Daley, James Madison University president Linwood Rose, and National Coordinator for Security, Infrastructure Protection and Counter-Terrorism Dick Clarke, answered questions about computer and network security.

JOHN PODESTA: "And just as in the 1950s when we were building an economy based on a new transportation system, a new interstate highway system and we put guardrails on that transportation system, we're here today to talk about how we can better protect the information technology and infrastructure of the information technology economy—not only for the government, but for the private sector, as well. . . .

". . . It's not just computers; it's the electric power grid, it's the other things that we learned so much about during our run-up to Y2K. The banking, financial industry—increasingly every single sector of the economy is tied in, linked through e-commerce, through the use of computer technology, to this kind of critical infrastructure that has developed over the course of the 1970s, 1980s and 1990s.

SECRETARY DALEY: ". . . no question, we have a new economy and we have an economy that is much more dependent, as we enter this next century, on information technologies. So our defending of this economy is most important to us. . . .

One of the consequences of leading this e-world is that we, as I mentioned, are more dependent on information technologies in our country, and therefore we're more subject to new and different kinds of threats.

Q: "What's the biggest threat that you're trying to guard against? Is it hackers and vandalism? Is it criminals? Or is it domestic or foreign terrorism?"

MR. CLARKE: "I think it's all of the above. There's a spectrum, from the teenage hacker who sort of joy rides through cyberspace, up through industrial espionage, up through fraud and theft. And up at the far end of the spectrum, to another country using information warfare against our infra-structure."

SECRETARY DALEY: "This is the first time in American history that we in the federal government, alone, cannot protect our infrastructure. We can't hire an army or a police force that's large enough to protect all of America's cell phones of pagers or computer networks—not when 95 percent of these infrastructures are owned and operated by the private sector."

Picking up on themes of critical dependencies on information networks, endorsement for moves to securitize comes not only from government authorities or other representatives of public interest but from corporate owners of intellectual property. They have tried, with some success, to hitch their star to the security wagon by claiming not only that rampant unauthorized copying and distribution of proprietary works poses an existential threat to their business but by presenting their possible demise as a dire threat to the U.S. economy. They have singled out as the "danger-ous" activity from which we ought to be protected out-of-control peer-to-peer file sharing.[17]

The Net itself has been presented as a potential battlefield for compre-hensive attack on the state.[18] According to this picture, warfare waged online through computer viruses, worms, and other malware could serve an enemy's strategic ends by disrupting "access or flow of forces" to a sen-sitive region.[19] A similar notion is embodied in remarks by Secretary of Defense Donald Rumsfeld at a June 6, 2001 meeting of the NATO Council, where he referred to the dangers of "attacks from cyberspace." This rather murky reference, nevertheless, conveys a sense of cyberspace as potentially an embattled frontier.[20] Imparting a sense of the magnitude and serious-ness of cyberthreats, Curt Weldon, chairman of the National Security Committee's subcommittee on military research and development, invokes a powerful national memory, "It's not a matter of if America has an electronic Pearl Harbor, it's a matter of when."[21]

For those who warn of cyberspace as a staging ground for an aggressive attack on the nation, another reason not to underestimate the dangers inherent in the networked information infrastructure is asymmetry. The Net enables a magnitude of damage hugely disproportional to the size and relative strength—measured in conventional terms—of an attacker. Expe-rience has shown that even a single, not especially skilled, attacker can cause considerable inconvenience, if not outright damage. This means that the United States must guard against the usual array of world powers as well as all adversaries with sufficient technical know-how. In official statements about cybersecurity adversaries of many types are mentioned, ranging from malevolent teenagers, common or organized criminals and terrorists, to hostile nations. According to Bendrath, successive U.S. administrations under Bill Clinton and George W. Bush have cycled through opinions over the source of greatest concern, whether organized criminals, terrorists, or hostile states. For a country like the United States, which is in a position to draw confidence from its size and strength, the notion of a small but disproportionately destructive "asymmetric threat" challenges national security orthodoxy and deepens collective worry.

Contrasts

The point of the discussion so far has been to educe contrasts between the conceptions of security information technical security and cybersecurity, respectively. There are several sources of difference. One is the degree of severity and the nature of the perceived threats. Technical security acknowledges a broader variation in both degree of harm and its type, including damage to property, incursions on autonomy, privacy, and productivity. Cybersecurity, in moves to securitize various threats, posits them as dire, possibly existential. A second difference is due to differences in the prototypical referent object. The former seeks security primarily for individual notes (people, agents, institutions), while the latter focuses on collective security (state or nation). A third difference, discussed in the next section, is due to divergent paths each conception carves for actions taken (preemptive or punitive) in the name of security.

The Practical Importance of Securitization

Both conceptions are intended to carry moral weight, that is, they serve as a source of justification for thinking that computer security is important and worth doing something about. They do so, however, in different ways, and this difference matters. The conception that informs technical computer security suggests an array of responses that would normally be recommended for a range of unethical (including criminal) actions. More will be said about this later. By contrast, the logic of national security, which informs those who move to securitize online threats, calls for extraordinary responses; security discourse not only heightens the salience and priority of designated threats but also bestows legitimacy on a particular range of reactions.[22] As observed by James Der Derian:

> No other concept in international relations packs the metaphysical punch, nor commands the disciplinary power of "security." In its name peoples have alienated their fears, rights and powers to gods, emperors, and most recently, sovereign states, all to protect themselves from the vicissitudes of nature—as well as from other gods, emperors, and sovereign states. In its name weapons of mass destruction have been developed which transfigured national interest into a security dilemma based on a suicide pact. And, less often noted in IR, in its name billions have been made and millions killed while scientific knowledge has been furthered and intellectual dissent muted.[23]

Similarly Buzan, Waever, and Wilde write, "What is essential (to securitization) is the designation of an existential threat requiring emergency action or special measures and the acceptance of that designation by a significant audience."[24] These "special measures" typically involve bending rules of normal governance, and as matters of national security they are lifted—presumably temporarily—outside, or beyond the bounds of political procedure.[25] In the face of securitized threats and times of national crises, even liberal democracies accept breaks from "business as usual," including (1) reduced restraints on government powers, frequently manifested in the curtailment of civil liberties. In the USA PATRIOT Act, for example, some have seen a worrying move to extend wide-ranging, less-restricted powers of national security agencies into the domestic realm as necessary for the fight against terrorism; (2) breaks from normal democratic procedure, including government secrecy normally not tolerated by citizens. (This, too, has been seen in the period following the September 11 attacks.)[26] Other breaks occur when, in the name of security, officials circumvent normal principles of justice, such as the routine use of racial profiling, officially forbidden in domestic law enforcement;[27] (3) steep incremental funding for security agencies and infrastructures. Although questioned in some quarters, most public leaders and citizens seem to accept national defense as having a high (perhaps the highest) priority claim on collective resources, even channeling resources away from other valued public goals.[28]

Implications for Computer Security

I began the chapter by claiming that distinct conceptions of computer security could steer practical efforts along diverging paths, spelling tension in future political and technical decision making. How this tension will be resolved is not clear, though our survey has illustrated support for both conceptions among political leaders, technical experts, industry lobbyists, heads of security agencies, and the media.[29] Moves to securitize are clearly evident but not endorsed by a critical enough mass to outweigh competing conceptions.[30] In the concluding sections of this chapter, the goal is not to settle the question whether technical computer security or cybersecurity (and securitization) prevails, or which will prevail in conceptualizing online threat (a great deal more empirical study would be needed) but briefly to outline the distinct futures we face if one or the other does.

To map out the possibilities, consider a hypothetical neighborhood that has experienced a sharp rise in break-ins and household burglaries. Gathered to discuss security strategies, worried residents are split between two alternatives: in strategy A, public funds will fit each household with state-of-the-art locks, motion detection systems, and burglar alarms linked directly to the local police station. Residents would also subscribe to a neighborhood watch program. In strategy B, public law enforcement agencies will be brought in to install floodlights in all public spaces as well as centrally managed networked surveillance cameras fitted with facial recognition systems. Checkpoints staffed with private security officers as well as, occasionally, police will be posted at key intersections.[31] While common sense tells us that A and B will both reduce the incidence of crime in the neighborhood, their designs for doing so are quite distinct.[32]

Applying this case to the context of computers and information networks, we find strategy A closer to the heart of technical computer security; it seeks to protect individuals by fortifying individual (or institutional) nodes on the network. It is less concerned with identifying and stopping attackers before they act and more focused on strengthening protections for potential targets of such attacks as may occur. This approach is similar to recommendations from a February 2003 report of the Bush administration, *The National Strategy to Secure Cyberspace*, which seeks to reduce weaknesses in protocols and applications that open end-users to destructive attacks such as viruses and worms, destructive miniapplications, and denial of service. Similarly, in a statement to a Subcommittee of the U.S. Senate, Amit Yoran, Director of the National Cyber Security Division of the Department of Homeland Security, recommended a "threat-independent" approach focused on reducing vulnerabilities rather than on identifying and undermining specific threats.[33] His argument, which is compatible with recommendations of *The National Strategy to Secure Cyberspace*, was that limited resources would be more effectively applied to shoring up vulnerabilities and known system weaknesses.[34] How to reduce vulnerability is a technical question that leads us back to precepts of technical computer security.

Strategy B, with its checkpoints and surveillance, differs from A in at least two respects: one, in casting all passers-by within a net of suspicion, and second, in vesting greater control in the hands of centralized authorities. These moves are compatible with securitization because, by anticipating dire and imminent attack, it makes sense to seek to stop it before it occurs. This is best done by knowing who everyone is and what they are doing. Technical barricades that prevent access by all but authorized entities are the online equivalents of checkpoints. Although authorization *could* be tied to qualifying but nonidentifying features, such as reputation and account status, the trend seems to be toward full identification, for example, in the energetic embrace of biometric identification, flight passenger profiling systems, and even road toll systems in the United States such as EZ Pass. Floodlit, biometric-enhanced video surveillance find parallels online in mechanisms that monitor and filter information flows, such as DCS1000 (previously, Carnivore), intrusion detection systems monitoring unusual activity, and regulation to extend the CALEA (Communications Assistance for Law Enforcement Act) requirement of ability to tap phone lines to voice-over-IP. The USA PATRIOT Act seeks to give law enforcement and security personnel greater powers to scrutinize online postings and communications.[35] Also predicted by the model of securitization are the persistent calls for large increases in funding for computer security, security research, and cybercrime units.[36]

In the case of the neighborhood, as in the case of computers and networks, the choice is difficult partly because it is contingent not only on the facts of the matter, which are not all that well understood, but also on preferences and values, which are contested. A neighborhood resident, enthusiastic about the virtues of both A and B, might suggest doing both (surely there's no such thing as too much security). The problem with this solution is that even if it were affordable, it overlooks inherent incompatibilities in underlying values. In the online context, the incompatibilities between the parallels to strategies A and B are not only evident in the dimension of values but also materially. Technical computer security demands protection for individuals from a variety of harms, including breaches of confidentiality and anonymity and a chilling of speech, action, and association. Strategies of type B involve scrutiny, individual accountability, transparency, and identifiability, which often are antithetical to the variety of individual liberties and self-determined choices protected in the alternative strategy.

The considerations laid out above follow well-trodden paths in the theory and practice of politics, which in liberal democracies have resulted in familiar compromises such as rule-bound procedures for criminal investigation, prosecution, punishment, and governance generally. These issues extend well beyond the scope of this chapter; our business here is merely to point out that design specifications for computer security may embody commitments to one understanding—technical computer security focused on the "ordinary" security of individuals—or another—cybersecurity responding to threats that have been securitized.

If the securitization of online threats succeeds, the former might seem "too little, too late." But the extraordinary responses that securitization allows pose dangers of a different kind. By removing from individuals the cover of anonymity and confidentiality, and investing governmental and other authorities with greater power and discretion over their online activities, we expose their vulnerability to the tyranny of corrupt officials or simply the excessive control of overreaching authorities. Strategies of type B work in the face of dire and urgent threats, among other things, by suppressing harmful attacks, but they open a population to the risk that suppression extends beyond its target in ways mentioned above. Moves to securitize should therefore be carefully scrutinized.

Is Securitization Warranted?

In developing their framework, Buzan and Waever are preoccupied primarily with the construction of securitization and not with the question a realist might ask: when is securitization legitimate or warranted? They do not altogether ignore this question, recommending as a general rule that a society (nation, state, etc.) set a high threshold for accepting securitizing moves on the grounds that removing important issues from the realm of public deliberation, and allowing leaders to work outside the constraints of cherished political principles, has potentially high costs.[37] I would like to give their recommendation greater specificity, perhaps pushing beyond the boundaries that a constructivist might set. To answer the question of the warrant of securitization, guided by the precepts of the framework and a skeptical stance, we must set about discovering how dire, how imminent, how total the presumed threats are. We should question the appropriateness of the proposed measures and their proportionality to the threats.

In the context of computer and online security, the question of how dire and imminent the threats are calls for data and analysis that are not readily available to the broader public. One reason for the difficulty is that although many of the top technical security experts (computer scientists and engineers) pursue research into technical vulnerabilities, that is, the *possibilities* for attack and damage, they do not seem to have a holistic picture of their *probabilities*, the general incidence, of that actual damage. This calls for more than technical analytic understanding. Sporadic stories of attacks in publicly available sources and even the direct experience by ordinary users are insufficient for drawing wise conclusions. Certainly, they do not constitute a sufficient basis for choosing between the models constructed by technical security and cybersecurity, respectively. Those who follow these issues also learn that much is withheld or simply not known, and that estimates of damage are strategically either wildly exaggerated or understated.

In looking for supporting evidence for one of the two competing conceptions, a problem beyond the scarcity of relevant data and analysis is how to interpret (or read the meaning of) attacks that we do hear about. A virus attack on the Internet that corrupts thousands of computer systems, interpreted within the technical security model, is presented as a criminal attack against thousands of individuals and is the business of domestic law enforcement, constrained by the relevant protocols of investigation, arrest, and so forth. This same attack, within the cybersecurity model, may be construed as an attack against the nation and count as evidence for securitization. The importance of meaning attributed to an event was evident in the minutes and hours following the attacks on the World Trade Centers—conceived of not as crimes against the many *individuals* killed and injured but as a transgression against the United States—not by particular individuals, but by the terror organizations and nations constituting the "axis of evil." Corporate owners of intellectual property have been particularly adept at reading broad meanings into unauthorized uses and distribution of copyrighted materials, lobbying with relative success to pose these activities as deeply threatening not only to them but to the U.S. economy. Their efforts have paid off in predictable ways (according to the Copenhagen School), namely, measures that many legal scholars argue are extraordinary, including quite general attacks on P2P file-sharing, which they pose as a threat to law and order.[38] These lobbies have also successfully achieved incremental appropriations of government funds for law enforcement efforts to stem unauthorized exchanges, such as a $32 million increase in spending in 2001 for FBI cybercrime units and equipment.[39] Further, not only has there been a significant ramping up of punishment regimes, but also a worrisome weakening of requirements of due process (for example, subpoenas in abridged form that need only the signature of a clerk of the court rather than a judge or magistrate).

Conclusion

This chapter has argued that the way we conceptualize values can influence the shape of technical design and related public policy. In the research, design, development, and regulation of computer security, it is clear that strong commitment to the underlying value of security motivates much of its attraction and public support. But what I have tried to show is that at least two quite distinct and incompatible conceptions of security vie for public and expert support, and that which of the two ultimately dominates will make a difference for computerized, networked individuals and societies. How these differences play out through law, policy, and budget appropriations is important, but I have sought particularly to indicate the potential of the two conceptions for shaping technical design. The reason for this focus is not that the realm of system design and development is more important, but because it is all too often neglected as a site for resolving political and ethical conflict. Further, once standards are adopted, constraints and affordances built, technical systems are less tractable than other forms of policy resolution.[40]

In laying out some of the differences between the two conceptions of security, I have tried to show what is at stake in the selection of the one over the other. If those who subscribe to a conception of security as cybersecurity are right, particularly if the magnitude of the threat is as great as those on the extremes claim, then an extraordinary response (strategy B in the hypothetical neighborhood) is warranted despite its chilling effects. In the context of airports, we seem to have accepted such conditions: virtually ubiquitous informational and visual surveillance with highly controlled patterns of movement.[41] Presumably, nuclear power plants and high-security prisons limit the freedom of action in similar ways, and justifiably so.

I am inclined to resist a move to frame computers and networked information and communications systems in these ways, as so dangerous that they warrant extraordinary treatment of this kind. This inclination has less to do with efficacy than purpose. As long as we value our networked information infrastructure for its contribution to public communication, community, political organization, association, production and distribution of information, and artistic creation, its security is best pursued under the conception I called "technical computer security." Just as the residents of our hypothetical neighborhood might agree that improvements in safety would be greater with strategy B, they may nevertheless choose A because they prefer the type of neighborhood that would follow as a result. Similarly, securitization might make the Net safer but at the expense of its core purpose as a realm of public exchange. It makes no sense to make security the paramount value when this essential purpose is undermined. Aquinas recognized this point when he advised, "Hence a captain does not intend as a last end, the preservation of the ship entrusted to him, since a ship is ordained to something else as its end, viz. to navigation;"[42] or in Goodin's paraphrase, "if the highest aim of the captain were to preserve his ship, he would keep it in port forever."[43]

NOTES

1. This chapter has been on the drawing boards for longer than I dare to admit. Along the way, many have helped its development by generously sharing their wisdom: James Der Derian, Niva Elkin-Koren, Ed Felten, Batya Friedman, Lene Hansen, audiences at CEPE, TPRC, the Yale Cybercrime and Digital Law Enforcement Conference, the Watson Institute's Symposium in Dis/Simulations of War and Peace," and the University of Newastle, Computer Science Department. It has also benefited from the excellent editorial work of Sam Howard-Spink. An earlier version was published in *Ethics and Information Technology*, Vol. 7, No. 2, June 2005, 61–73.

2. Langdon Winner, *"Do Artifacts Have Politics?" The Whale and the Reactor: A Search for Limits in an Age of High Technology* (Chicago: University of Chicago Press, 1986).

3. B. Pfaffenberger, "Technological Dramas," *Science, Technology & Human Values*, 17(3): 282–312, 1992.

4. See the project "Value in Technology Design: Democracy, Autonomy, and Justice," available at: http://www.nyu.edu/projects/valuesindesign/; B. Friedman, P.H. Kahn Jr., and A. Borning, "A Value Sensitive Design and Information Systems," forthcoming in *Human-Computer Interaction in Management Information Systems: Foundations* (P. Zhang and D. Galletta, eds.) (New York: M. E. Sharpe); L. J. Camp, "Design for Trust," in *Trust, Reputation and Security: Theories and Practice: Aamas 2002 International Workshop, Bologna, Italy, July 15, 2002: Selected and Invited Papers (Lecture Notes in Artificial Intelligence)*, (Rino Falcone, ed.) (Berlin: Springer-Verlag, 2003); L. J. Camp & C. Osorio, "Privacy Enhancing Technologies for Internet Commerce," in *Trust in the Network Economy* (Berlin: Springer-Verlag, 2002); Mary Flanagan, Daniel Howe, and Helen Nissenbaum, "Values in Design: Theory and Practice," Jeroen vanden Haven and John Weckert (eds.), *Information Technology and Moral Philosophy* (Cambridge: Cambridge University Press, forthcoming 2007); H. Nissenbaum, "Will Security Enhance Trust Online, or Supplant It?" in *Trust and Distrust in Organizations: Dilemmas and Approaches*, Volume VII in the Russell Sage Foundation Series on Trust (M. R. Kramer & S. K. Cook, eds.) (New York: Russell Sage Foundation, 2004); Y. Benkler & H. Nissenbaum, "Commons-Based Peer Production and Virtue," forthcoming.

5. National Research Council, *The Internet under Crisis Conditions* (Washington, D.C.: National Academies Press, 2003); L. J. Hennessy, A. D. Patterson and S. H. Lin (eds.), *Information Technology for Counterterrorism* (Washington, D.C.: National Academies Press, 2003); R. Baskerville, "Information Systems Design Methods: Implications for Information Systems Development," 25(4) *ACM Computing Surveys*, 375–414, 1993.

6. "Trust in Cyberspace," Committee on Information Systems Trustworthiness, National Research Council (1999), *available at* http://www.nap.edu/readingroom/books/trust/; see the society's dependability's definition by the DIRC project, *available at* http://www.dirc.org.uk/overview/index.html.

7. R. Bendrath, "The American Cyber-Angst and the Real World—Any Link?" In R. Latham (ed), *Bombs and Bandwidth: The Emerging Relationship between Information Technology and Security* (New Press, 2003), 49–73.

8. According to the February 2003 "National Strategy to Secure Cyberspace" (*available at* http://www.us-cert.gov/reading_room/cyberspace_strategy.pdf), cyberattacks on U.S. information networks can have serious consequences such as disrupting critical operations, causing loss of revenue and intellectual property, or loss of life; see also United States Senate, Committee on the Judiciary, Testimony of Mr. Keith Lourdeau, FBI Deputy Assistant Director, Cyber Division, February 24, 2004 (*available at* http://judiciary.senate.gov/testimony.cfm?id=1054&wit_id=2995).

9. R. Arthur, "Prohibition and Preemption," in 5 *Legal Theory*, 235–263 (Cambridge: Cambridge University Press, 1999).

10. R. Anderson, "Cryptography and Competition Policy—Issues with Trusted Computing," in *Proceedings Workshop on Economics and Information Sector*, 1–11 (May 2003).

11. For a description of this approach to security studies, I have used B. Buzan, O. Wyer, J. D. Wilde, and O. Waever, *Security: A New Framework for Analysis* (Boulder: Lynne Rienner, 1997); O. Waever, *Concepts of Security*, Ph.D. dissertation, Institute of Political Science, University of Copenhagen, 1995.

12. Buzan, Wyer, Wilde, and Waever, *supra*, note 11, 32.

13. J. Kelley, "Terror Groups Hide behind Web Encryption," *USA Today* (February 6, 2001), discussed in D. McCullagh, "bin Laden: Steganography Master?" *Wired News* (February 7, 2001), *available at* http://www.wired.com/news/print/0,1294,41658,00.html.

14. Bendrath, *supra*, note 7, 49–73.

15. S. Gaudin, "The Terrorist Network," *NetworkWorldFusion* (November 26, 2001), *available at* http://www.nwfusion.com/research/2001/1126featside4.html.

16. D. Jehl and D. Rohde, "Captured Qaeda Figure Led Way to Information behind Warning," *New York Times* (August 2, 2004).

17. For example, the testimony of Jack Valenti, president and CEO of Motion Picture Association of America, before the Subcommittee on Courts, the Internet, and Intellectual Property Committee on the Judiciary U.S. House of Representatives, "International Copyright Piracy: Links to Organized Crime and Terrorism" (March 13, 2003), *available at* http://www.house.gov/judiciary/valenti031303.htm.

18. An official rendering of threats and vulnerabilities in the context of national security concerns can be seen in *The National Strategy to Secure Cyberspace*, February 2003, a report by President George W. Bush's Critical Infrastructure Protection Board (headed by Richard A. Clarke), especially the chapter "Cyberspace Threats and Vulnerabilities: A Case for Action."

19. Bendrath, *supra*, note 7, 56, quoting Admiral Thomas R. Wilson's comments during a hearing of the Senate Select Committee on Intelligence, February 2001.

20. Bendrath, *id.*, 57.

21. K. Mitnick, "Hacker in Shackles," *Guardian* (London) (August 10, 1999).

22. L. Hansen, "The Little Mermaid's Silent Security Dilemma and the Absence of Gender in the Copenhagen School," 29(2) *Millennium*, 285–306.

23. James Der Derian, "The Value of Security: Hobbes, Marx, Nietzsche, and Baudrillard," in D. Campbell and M. Dillon (eds.), *The Political Subject of Violence*, (Manchester: Manchester University Press, 1993).

24. Buzan, Wyer, Wilde, and Waever, *supra*, note 11, 27.

25. *Id.*, especially 23–25.

26. For more on the subject of government secrecy, *see* M. Rotenberg, "Privacy and Secrecy after September 11," in Bendrath, *supra*, note 7, 132–142.

27. The point is derived from Will Kymlicka, "Justice and Security in the Accommodation of Minority Nationalism, Comparing East and West," draft paper presented at Princeton University, 2001, especially 16–21.

28. For a critical discussion of this practice, *see* R. Goodin, *Political Theory and Public Policy* (Chicago: University of Chicago Press, 1982), chapter 11, "The Priority of Defense."

29. A similar connection but with motion in the other direction is pointed out by Birnhack and Elkin-Koren in an important paper on the ways security concerns have allowed the state to reenter governance of the Net by collaborating with private actors. M.D. Birnhack and N. Elkin-Koren, "The Invisible Handshake: The Reemergence of the State in the Digital Environment," 8 *Virginia Journal of Law & Technology*, 6 (2003). Attorney-General John Ashcroft stressed the possible dangers to society as a result of intellectual property infringement: "Intellectual property theft is a clear danger to our economy and the health, safety, and security of the American people." "Attorney-General John Ashcroft Announces Recommendations of the Justice Department's Intellectual Property Task Force." October 12, 2004, *available at* http://www.usdoj.gov/criminal/cybercrime/ AshcroftIPTF.htm. The possible relation between security and intellectual property theft was recognized in the task force report itself: "those who benefit most from intellectual property theft are criminals, and alarmingly, criminal organizations with possible ties to terrorism." *See* U.S. Department of Justice, *Report of the Department of Justice's Task Force on Intellectual Property*, October 2004, 7, *available at* http://www.usdoj.gov/criminal/cybercrime/IPTaskForceReport.pdf.

30. Evidence of disunity comes, for example, from the Federal District Court in Manhattan ruling in *Doe v. Ashcroft*, 334 F. Supp 2d, 471 (2004), striking down, on constitutional grounds, a section of the USA PATRIOT Act that would have allowed government security agencies to subpoena personal information from Internet Service Providers without having to obtain a court order.

31. Obviously, these are paradigmatic and designed to illustrate alternatives at two ends of a spectrum which offers many variations in between.

32. Discussions with Ed Felten greatly influenced the conception of this example.

33. Statement by Amit Yoran, Director National Cyber Security Division Department of Homeland Security, before the U.S. Senate Committee on the Judiciary Subcommittee on Terrorism, Technology, and Homeland Security, February 24, 2004.

34. *The National Strategy to Secure Cyberspace*, Bush Administration, final draft released February 14, 2003, *available at* http://www.whitehouse.gov/pcipb/.

35. E. Lipton and E. Lightblau, "Online and Even Near Home, a New Front Is Opening in the Global Terror Battle," *New York Times*, September 23, 2004, A12.

36. *See, for example*, the CIA and National Science Foundation joint project, "Approaches to Combat Terrorism: Opportunities for Basic Research," aimed at finding ways to monitor online chat rooms. For more information about this project and additional ones, visit the EPIC website at http://www.epic.org/privacy/wiretap/nsf_release.html. *See also* the "EFF Analysis of the Cyber Security Enhancement Act," *available at* http://www.eff.org/Privacy/Surveillance/?f=20020802_eff_csea_analysis.html.

37. Buzan, Wyer, Wilde, and Waever, *supra*, note 11, discussion on 29–30.

38. Digital Millennium Copyright Act of 1998 (DMCA), Pub. L. No. 105-304, 112 Stat. 2860, Codified as 17 U.S.C. §§1201–1205; for commentary review, *see* J. Litman, "The Exclusive Right to Read," 13 *Cardozo Arts & Ent. L. J.*, 1994, 29; P. Samuelson, "Intellectual Property and the Digital Economy: Why the Anti-Circumvention Regulations Need to Be Revised," 14 *Berkeley Tech. L. J.*, 1999, 519. *See also* the pending legislation: S. 2560, The International Inducement of Copyright Infringement Act of 2004 (The INDUCE Act), presently "on hold."

39. "House Gives Final Approval to FY 2002 Commerce, Justice, State and Judiciary Spending Bill," *CJIS Group News* (November 14, 2001), *available at* http://www.cjisgroup.com/aboutCJIS/newsBudget111401.cfm

40. L. Winner, *Do Artifacts Have Politics? The Whale and the Reactor: A Search for Limits in an Age of High Technology* (Chicago: University of Chicago Press, 1986).

41. *See, for example*, the attempt to create passenger profiling as part of the Secure Flight passenger prescreening program. The Transportation Security Administration has ordered airlines to turn over a month's worth of passenger data, which will allow the creation of passenger profiling. For more information about this step and the attempt to prevent such profiling in the name of privacy rights, visit the Electronic Privacy Information Center (EPIC) website, *available at* http://www.epic.org/privacy/airtravel/profiling.html.

42. Thomas Aquinas, *Summa Theologica*, Part I of II, Question 2, Article 5.

43. R. Goodin, *Political Theory and Public Policy* (Chicago: University of Chicago Press, 1982), 233.

Part II

New Crimes
Virtual Crimes of the Information Age

5

Real-World Problems of Virtual Crime

Beryl A. Howell

Theoretical debates about how best to address cybercrime have their place but, in the real world, companies and individuals are facing new harmful criminal activity that poses unique technical and investigatory challenges. There is nothing virtual about the real damage online crime can inflict offline to victims. At the same time, technology is inviting uses that may result in significant, though sometimes inadvertent, criminal and civil liability. The law is not always crystal clear about whether specific conduct is a crime and about which tools investigators may use to collect evidence identifying the scope of the criminal activity and the perpetrator. In this essay, three stories based on real-life cases are described that highlight murky areas of the law.

At the risk of spoiling the suspense, let me make the moral of these stories plain at the outset: specific laws directed to specific problems are important, both as guidance to law enforcement on how investigations may be conducted, with appropriate safeguards for civil liberties and privacy, and to alert people where legal lines are drawn as a caution against crossing them.

Does this require endless effort to update the laws to keep pace with technology? Yes, but the Congress returns every year with the job of making new laws. Will the pace of legal changes always be behind technological developments? Yes, but in my view the correct pace is a "go slow" one. By the time a proposal has gone through the legislative process, the problem it seeks to address will have ripened into better definition. The better defined a problem is, the better policy makers are able to craft a narrow and circumscribed law to address the problem, while minimizing the risk of excessive breadth that could chill innovation and technological development.

The first story arises from a computer investigation that was conducted in 2004 within the Committee on the Judiciary of the U.S. Senate. This story could appropriately be named The Case of the Snooping Staffers and Peeking Politicos. The facts of this case are quite simple. In November 2003, conservative papers and a website—the *Wall Street Journal* editorial page, the *Washington Times*, and the Coalition for a Fair Judiciary—published excerpts from nineteen internal staff memoranda to Democratic members on the Senate Judiciary Committee.[1] As is frequently the case with computer security breaches, the scope of the breach is usually far more serious than the initial problem suggests. Indeed, these nineteen leaked memoranda were just the tip of the iceberg.

The Senate Sergeant of Arms conducted a limited "administrative, fact-finding inquiry" at the bipartisan request of the Chairman of the Judiciary Committee and Senior Democratic Members into the circumstances surrounding the theft of the Democratic staff memoranda.[2] The report of the inquiry revealed that a staffer for Senator Hatch and a staffer for Majority Leader Frist had for almost eighteen months on a daily basis methodically accessed files of targeted Democratic staffers working on judicial nominations and taken almost 4,700 documents.[3] Evidence was uncovered that the Hatch and Frist staffers took steps to cover their tracks and conceal their theft of the Democratic staff memoranda, keeping the stolen documents in a zipped (i.e., compressed), password-protected folder on the Hatch staffer's computer.[4]

The Committee file server was shared by both Democrats and Republicans, with each staffer having his or her own account associated with a personal electronic folder for storage of documents or other data. Staff working for the same senator had permission to share certain files among themselves, but no other members' staffs were permitted to see these files.[5] At least that is how the permissions had worked, were understood to work, and were supposed to work. When a new systems administrator was hired in 2001, he did not set the permissions correctly for over half of the staff on the Committee, so the files in those accounts were accessible to any user with access to the server.[6]

One might think the discovery that Republican staffers were spying on the internal and confidential memoranda among Democratic staff and members would have the effect of throwing gas on an already simmering partisan fire. Interestingly, that is not what happened. Instead, virtually every Committee member from both sides of the aisle agreed that this spying was an appalling breach of confidentiality and custom on the Committee.

There has been public debate, however, about whether a crime has been committed, which is somewhat ironic since this incident involved the Committee responsible for crafting the original Computer Fraud and Abuse Act (CFAA) and every amendment to that law for the past decade.[7] Was the unauthorized access by the Republican staffers simply immoral or was it a crime?

Former White House Counsel C. Boyden Gray, the Chairman of the Committee for Justice, former Majority Leader Trent Lott, and others, have asserted that no crime was committed since the improperly configured security settings on the Committee file server provided easy access.[8] The Committee for Justice promulgated a "fact sheet" asserting that no crime occurred because there was no "hacking."[9]

Yet, by its plain terms, the CFAA prohibits both unauthorized access, which is colloquially called "hacking," and exceeding authorized access of "protected computers."[10] "Hacking" is not a defined term nor even used in the law. The term "unauthorized access" is also not defined in the law, while the term "exceeds authorized access" is broadly defined to mean "to access a computer with authorization and to use such access to obtain or alter information in the computer that the accessor is not entitled so to obtain or alter."[11] The CFAA contains absolutely no requirement that data be secured and rendered inaccessible to unauthorized users to enjoy the protection of the statute.[12] On the contrary, this statute imposes misdemeanor criminal liability for merely obtaining information stored on a computer system by accessing a computer without authorization or by exceeding authorized access.[13]

The shrill partisanship voiced by some senators who do not serve on the Judiciary Committee, and by outside groups, obscured the fairly simple legal questions posed in the Peeking Politicos debacle, including: (1) did the surreptitious accessing, reading, and copying of Democratic staff memoranda on multiple occasions over a period of months by Republican staff constitute "obtaining information" within the meaning of the CFAA? (2) did this activity by Senator Hatch's staffer, who was authorized to use the Senate Judiciary server, fall within the CFAA's prohibition of exceeding authorized access? and (3) did directions by Majority Leader Frist's staffer to Senator Hatch's staffer to engage in this activity run afoul of the CFAA's prohibition on unauthorized access?

The plain terms of the statute appear to provide affirmative responses to these questions, a conclusion corroborated by explanations of the intended scope of the law found in the legislative history. Since the mid–1980s, the CFAA has undergone several significant amendments that have expanded the law's scope from government and financial institution computers to cover virtually every computer connected to the Internet, and added a civil cause of action as an enforcement mechanism to supplement the criminal penalties for significant breaches. As originally enacted, in 1984 the CFAA penalized knowingly obtaining classified information,[14] and financial records or credit histories in financial institutions,[15] and using, altering, or destroying any government information,[16] by accessing a computer without authorization or "having accessed a computer with authorization, us[ing] the opportunity such access provided for purposes to which such authorization does not extend."[17]

The conduct prohibited by "unauthorized access" is "analogous to that of 'breaking and entering.'"[18] By contrast, the conduct barred by exceeding authorized access was intended "to make it a criminal offense for anyone who has been authorized to use a computer to access it knowing the access is for a purpose not contemplated by the authorization. As a result, it prohibits access to a computer to obtain the described data when the perpetrator knows that the access is not authorized or that it is not within the scope of a previous authorization."[19] On the other hand, information obtained only incidentally, "pursuant to an express or implied authorization," or in accordance with "normal and customary business procedures and information usage" is not covered.[20]

The cumbersome phrase used in the original CFAA—"having accessed a computer with authorization, uses the opportunity such access provided for purposes to which such authorization does not extend"—was condensed to the current language of "exceeds unauthorized access" in order "merely to clarify the language in existing law"[21] and "simplify the language."[22] Inadvertent or mistaken access to computer files, which a person is not authorized to view, does not run afoul of the law. The Senate Judiciary Committee acknowledged that distinguishing "between conduct that is completely inadvertent and conduct that is initially inadvertent but later becomes an intentional crime" may be "a difficult line to draw in the area of computer technology because of the possibility of mistakenly accessing another's computer files."[23] Yet both Judiciary Committees authorizing this criminal statute made clear that exploiting access that was unauthorized would not be excused, even if the initial discovery of the means to such access was inadvertent or accidental. The Senate Judiciary Committee explained,

> [T]he Committee would expect one whose access to another's computer files or data was truly mistaken to withdraw immediately from such access. If he does not and instead deliberately maintains unauthorized access after a non-intentional initial contact, then the Committee believes prosecution is warranted. The individual's intent may have been formed after his initial, inadvertent access. But his is an intentional crime nonetheless, and the Committee does not wish to preclude prosecution in such instances.[24]

The conduct covered by the term "obtaining information" has been consistently interpreted to include "mere observation of the data. Actual asportation, in the sense of physically removing the data from its original location or transcribing the data, need not be proved in order to establish a violation of [18 U.S.C. § 1030(a)(2)]."[25]

The plain terms of the CFAA, as informed by the legislative history, supports the analysis of the Peeking Politicos' activity. As the Pickle Report noted, the "practice in the Judiciary Committee is to 'share' certain files among staff working for the same Senator."[26] Each user also "should have exclusive access to his or her own directory."[27] In short, a Committee staffer is authorized to access his or her personal folder as well as shared files archived or stored on the server by staff employed by the same member for whom that staffer is employed. This authorization is limited and does not cover access to, let alone the copying, transfer within the Senate, and dissemination outside the Senate of private, confidential information from the archived files of other senators' offices. The latter activity would exceed any such limited authorized access to the Committee server and would likely constitute a misdemeanor violation of section 1030(a)(2) of the CFAA.

Moreover, directions or requests by a Frist staffer without access rights to a Hatch staffer with only limited access rights to exceed that authority for purposes of obtaining data on a Committee server, as the Pickle Report indicated that the Majority Leader's staffer did, may, at a minimum, warrant aiding and abetting liability, or be sufficient to constitute obtaining unauthorized access. The fact that both staffers worked for the Senate is not a mitigating factor. The prohibition on unauthorized access to federal government computers does not only apply to persons entirely outside the government. On the contrary, as the Committees authoring the CFAA explained, "The Committee does not intend to preclude prosecution under this subsection if, for example, a Labor Department employee authorized to use Labor's computers accesses without authorization an FBI computer. An employee who uses his department's computer and, without authorization, forages into data belonging to another department, is engaged in conduct directly analogous to an 'outsider' tampering with Government computers. In both cases, the user is wholly lacking in authority to access or use that department's computer. The Committee believes criminal prosecution should be available in such cases."[28]

In addition to facing a possible misdemeanor violation, the activity of the Peeking Politicos may have potential civil liability repercussions as well. The CFAA authorizes civil actions for compensatory damages or injunctive relief by any person who suffers (1) any "damage," which is defined to mean any impairment to the integrity or availability of data,[29] or (2) any "loss," which is defined to mean any reasonable cost of responding to an offense, conducting a damage assessment and restoring data, any revenue lost, cost incurred, or other consequential damages incurred because of interruption of service.[30] The staffers who obtained unauthorized access to the Democratic staff memoranda may be subject to civil suit for damages, including by the Senate, which has incurred expenses in the investigation into what happened, including the costs of personnel diverted from other duties in the office of the Sergeant of Arms to focus on the investigation and of consultants hired to conduct forensic examinations of the systems involved.

The scope of the activity covered by the terms "access without authorization" and "exceeds authorized access" ranges from simple snooping by authorized users of a network, such as employees inappropriately accessing confidential personnel files of other employees or students accessing or altering grades, to seriously damaging activity, such as the theft of trade secrets or other confidential information. This leaves enormous discretion to prosecutors. In a politically charged matter, such broad discretion may be both an unwelcome and uncomfortable circumstance. One commentator recently noted, "If it is widely believed that some conduct may technically fall within the language of the CFAA but should in fact not be criminal, the law should be amended. Reliance on the 'reasonable exercise' of prosecutorial discretion is not an adequate response. The text of the statute should reflect such limits."[31]

The Pickle Report stopped short of making any recommendations for referral of individuals for criminal violations, but did outline the relevant elements of potentially applicable criminal offenses.[32] The matter has now been referred to the Justice Department by a bipartisan group of members. The ending to this story must await the prosecutors' decision as to whether a crime was committed.

In some situations, there may be no question that the computer activity at issue is a crime, but the technology creates issues about whether the crime was committed by the computer user or the computer program. This was the conundrum confronted in The Case of the Parental Nightmare.

It starts one morning over a year ago, when a suburban mom had her morning coffee interrupted by a knock at the door. It was FBI agents announcing they were there to question, and possibly arrest, the child pornography distributor living and using a computer in the house. They determined the computer being used to distribute child pornography—which is a felony to possess and to distribute—was in the teenage son's room. Like over 60 million other people,[33] he had installed the file-sharing software program KaZaa on his computer. The teenager had then gone searching for erotic material, which he downloaded into his shared KaZaa folder. Included in this material were child porn images, which many other KaZaa users then located and downloaded from his home computer.

In fact, unbeknownst to the teenager, his machine had been turned into a supernode on the peer-to-peer (P2P) system. He was unaware of the option buried in the software to prevent this from happening and did not change the default settings, which permitted it. So his machine was being used by many clients and other supernodes to point to files on his and other hard drives available for sharing, including child porn. The teenager technically did not have all the child porn files on his computer—enough for a felony—but he had an index pointing to other locations with child porn. This also made his machine a much bigger target for law enforcement looking for online child porn distributors.

P2P file-sharing programs make distribution a passive act, but no less subject to criminal liability. People do not fully realize that the simple act of selecting files or folders to share on KaZaa makes them a distributor of all those files, and that the act of distribution, even if initiated by other users, carries with it hefty criminal and civil liability under criminal copyright laws, child porn laws, and laws restricting the distribution of obscene materials to minors.[34]

This was just the beginning of the parents' problems. They then wanted to find out exactly what the evidence was on their son's computer. Was he actively sending child porn as email attachments to others? Was he merely viewing child porn images online or intentionally storing those images on his computer? Was he actively posting or uploading child porn images to any sites? Or, instead, was he merely a passive distributor by virtue of having downloaded the illegal images into a KaZaa shared folder, with the program doing the active work? The answers to these questions could provide a more complete picture of the nature of the teenager's computer activity and a context for the activity involving the illegal child porn images that could be helpful in the defense of their son and to persuade a prosecutor not to charge him. Finding those answers required the analytical services of a computer forensic examiner.

The child porn possession crime is so strict, however, that forensic examiners and even attorneys have to be careful not to have such images in their possession. The law treats child porn essentially like heroin—the mere possession, even on behalf of a client to assist in an investigation or defense—is no exception to the crime.[35] As one court put it: "Child pornography is illegal contraband."[36] Special protocols have to be followed for forensic examiners to handle matters involving child porn. These protocols may, in appropriate circumstances, be negotiated with the investigating law enforcement agency and may require specific direction from the court.[37] Stringent controls may be placed on the computer forensic examiner that limit the location where the examination takes place, the extent of any copying of the images, and the removal of any work product resulting from the examination.

Significantly, even if a forensic examination of a computer reveals that child porn images were not manually downloaded or saved but, as a result of the computer user viewing the images online or receiving pop-up advertising with the images, were stored only in a temporary Internet file on the computer, the user faces criminal liability for possession. Images searched out, found, and viewed on web pages are automatically saved by the computer's web browser in a browser cache file and stored on the hard drive, until the contents of that file are deleted by the user. Courts have upheld convictions for possession of child pornography for viewing illegal images accessed online, without any manual downloading or saving of the images onto the computer.[38]

While we still do not know the end of the story of the Peeking Politicos, the story of the Parental Nightmare was a happy one, since the prosecutor declined to prosecute the juvenile. Our forensic examination of the teenager's computer confirmed that he did not actively distribute the child porn images, which were nevertheless accessed and uploaded by other KaZaa users.

Changes are already developing in P2P networks to get around the liability risks of possessing and distributing illegal material. One such system involves encrypting the files that a user wants to share, pushing the encrypted files onto another client machine, and then making the decryption key available at "Free sites," along with pointers to where the material may be found.[39] The keys are distributed, not the material, and the person in possession of the encrypted material has deniability about what the subject matter of the encrypted file is. Some in law enforcement are already anticipating a need for new laws to make it illegal to possess a deliberately stored decryption key that the user knows relates to an illegal file.[40]

P2P networks actually make the work of investigators fairly easy, since they can track who is sharing illegal files and how much distribution is occurring.[41] In the digital world, users of peer-to-peer networks may find that the technology has taken them for a ride across legal lines imposed by strict liability laws for possession and distribution of certain materials, including child porn and infringing copyrighted works.[42]

The opportunities presented by wireless technologies to conceal the origin of communications may make finding perpetrators of computer crime more difficult, as demonstrated by the final story of The Case of the WiFi Spoofer. For about two years a company was the target of embarrassing emails containing derogatory and sexually explicit patents as attachments. These emails were not sent to the company, but worse, they were sent to the company's clients with spoofed (i.e., faked) email addresses to make the emails appear to have come from senior executives within the company. The company's clients did not want to receive these disturbing spoofed emails, and the company risked the loss of their business unless the harassing emails were stopped.

The email header information on the emails showed the originating IP addresses, which the FBI attempted to trace. The traces, however, did not lead back to the perpetrator, but to random home users' wireless access points to which the perpetrator had gained access. This access was gained by a practice known as "war driving." The perpetrator would drive his car around residential neighborhoods with a laptop equipped with a WIFI card and antenna, searching for unprotected wireless access points to which he could connect. A typical home wireless access point will transmit its signal from several hundred feet, well beyond the home's walls. By the time the FBI was able to obtain the subscriber information and location of the WiFi point used by the perpetrator, the perpetrator was, of course, long gone. Wireless access point equipment is sold with no security features enabled to block unauthorized access as the default setting. Many users do not bother, do not wish, or do not know how to change the default settings on the equipment to block such unauthorized access. This equipment has the capability to maintain a log identifying the MAC address of every computer accessing the Internet through the WiFi point, but again this log must be activated by the user. Even when homeowners have permitted examination of their access points that the perpetrator had co-opted, there were no logs of his particular computer having connected to them. This provided a perfect method for the perpetrator to ensure the anonymity of his email messages.

In addition to war driving, this perpetrator also sent spoofed emails from computer labs at various universities in the D.C. area, after gaining access to the computers using false or stolen student accounts. He used the hijacked student accounts to access a proxy server to conceal the originating IP address of the computer he was using within the university computer lab, and used that proxy server to access email accounts, to which he had obtained unauthorized access at AOL and Yahoo, from which he sent spoofed emails. This made him difficult to trace.

Almost two years into this expensive harassment, the company turned to my firm for assistance. At that point, the company did not know whether the WiFi Spoofer was one person or a group, a malicious insider or outsider, what the person/persons wanted or what was motivating the harassment. Most of all, the company wanted the damaging email campaign to stop.

Extensive computer forensic analysis of the company's computers and systems helped to rule out a malicious insider as the perpetrator of the email campaign. This analysis revealed, however, a number of unauthorized log-ins to the company's server over a four-month period in 2003 with originating IP addresses that were traced to a local university. Steps were taken to lock down the security of the company's network.

Sometimes technology has to take a back seat to good old gumshoe work. Through a combination of interviews with people in the industry, including competitors of the targeted company, and government agency personnel involved in patent file production, plus use of a clinical psychologist with expertise in developing detailed profiles based upon text and emails, a primary suspect was identified within several weeks.

Over the course of the investigation, we discovered that senior executives at a sister company of the targeted company had received emails from a person complaining about the targeted company. Textual and psychological analysis by the clinical psychologist demonstrated that the author of the spoofed emails was the same author sending the complaining emails (under a fake name) to the sister company. He further determined that a single author, not a group, was involved. But who was this person and how were we going to determine whether it was the primary suspect?

We sent the complainer an email to see if he would reengage in communications with representatives of the sister company. In order to find out the IP address of the computer where the email was opened, a technical tool, called a web bug, was used to capture the IP address of the computer where the email was opened.[43] In addition, this tool provides related information about when the perpetrator opened the email, how long the email was kept open, and how long it took the perpetrator to respond after opening the email. This information is relevant to building a profile of the perpetrator and anticipating how to interact with him in an effective manner to identify him.

Web bugs such as the one used in this case capture information generated by the computer system itself, not content that is generated by the computer user. The CFAA was intended to protect the privacy and security of computer content and therefore does not cover computer system information such as IP addresses. Yet, absent a definition of "information" in the statute, the blurry lines in the scope of the CFAA's coverage of such computer-generated system information must be navigated by aggressive investigators choosing the technical tools necessary to investigate cybercrime.

After a carefully calibrated series of exchanges, the WiFi Spoofer sent a multimillion-dollar extortion demand threatening to unleash a denial-of-service attack that would be made to appear to come from the targeted company and that would use as a "payload" confidential information on the company and its clients that he had obtained through "dumpster diving" of the company's trash bins. The perpetrator revealed many additional details that were consistent with the information on the primary suspect we had already identified. At the same time, the primary suspect was put under surveillance, which resulted in placing him in the same place—at a university computer lab—where certain incriminating emails originated.

The FBI then arrested him. When the defendant's house in Maryland was searched they found not only computers and other items related to the attempted extortion, but also firearms, components for hand grenades, and the formula and items necessary for making Ricin, a deadly toxin. He was detained pending trial and pleaded guilty in June 2004 to a violation of the CFAA provision prohibiting online extortion. As noted before, often in cybersecurity investigations, the threats that the victims are aware of usually are just the tip of the iceberg.

The story of the WiFi Spoofer had a happy ending, at least from the perspective of the targeted company. After almost two years of being victimized, it took the concerted investigative effort of the FBI, the U.S. Attorney's office, and a private cybersecurity firm to track this perpetrator, through use of technical tools, physical surveillance, a clinical psychologist, and good interviewing techniques.

This story also points out how the CFAA may stymie legitimate self-help efforts to identify perpetrators of harmful online crimes, and brings to full circle the question of the scope of this statute. From the perspective of the Peeking Politicos in the case of the Senate Judiciary Committee server spying case, and of the investigators in the case of the WiFi Spoofer, the reach of the CFAA was a puzzle that had to be carefully scrutinized. This should be a cautionary note in future policy debates, including, for example, over "spyware." Care must be taken to ensure that legitimate and other self-help activities are not impaired by regulatory measures written so broadly without clear malicious intent requirements that they suffer from the same scope questions raised by the CFAA.

Rapid technological developments in communications technologies are providing new opportunities for violators to cover their tracks, new techniques for investigators to pursue them, and new traps of liability for the reckless computer user. Tensions are inevitable as these developments test the reach of current laws and the circumstances in which putative defendants may find themselves liable and victims may engage in self-help without themselves crossing ill-defined legal lines. It would be ironic, indeed, if the concern over harmful online activity results in over-regulation of the use of certain technologies, with the effect of hamstringing victims and investigators from using those or similar tools to stop or prevent the harmful conduct.

NOTES

1. *See, e.g., Review & Outlook,* WALL STREET JOURNAL (November 14, 2003); The Committee for Justice, *Fact Sheet: The Democratric Judicial Memo Investigation* (January 22, 2004), *available at* http://committeeforjustice.org/cgi-data/press/files/10.shtml.

2. REPORT TO THE U.S. SENATE COMMITTEE ON THE JUDICIARY BY SERGEANT OF ARMS BILL PICKLE (2004), at p. 7 (hereafter "PICKLE REPORT"). The inquiry was necessarily limited since the Sergeant of Arms has no subpoena powers.

3. Pickle Report, at p. 9.

4. *Id.*, at p. 8.

5. *Id.*, at p. 18.

6. *Id.*, at p. 11.

7. 18 U.S.C. § 1030.

8. C. Boyden Gray, *Faulty Judiciary Network: Let's Establish the Facts,* WALL STREET JOURNAL (December 23, 2003), quoting Mr. Gray as stating, "The Democrats designed a faulty 'shared network' where files could be accessed freely by staffers of either party; if you had material you wanted kept completely confidential, you were advised to store it on your own hard drive. No one exceeds their authority when they log on and access files on their own computer's desktop. Democrats, in other words, were the ones who disclosed their own documents, which were in fact entirely unrestricted." See also Charlie Savage, *GOP Downplays Reading of Memos,* BOSTON GLOBE, January 23, 2004, *available at* http://www.boston.com/news/nation/articles/2004/01/23/gop_downplays_reading_of_memos/; Alexander Bolton, *Leak Staffer Ousted; Frist aide forced out in an effort to assuage Dems,* THE HILL, Feb. 5, 2004, *available at* www.hillnews.com/news/020504/leak.aspx, quoting Senator Trent Lott (R-Miss.) as stating, "Right now I think that was pretty unfair. . . . I don't have the impression he did anything wrong. . . . I don't know the details, but I would not be a friend in firing a highly qualified staffer." Geoff Earle, *Leak Probe Expands; Santorum assails signs investigation targets GOP aides,* THE HILL, Feb. 11, 2004, *available at* http://www/hillnews.com/news/021104/probe.aspx, quoting Senator Santorum as stating, "If there's anything criminal, it's the behavior of the Democrats." Dahlia Lithwick, *Memogate,* SLATE MAGAZINE, Feb. 19, 2004, *available at* http://slate.msn.com/id/2095770, "some conservative groups claim that no crime occurred."

9. The Committee for Justice, *Fact Sheet: The Democratic Judicial Memo Investigation* (January 22, 2004), *available at* http://committeeforjustice.org/cgi-data/press/files/10.shtml, regarding the appropriateness of the Sergeant of Arms' investigation. "It was a mistake to give credence to the Democrat complaint that any impropriety had occurred with regard to the disclosure of these documents to the press. . . . If Senate computers were hacked into, a law might have been violated. . . . Was there a 'hacking'? No, it appears not. . . . The documents in ques-

tion were inadvertently disclosed and obtained off an unsecured shared network accessible to both Democrat and Republican Judiciary Committee staff. . . . In short, there was no breaking and entering. Staffers were entitled to access their own desktop computers and the committee network on which the documents were inadvertently disclosed."

10. *See* 18 U.S.C. § 1030 (e)(2).

11. 18 U.S.C. § 1030 (e)(6).

12. The Computer Fraud and Abuse statute, in pertinent part, bars (1)intentionally accessing a computer; (2) to obtain information from "any department or agency of the United States," which is defined, in 18 U.S.C. § 1030(e)(7), to include "the legislative or judicial branches of the Government"; (3) "without authorization" or by "exceeding authorized access," which is defined, in 18 U.S.C. § 1030(e)(6), to mean accessing a computer with authorization but to use such access to obtain or alter information in the computer that the accesser is not entitled to obtain or alter.

13. 18 U.S.C. §1030 (c)(2)(A). This illegal activity may also be a felony offense with up to five years' imprisonment if committed for commercial advantage, private financial gain, in furtherance of any criminal or tortuous act, or if the value of the information exceeded $5,000.

14. 18 U.S.C. § 1030(a)(1)(1984), enacted as part of the Comprehensive Crime Control Act in Continuing Resolution 648 (P.L. 98-473).

15. *Id.*, at (a)(2).

16. *Id.*, at (a)(3), penalized "Whoever . . . knowingly accesses a computer without authorization, or having accessed a computer with authorization, uses the opportunity such access provides for purposes to which such authorization does not extend, and by means of such conduct knowingly uses, modifies, destroys, or discloses information in, or prevents authorized use of, such computer, if such computer is operated for or on behalf of the Government of the United States and such conduct affects such operation."

17. *Id.*, at (a)(1)–(3).

18. H. REP. No. 99-894, "Counterfeit Access Device and Computer Fraud and Abuse Act of 1984," at p. 21 (1984) (hereafter "1984 HOUSE JUDICIARY REPORT").

19. *Id.*, at p. 21.

20. *Id.*

21. H. REP. No. 99-612, "Computer Fraud and Abuse Act of 1986," at p. 11 (1986) (hereafter "1986 HOUSE JUDICIARY REPORT").

22. S. REP. No. 99-432, "Computer Fraud and Abuse Act of 1986," at p. 9 (1986) (hereafter "1986 SENATE JUDICIARY REPORT"). The CFAA was first significantly amended in the very next Congress after its initial passage, including by (1) changing the scienter requirement from "knowingly" to "intentionally" for the prohibitions in sections (a)(2) and (3) to make amply clear that only intentional acts were covered and not "mistaken, inadvertent or careless ones." *Id.*, at p. 5; (2)

removing from the prohibition in section (a)(3), which bars unauthorized access to government computers, coverage of insiders in order to protect whistleblowers and leaving intradepartmental trespass to be handled by other applicable laws. *Id.*, at pp.7–8, 20–23 (Additional Views of Messrs. Mathias and Leahy); and (3) adding three new offenses in new subsections (a)(4), (5), and (6). While subsection (a)(3) continues only to apply to outside hackers, subsection (a)(2), which bars both outsiders and insiders from unauthorized access to "protected computers" to obtain information, was amended in 1996 by the National Information Infrastructure Protection Act, S. 982, sponsored by Senators Kyl, Leahy, and Grassley, to cover federal government computers within the definition of "protected computer." The purpose of this amendment was to increase privacy protection for information stored on government computers in the wake of public and congressional reports on "Government employees who abuse their computer access privileges by snooping through confidential tax returns, or selling confidential criminal history information from the National Crime Information Center." 142 CONG. REC. S10889 (daily ed. Sept. 18, 1996) (statement of Sen. Leahy).

23. 1986 SENATE JUDICIARY REPORT, at p. 14.

24. 1986 SENATE JUDICIARY REPORT, at p. 14; *see also* 1986 HOUSE JUDICIARY REPORT, at p. 10 ("the Committee does not intend to prevent prosecution of a person under this subsection whose initial access was inadvertent but who then deliberatively maintains access after a non-intentional initial contact").

25. 1986 SENATE JUDICIARY REPORT, at p. 6–7; *see also* 1986 HOUSE JUDICIARY REPORT, at p. 10 ("There was some concern evidenced . . . by the Department of Justice and others that the term 'obtains information' . . . makes this subsection something other than an unauthorized access offense. The Committee disagreed with this interpretation and states that the term included 'observing' or 'accessing' the protected information"); S. REP. No. 104-357, "The National Information Infrastructure Protection Act of 1995," at p. 7 (1996) ("1996 SENATE JUDICIARY REPORT") (as used in subsection 1030(a)(2), "the term 'obtaining information' includes merely reading it. There is no requirement that the information be copied or transported. This is critically important because, in an electronic environment, information can be stolen without asportation, and the original usually remains intact").

26. PICKLE REPORT, at p. 18.

27. *Id.*

28. 1986 SENATE JUDICIARY REPORT, at p. 8. *See also* 1986 HOUSE JUDICIARY REPORT, at p. 11 ("the Committee does not intend to exclude under 1030(a)(3) conduct by a Federal employee who is an authorized user, for example, of a Department of Labor computer but without authority accesses a Department of Defense computer while at work or in a similar fashion using his own personal computer at home to access without authority a Department of Justice computer system").

29. 18 U.S.C. §1030(e)(8).

30. 18 U.S.C. §1030(g) and 1030(e)(11). Notably, the CFAA requires proof of more elements for civil liability than for criminal liability. The same conduct that may constitute a misdemeanor criminal charge may not support civil liability, which requires the plaintiff to show damage to the availability of data or financial loss.

31. Assistant Professor Joseph Metcalfe, *District Court Concludes That Obtaining Access to a Password-Protected Website Using Another Person's Password Is a Violation of the Computer Fraud and Abuse Act* (March 22, 2004), *available at* http://hermes.circ.gwu.edu/cgi-bin/wa?A2=ind0403&L=cybercrime&F=&S=&P=70.

32. PICKLE REPORT, at pp. 13, 59–62.

33. *See* KaZaa website, http://www.kazaa.com.

34. 18 U.S.C. §1470.

35. 18 U.S.C. §2252(a)(5)(B), bars possession of any child porn, with punishment up to five years' imprisonment. The law provides an affirmative defense if the defendant (1) has fewer than three child porn images, and (2) took prompt steps, without retaining or allowing any person other than a law enforcement agency to access the image, to destroy each image or report the matter, and allow access, to law enforcement.

36. United States v. Kimbrough, 69 F.3d 723, 731 (5th Cir. 1995).

37. *Id.*, at 731 (government refused to allow defendant to copy charged images of child pornography and defense expert was allowed to examine the child porn at the offices of the Customs Service, U.S. Attorney's office, or defense counsel's office); Rogers v. State, 113 S.W. 3d 452, 458–59 (TX Ct. of App. 4th Dist., 2003) (despite state court direction that defense expert be given access to and allowed to prepare a cloned copy of the defendant's hard drive in a child pornography possession prosecution, the local federal prosecutor advised defense counsel that "obtaining and retaining the mirror image would be grounds for federal prosecution because federal law did not contain an exception for discovery in criminal cases;" defense expert conducted examination in sheriff's office). Glenn Puit, *Arrest Threat: Child Porn Copies Lead to Conflict*, LAS VEGAS REVIEW-JOURNAL (July 28, 2003), (local prosecutor threatened to arrest defense counsel for possession of child porn images even though judge had previously authorized counsel to possess the images in order to assist his client's defense).

38. Commonwealth v. Simone, 2003 Va. Cir. LEXIS 215 (Portsmouth, VA Cir. Court) (child porn images recovered from temporary Internet file on defendant's computer after he viewed but did not manually save images sufficient for conviction since he reached out for and controlled the images at issue). United States v. Tucker, 305 F.3d 1193, 1198 (10th Cir. 2002), *cert. denied*, 537 U.S. 1123 (2003) (conviction upheld for possession of files automatically stored in a browser cache because defendant's "habit of manually deleting images from the cache files estab-

lished that he exercised control over them"); *but see* United States v. Perez, 247 F. Supp. 2d 459, 484 fn. 12 (S.D.N.Y. 2003) (court raised without resolving "the issue of whether images viewed on the internet and automatically stored in a browser's temporary file cache are knowingly 'possessed' or 'received'"); United States v. Stulock, 308 F.3d 922, 925 (8th Cir. 2002) ("one cannot be guilty of possession for simply having viewed an image on a web site, thereby causing the image to be automatically stored in the browser's cache, without having purposely saved or downloaded the image").

39. Geoff Fellows, *Peer-to-Peer Networking Issues—An Overview*, Digital Investigation (2004), vol. 1, at pp. 3–6.

40. *Id.*, at p. 6.

41. *Id.*, at p. 4 ("The structure of peer-to-peer networks presents opportunities to law enforcement for proactive investigation. . . . This results . . . in prosecutions not for the mere possession of obscene images but rather for distribution, a much more serious offense.").

42. While criminal copyright liability requires a "willful" intent, civil infringement liability is strict.

43. An IP address is the unique address assigned to every machine on the Internet and consists of four numbers separated by dots. A web bug, or pixel tag, is embedded in an HTML-formatted email message sent to the perpetrator. When the email message is opened, the image tag refers the user's browser to a 1x1 pixel transparent picture stored on a web server under the control of the party embedding the image tag. The web server then keeps a log of all requests for that image and logs the IP address of the browsing host, the time and date of the request and also, in these cases, a referring URL that shows the last URL loaded by the browser so that we can track what site referred the browser to the web server. This type of image tag works similarly to the default logging of a web server, that is, when a user visits a website, the website collects information on the IP address of the visitor's web browser and the date and time when the visit occurred. This type of logging is widely used by websites to track web page activity for security purposes. Just as a website tracks the IP address of browsers accessing the website, the web bug tracks the IP address of browsers on computers where the tagged email message is opened and provides information on when the person opens the email message, the IP address of the browser used to open the email, and what type of browser was used (e.g., Microsoft's Internet Explorer, Netscape, or Mozilla). It is less intrusive than a cookie, which websites place directly on a visitor's hard drive and may be used to monitor web surfing activities of a user and to capture personally identifiable data about unsuspecting computer users. Such use of cookies have been found to raise viable claims of violations of the Electronic Communications Privacy Act (ECPA), 18 U.S.C. § 2701, though not of the CFAA. *See In re Pharmatrak, Inc. Privacy Litigation*, 329 F.3d 9 (1st Cir. 2003) (district court's summary judgment finding defendants' use of web bugs that col-

lected personal information about website visitors by planting cookies on the visitors' computer hard drives was not in violation of ECPA was reversed, but district court judgment of no CFAA violation was not disturbed). *In re Intuit Privacy Litigation*, 138 F. Supp. 2d 1272 (C.D. CA 2001) (plaintiff computer users who visited website, www.quicken.com, and had cookies surreptitiously embedded on their hard drives in order to track and record a particular user's movements across the web failed to show any economic damage as required under 18 U.S.C. § 1030(g) and that claim was dismissed, but claims under the ECPA survived motion to dismiss).

Part III

New Cops
Rethinking Law Enforcement in a Digital Age

6

Designing Accountable Online Policing

Nimrod Kozlovski

The transition to an information society increases dependence on communication and computation infrastructure. While the new online environment introduces great opportunities for contemporary society, it also creates unforeseen vulnerabilities and changes the types of risks we face. Our information infrastructure was designed with a particular sense of security—ensuring the survivability of the network—but has limited built-in guarantees for confidentiality and integrity of information or assurances of services' availability. Most legal systems have amended their laws to criminalize attacks against availability, confidentiality, or integrity of information systems (which I will refer to collectively as "computer crimes") and shaped their procedural laws to better serve online law enforcement. Nevertheless, by observing the exponentially growing incidence of computer crimes, we can conclude that the law has gained only limited deterrent effect. Computer crimes demand innovative thinking when it comes to the efficient design of law enforcement systems. The technological and social conditions of criminal activity have changed and the conventional law enforcement response to crime is ill-equipped to address these changing conditions.

Law enforcement offline is mainly a reactive system, relatively centralized, publicly managed, and rooted in human discretion. The emerging system of online law enforcement is different: it is mainly preventive, highly decentralized, a hybrid of public and private enforcement, and highly automated. It is informed by information security strategies. It is much more pervasive than offline governmental law enforcement. It calls for the ubiquitous policing of online activities to monitor, control, deter, deflect, detect, prevent, or preempt risky and potentially malicious activities. Practically, this new system of policing is emerging with no clear legal structure. It seeks the enactment of new legislation, adapted to the online environment, to embrace this model of policing. Doing so will restructure the nature of criminal law, its role in society, its subjects of regulation, and its attitude toward innocents at the scene of the crime.

The strengths of the emerging model derive from employing alternative strategies of law enforcement. It is dynamically adaptive to a digital crime scene. Yet many of the model's features escape those restraints that limit the use of policing power. The legal, institutional, and technological settings of conventional law enforcement are based on the conditions of physical crime scenes and fail to transfer smoothly to online ones.

This essay argues that it is time to study the new policing model and to understand why it escapes the restraints that society deemed necessary to tame the power to police. It further argues that it is possible to have a more secure environment, one which at the same time enhances liberty— but in order to achieve these goals, it is imperative to design an accountable policing model.

In a democratic society, those invested with policing power—either public or private—must be held accountable. Accountability manifests itself in responsibility to account for actions taken and actions not taken, and to explain or justify them. It is the duty to expose oneself to review and the possibility of sanctions. Accountability mechanisms are essential to protect civil liberties, deter those who police from abusing their power, promote efficiency, and open a democratic dialogue.

Accountability is a relational concept. It gains its meaning through interactions, reciprocal rights, and obligations within given relations. To understand the nature of online accountability, we need to acknowledge the presence and effects of the new information intermediaries: the service providers and information gatekeepers (whom I will refer to as "third parties"). The accountability of the individual, of the law enforcer, and of omnipresent online third parties all interact with each other. These connections of reciprocal accountability of all parties exist in a dynamic equilibrium which balances liberty and security in society. Currently there is a race to the bottom, as the new environment enables all parties to evade accountability. We experience an accountability deficit, but such a situation is unstable. My proposed solution links users' traceability with the accountability of police and offers a viable equilibrium in which liberal democratic values can be secured.

Now—when the technology for the new policing model is still being developed—is the time to design the measures that will ensure accountable policing. The design stage must be informed by accountability values. The development of new technology invites the establishment of new institutions to supervise policing, and value-driven design may enable new legal procedures that are better equipped to hold policing accountable. It is in our hands to design a desirable policing system.

I. A Paradigm Shift in Online Policing

The rise of a new policing system can be primarily attributed to features of the online environment: digitization, anonymity, connectivity, mobility, decentralization, and interdependence.[1] The new environment requires law enforcement to reassess vulnerability and risk[2] and to reconsider effective points of intervention. By abusing common vulnerabilities, wrongdoers can pose asymmetric risks to other users and cause cascading damage, while potentially remaining untraceable and out of the reach of law enforcement. The technological structure of the network makes omnipresent third parties, such as Internet Service Providers (ISPs) and DNS servers, essential to the operation of policing. It further introduces powerful gatekeeping nodes, such as portals, search engines, and dominant websites which can be utilized for law enforcement. The challenge is to find effective centralized intervention points in a decentralized environment. Although technology is constantly evolving to facilitate crime prevention,[3] it must work within existing legal constraints and demonstrates weakness in tracing criminals and in facilitating prosecution.

Lessons from offline enforcement have also led to innovative thinking about designing a policing regime for the online environment. Disillusion with the traditional deterrence model, disengagement from notions of rehabilitation, and the development of community policing theories all inform the design of online policing. The new environment in its formative stage can be understood as an experimental ground in which constant trials of alternative policing methods are studied.

These developments are leading to a distinct system of law enforcement. Fundamental notions in the operation of law enforcement are being gradually abandoned: its basis as a public operation run primarily by the government, limits on private parties' use of force, the goal of bringing criminals to justice, the centrality of human discretion, reluctance to require reporting of crimes, and a traditional unwillingness to use criminal law as a prior restraint. To fully understand virtual law enforcement, we need to relax our assumptions of traditional law enforcement and recognize that the new features of online law enforcement form a system of policing that is substantially different from traditional offline enforcement.

Prevention through Patterns

The new policing aims to prevent and preempt crime rather than to prosecute it. By predicting when, how, and by whom a crime will be committed, it aims to enable efficient intervention. Automated tools constantly monitor the environment to match users' risk profiles against dynamically identified patterns of criminal behavior. Patterns of previous computer crimes are coded as "crime signatures." These "signatures" can refer to a pattern of user behavior, a suspicious protocol structure, a distinguishable application pattern, or the semantic structure of a message. Automated tools screen packets in real time and raise an alert when a signature match is found. Further, they monitor for anomalies or deviations from "normal" behavior. The patterns of "normal" behavior are coded and an algorithm watches for a certain level of deviation from them. These systems aim to be able to disarm the attacker, redirect his actions to a "safe zone," block or modify his communication, or even strike back.

Alternative Restraints to Crime

The new policing relies heavily on nonlegal restraints. Scholarly work, supported by a growing body of empirical studies, has detailed the role of architecture (physical as well as virtual), social norms, and markets in regulating human behavior. Accordingly, law enforcement has recognized in virtual space a toolkit of restraints on criminal behavior. These restraints include law, technological features, network topology, and the social construction of particular uses of computers. Therefore, law enforcement shifts to affect the design of the technological environment.[4] It aims to set up systems which will disable the potential for crime, make it costlier, reduce its potential gain, or make it traceable. Law enforcement also aims to shape the social conditions of computer use to strengthen community control, to prevent the association of criminals, and to support social mechanisms of trust. It aims to establish market dynamics which are conducive to law enforcement and to thwart market initiatives which facilitate crime.

Private Public Policing

The new policing operates as a hybrid of public and private enforcement. There is a growing tendency to rely on the private sector's efforts.[5] The shift toward the private sector is conducted through partnership, delegation, the imposition of responsibilities, and full privatization. Instead of notions of a necessary separation between public enforcement and private beneficiaries, we see an increasing sense of mutual responsibility and joint operation. The line between private "security" and public law enforcement is blurring as private parties monitor the "public" flow of information and "secure" essential information junctions. New policies have been specifically tailored to increase private policing efforts and to enjoy their relative advantage. In this transition toward private enforcement, the regulation of the use of force shifts from public law to contractual arrangements between private service providers and their users. The extent and methods of this private policing are determined by contractual terms.

Decentralized versus Centralized Design

The new policing is shifting to a hybrid architecture that enjoys the benefits of both decentralized and centralized network topologies by optimizing the allocation of responsibilities between the center and the edges. This combination allows law enforcement to enjoy the relative advantage of the edges in sensing their local environment, analyzing risk in context, and using force in real time to mitigate damage. The edges are empowered and unchained from the rigid hierarchal constraints of conventional policing. At the same time this structure also empowers the center by using real-time communication to enable centralized defense mechanisms, such as the segregation of infected areas, blockage of certain domains, or centralized distribution of updated defense tools. The abundance of decentralized sensors enables the center to take a comprehensive view of the network and to make systemwide operational decisions. In addition, a fully distributed private architecture—a peer culture of security—is emerging to facilitate correlated vulnerability assessment and joint defense strategies.

Regulating Victims and Third Parties

The regulation of criminal behavior is shifting toward greater regulation of the behavior of victims and third parties.[6] It aims to create optimal behavior on the part of potential victims and to employ third parties for crime prevention and detection, damage mitigation, and evidence gathering. Sympathy for defenseless victims is replaced by a growing legal body of active obligations for self-defense. Criminal sanctions penalize the failure to follow these obligations when innocent third parties' interests are at stake.

The law further recognizes the unique role which third parties, including conduits, service providers, information gatekeepers, traffic routers, tool suppliers, and payment systems play on the digital crime scene and heavily regulates them. They may face liability, either direct (e.g., for clearing illegal transactions)[7] or secondary (e.g., notice and takedown requirements for illegal content). They may be subject to operational requirements, including requirements to design or adjust systems in order to facilitate enforcement,[8] to retain logs and traffic data,[9] to block illegal communication dynamically,[10] or to reroute traffic. They may also be given structural incentives, including the subsidization of enforcement-related operational costs, immunity from civil liability for enforcement-related activities, and gaining prioritized law enforcement treatment for cooperation.

With the regulation of third parties comes reassessment of the complex legal relations between the government, service providers, and users. Service providers in certain capacities are considered "partners" to the government in law enforcement. A common pattern in the regulation of third parties is to grant immunity for third parties vis-à-vis the users while simultaneously imposing new obligations vis-à-vis the government. Moreover, the regulation often assures the secrecy of interactions with law enforcement to secure the third parties' interest in nondisclosure.

Intelligence Architecture

New information-sharing architectures are emerging, informed by notions of open intelligence. Instead of the traditional separation of intelligence operations and law enforcement, we see joint operations and the dynamic allocation of priorities. Law enforcement shares intelligence information and raw output from decentralized sensors and dissolves reporting bottlenecks. Law enforcement opens bidirectional information channels to share policing-related information with the private sector, while also imposing new reporting obligations.

In addition, law enforcement opens information to upstream and downstream analysis, both public and private. Thanks to flexible sharing policies and tools of data anonimization, layer-specific and rules-based access authorization, information can be opened to variable levels of access depending on a user's needs, privacy, and trade secret interests.

Self-Help Sanctions

The new policing changes the essence of the use of force, redefining it in dynamic terms which acknowledge the diverse toolkit of means and the continuous nature of its imposition. The use of force, increasingly legalized, becomes routine through contracts. Instead of imprisonment or monetary fines imposed publicly through a judicial body following legal processes, online sanctions involve upfront exclusion or "virtual imprisonment,"[11] and are often imposed by private parties acting without judicial oversight, sometimes even invisibly.

Regulating Identification

The new policing focuses on connecting an online identity to a real-life person and therefore regulates the management of online identity. This focus on the identification process is based on an understanding of its potential vulnerabilities, as a successful misidentification by the criminal enables him to commit a chain of crimes. Currently, our contemporary society overrelies on identification processes, even those conducted with poor identification means not created for that purpose (e.g., social security numbers). This overreliance introduces a major security flaw, which current law enforcement initiatives try to tackle by identifying suspicious patterns of identification and by cross-checking that information with external sources.

The flexibility of online identity construction and the ease of impersonation create a challenge to security which requires consistent identification, trusted identities, and traceable users. Often, the attribution of online activity to a real-life person is the missing link in an investigation. Therefore, new laws aim to require a trace-back route to prevent misleading identification, and to limit the construction of multiple identities. Further, the law creates incentives to adopt more secure identification technologies, such as mandating digital signatures in transactions with the government or giving them a preferred evidentiary status.

Noncontent Analysis

Building blocks of data for crime analysis and investigation are being redefined by the new policing system. Data is structured in a way optimized for a wide range of new forms of analysis. Investigators increasingly focus on "noncontent" data such as traffic data and automated system logs, enabling them to create maps of associations, and to visualize nontrivial connections among events. While traditional content requires intense human interpretation and manual analysis to extract intelligence, noncontent data is tailored for automatic analysis. Even when the content is encrypted, the associated channel information and metadata can supply invaluable intelligence. Because such information is regularly in the possession of third parties, it can be retrieved without alerting suspects or allowing them to manipulate it. Emphasizing the importance of noncontent data, law enforcement organizations frequently advocate for new regulations that require service providers to retain traffic data for lengthy periods.

Taken together, these features form a new policing model which has noticeable advantages and disadvantages.

THE EMERGING POLICING MODEL
WITHSTANDS PERFORMANCE CHALLENGES

The new model of policing is relatively efficient, strategically employing the most effective tools, intervention points, and institutional settings for any given situation. It enables a flexible continuum of policing interventions which replace the rigid tools of physical enforcement. It creates a policing pattern which is responsive in real time to changing conditions to evolving risk patterns. It fits with digital information and takes advantage of flexibility in analyzing such information. It is capable of correlating identification patterns, behavioral patterns, association patterns, and application patterns to produce a unified comprehensive risk analysis.

Furthermore, the new model reduces the costs of policing and more effectively compels relevant parties to internalize the policing costs of their activities. Moreover, it invites relevant stakeholders to be involved in their policing effort and enables them to register their preferences in its design.

The new model regains the deterrence lost in the transition to the online environment and makes it scalable and applicable to other crimes.

This model also enables the creation of local policing with localized norms, avoiding the problem of extrajurisdictional effects. By employing local players and personalizing intervention, it has the potential to target policing to the relevant subjects while leaving other users unaffected. Moreover, the model, if designed with democratic values in mind, can actually enhance privacy by minimizing the collateral effects of policing. It can lead to more precise and focused interventions that replace the rough tools of current policing. Instead of interfering with innocent traffic to spot criminals, it can filter out only potential criminals, leaving other traffic untouched.

To conclude, the emerging model is better suited to the new information environment than is traditional law enforcement, because it understands the nature of the change from atoms to bits, from space to flow, from presence to representation. Yet what are the possible implications and unintended consequences of this model, which may cause resistance to its wider usage?

II. Unaccountable Online Policing

The new model of policing may lead to severe infringements upon civil liberties. First, it invites the excessive use of power by private entities, which can create inequality in enforcement, disproportional and untamed use of force, and biased policing. Second, by using sophisticated sorting tools, it introduces the possibility of constant profiling and systematic exclusion of segments of society. Third, it might limit liberty and discipline behavior by establishing a "tyranny of the pattern," in which deviation from preidentified patterns of "normal" behavior leads to sanctions. Such punishment of deviation could stifle creativity and perpetuate existing power structures. Fourth, it exposes the individual to extensive surveillance and control. Fifth, it opens the door for hidden surveillance and the illegitimate, invisible use of force. Sixth, it enables the government to extend its regulatory reach beyond the boundaries of the law alone.[12]

Furthermore, the model enables the government to circumvent existing limitations on policing power by employing regulatory arbitrage to evade restraints on state power. The government can, for example, use personally identifying information collected by commercial entities while avoiding the constitutional and legal limitations that would regulate direct governmental surveillance. This evasion expands policing power and distorts the balance between policing and liberty.

A closer look at these objections reveals that they focus on its potential toward excessive policing and the expansion of power beyond democratically imposed limitations. The fear they express is that of overpolicing through hidden and unregulated modes of operation. Both the dehumanization of power encoded within technology and the privatization of power intensifies the outcry. Our instincts about freedom resist ubiquitous policing which is not transparent, not required to justify its decisions, and not held accountable for its actions. This is the objection to unaccountable policing.[13]

The core principle of a democratic society is that with power comes responsibility; power in democracy is interwoven with restraints. The emerging policing model evades such responsibility. While it shifts from the foundations of the traditional policing model to tackle the challenges of the new crime scene, it also escapes the net of accountability originally designed to keep policing in check.

Existing accountability measures fail to address the paradigm shift in law enforcement for legal, technological, and institutional reasons.

Why Does the Law Fail to Hold Policing Accountable?

Legally, the structure of accountable policing is based on the assumptions of offline models. It assumes a prosecution-based system, enforcement conducted mainly by public officials, judicial overview encoded into the procedure, and notification of the subject of enforcement as the interested party in objecting to the enforcement. The new model of policing places all these assumptions in question.

In the shift from a prosecution-based model to a preventive one, legal accountability is eroded. The current legal structure gives the prosecutor incentives to follow legal rules by excluding evidence obtained in breach of those rules. But this model has no bite when the enforcement effort is not aimed at prosecution.

The regulation of policing has not kept pace with the institutional tendency to shift toward private enforcement. The current legal structure assumes that the public officials who conduct law enforcement will be constrained by constitutional and legislative protections of individual rights. Where private entities serve as agents of public law enforcement, these same legal constraints are applied to them. But as policing shifts to the private sphere it transfers constraining authority from the realm of constitutional law to the contractual. Freedom of contract, coupled with asymmetric bargaing power, leads to the expansion of the contractual use of force. Users are commonly required in their contracts with service providers to waive rights that protect them vis-à-vis the government. Thus, for example, users consent contractually that their service provider will have the discretion to transfer personally identifying information to the government, thereby waiving their protection from warrantless governmental search. These contractual arrangements thus circumvent constitutional protections.

RIGID BINARY DOCTRINES

The binary structure of legal doctrines enables investigative techniques to evade accountability. A legal structure built on dichotomies—search or non-search, private or public, content or no consent, expectation of privacy or no expectation of privacy—leads to binary doctrines which are too rigid to handle the complexity of the new technological environment and too often deem a policing practice to be fully unregulated.

OUTDATED LADDER OF ACCOUNTABILITY

Technological changes have lowered the level of accountability which law enforcers need to withstand regulatory control. These lowered standards often imply that judicial review is replaced by more lenient administrative review processes. Criminal procedure is currently structured according to a ladder of accountability which imposes different thresholds of accountability on different investigatory activities. Different procedures lead to the issuance of different legal orders (e.g., a search warrant or a subpoena). The chosen threshold is based on various factors: the type of information (user information, noncontent data, or content), the potential infringement on civil liberties, the intrusiveness of the act, the entity which possesses the information, the severity of the crime, the scope of existing evidence, and the stage of the investigation. The erosion in accountability occurs when changes in technology, the institutional setting, or business practices enable the bar to be lowered for any given activity.

Thus, for example, the shift toward remote storage and e-services enables the government to acquire information from third parties with a subpoena rather than obtaining a warrant to search a user's computer. Similarly, the storage of access logs on a web server enables the government to acquire the stored information from a service provider rather than obtaining a wiretap warrant.

ALTERNATIVE POLICING RESTRAINTS

The law fails to hold accountable governmental actions that are intended as a form of policing but which are carried out through nontraditional mechanisms. Current law is ill-equipped to conceive of regulatory modalities such as system design as policing actions that require careful legal attention. Such intentional intervention is often perceived not as imposed regulation, but as the objective conditions of the environment. Even when the indirect manner of regulation is perceived as an intentional governmental action, we lack the legal tools to hold it to account. While direct regulation needs to withstand a process that assures public accountability, transparency, and public participation, such mechanisms are absent when the regulation is indirect.

ARTIFICIAL CONSENT

Liberal foundations of the law that protect autonomy and set the boundaries between the individual and society are turned on their head in the new environment and are used to subject the individual to power. Consent is a core legal concept that protects individual autonomy from external power. However, legal doctrines often deprive the individual of a meaningful choice over whether to consent to surveillance and policing. The doctrine of consent to search and seizure was devised as an exception to the procedural requirements that safeguard privacy. The law, however, has evolved into a regime in which consent is often fictitious: either no actual consent was given (e.g., consenting to a search of personal belongings in a shared apartment) or one in which one has no practical choice but to consent (e.g., residents of public housing projects being required to consent to police raids). In the Internet context, consent is legally assumed from the mere use of technology, which potentially reveals information to third parties. Consent is also upheld in situations of no meaningful choice, such as the consent given in standard Internet service contracts to allow police access to private information.

Why Does Technology Fail to Hold Policing Accountable?

Technologically, policing accountability structures have depended on the visibility of the enforcement effort and the transparency of the regulatory modes that the technology employs. When policing is visible, we can publicly hold law enforcement accountable. Visible use of force often leads to public outcry when the policing effort is perceived as brutal, disproportionate, or biased. Visibility enables the suspect or bystanders to present their version or to record the course of action for later review. Visibility further enables social mechanisms like reputation and shame to deter overzealous enforcement. In addition, transparency enables an understanding of policing methods and the tracing of coercive force. Transparency enables us to perceive a specific act as policing and to map the sources of force which affect us. It makes it possible to sort out intentional force from objective conditions of the environment. This visibility triggers resistance and requests to account for the use of force. Moreover, the deterrent effect of a policing tool—whether a policeman's club, a checkpoint, or handcuffs—is often tied to its transparency.

Digital cops, however, are invisible. In virtual space, policing often becomes invisible and the nature of force is no longer transparent. The user often cannot tell that there is a policing tool in the environment. Policing tools operate in the background and are normally deployed at strategic information junctions outside users' reach. Surveillance and information flow analyses are conducted without leaving traces on the original documents. Moreover, policing functionalities are embedded within systems that also provide other functionalities and cannot be separately noticed. Even extremely intrusive tools, such as keystroke loggers installed on the user's computer, can be disguised to appear innocent. Tools which are designed to detect such software are regularly disabled to prevent disclosure.

NONTRANSPARENT POLICING

The nature of the regulatory effect of the technology is not transparent. Technology can be visible and its installment can be publicly announced, yet we cannot immediately tell how it constrains our behavior. The technology is often installed as a black box. Closed-source software is transparent to the user in only a limited sense: he or she can observe only the interface and the functional results of the process. However, one cannot tell how it operates and what additional features are embedded inside. Furthermore, the user cannot differentiate between a merely technical response of the network and intentional policing. For example, when policing is conducted by rerouting HTTP requests to an error page, the user commonly perceives the error as website malfunction and not as policing.

Moreover, current legislation gives protection to security measures put in place to prevent users from seeing the relevant code. Freedom of information legislation fails to supply the public with the right to observe the design or configuration of surveillance technology.[14] Courts have formerly only been willing to disclose the code of surveillance devices to a privileged few, based on the proposition that further disclosure will render the technology ineffective and vulnerable to circumvention. Similarly, filtering tools which conduct core policing functions online are based on the premise that their filtering rules remain secret.

Why Does Institutional Structure Fail to Hold Policing Accountable?

Institutional structures establish accountability through disciplinary efforts. Hierarchy within organizations, operational walls between departments, and interorganizational collaborations open acts and omissions to review.

The internal organization of law enforcement was designed to foster a culture of accountability with joint responsibility for acts and omissions. Internal procedures obligate officers to subject their work to supervision and make supervisors responsible for the work of their supervisees. These notions are also reflected in requirements for approval from higher-ranking officers for certain investigative techniques, such as wiretaps. These procedures create a bidirectional accountability structure. Furthermore, by acting as initial authorizers, courts enforce compliance with internal authorization requirements. The court's own accountability acts as an additional safeguard. Since the court's proceedings are public, it will hesitate to function as a mere rubber stamp.

This internal accountability structure becomes questionable when policing shifts to a preventive mode, when technology reduces the procedural requirements for acquiring information, or when information is transferred voluntarily by third parties. Moreover, technology also serves to reshape hierarchal structures of command with embedded monitoring and control into flattened structures of operation that generate less internal review.

More importantly, the design of information systems in service of policing may alter the structure of accountability. Because a virtual institutional structure emerges around the organizational logic of the information systems, this structure will reflect, inter alia, access rules, authorization management, database design, query formats, and interorganization communication tools. Those accountability values which were among the considerations which informed the institutional design of policing will be absent online, unless we code them into the system.

OPERATIONAL WALLS

Operational separation between departments or functions within an organization can serve to fence the flow of information in an organization and to control the unwanted coordination of functions. Such operational walls are erected when there is an interest that calls for an intentional separation between departments or functions, to solve potential conflicts of interest, or to prevent unwanted concentrations of power. Institutional operation walls were traditionally erected to separate law enforcement from intelligence and to control information sharing between governmental bodies. The emerging policing model blurs these institutional lines, embraces joint operations, and facilitates information-sharing practices. Furthermore, the information and communication infrastructure in service of policing is currently being designed without encoding operational walls into the information architecture.

INEVITABLE COLLABORATIONS

Those who are required to collaborate with other people expose themselves to review, increasing their accountability. Collaborators can monitor their actions and can be called to testify in legal proceedings. When operational needs require the police to collaborate with other entities, the police are exposed to review and their operations are subject to increased possibilities of disclosure. For example, when interception of communication has to be conducted at the premises of service providers, the government has to disclose its operation to these providers. The service provider can potentially question the operation, challenge it, or be called to testify in legal proceedings in which the evidence obtained from the interception is examined.

Moreover, because new technological tools incorporate skills and resources which traditionally resided in different institutions, they enable law enforcers to refrain from forming collaborations which once seemed unavoidable. Furthermore, new tools enable opaque collaboration, in which the details of the collaboration are kept hidden from the collaborator. For example, existing technology enables remote database queries without revealing the details of the query to the database owner. The police can use a hashed form of a searched entry to match against a database, without disclosing the search details to the database owner unless a match is found. Alternatively, policing tasks which require massive computation can be performed without disclosing the details of the operation and with no requirement to have all the computation resources in-house. The use of distributed computation enables the decomposition of a large assignment into many small units without revealing the overall assignment to any of the individual processors.

Let's summarize the argument made thus far: the operation of policing has built-in assurances of accountability. These assurances operate in legal, technological, and institutional layers. Working in tandem, these layers form a complex net of accountability which restrains the use of policing power and makes it answerable. However, with the emergence of a new policing model for cybercrime, the setting for policing operation has changed and put in question the effectiveness of this network of accountability. When legal, technological, and institutional settings change, accountability measures are easily circumvented or become nonfunctional.

III. Accountability

Before we inquire deeper into the structure of accountability for the new policing model, it will be instructive to take a closer look at the concept of accountability itself. Accountability, as I see it, is answerability. Accountability mechanisms are the rules, processes, technologies, design principles, and institutional structures which hold an entity to account for its actions and inactions. In the context of policing, accountability mechanisms can take various forms: a legal requirement to report the use of surveillance technology in investigation, a requirement to notify the subject of a search, a procedure to produce evidence in open court to support prosecution, or a technological feature that reports to the subject of information when that information is accessed.

Accountability mechanisms assure answerability; they monitor compliance with substantive and procedural requirements and enable dynamic questioning of their ongoing efficiency and desirability. They deter enforcers from uncontrolled unilateral acts or abuses of power. Accountability mechanisms open a dialogue between the enforcer and its relevant supervisor or community. They function as a counterforce to authority and tame unbridled power. As such, these measures protect civil liberties and ensure that the democratically determined balance between security needs and civil liberties is observed. Accountability measures expose infringements of liberties hidden in the practical operation of policing, reveal gaps between declared rights and their fulfillment, and serve as a guard against unauthorized invasions of privacy. Moreover, they expose inequality and discrimination hidden in policing practices. Finally, they protect one's right to speak freely by requiring a censorial power to answer for the unauthorized act of blocking or disruption.

Accountability is essential for more than protecting rights. Accountability also promotes efficiency while enabling the measurement and assessment of performance, forcing judgment about the wisdom and fairness of decisions. It enables one to assess whether the social cost of policing is appropriate and proportional to the harm it prevents. It controls abuse and misuse while revealing the unauthorized use of power. In the context of law enforcement, accountability even promotes the security of the endeavor of enforcement itself by acting as a tool to monitor against potentially insecure policing systems or a potential counterintelligence effort.

Accountability measures can be embedded in the technological, legal, institutional, or social layers of a policing process. Accountability systems should be understood as a delicate puzzle in which each layer is assigned a certain role and operates and reacts to measures of accountability in other layers. The accountability effect is the overall outcome of the functioning of all elements. Accountability is a dynamic construct, and tuning or distortion of one measure may have a domino effect on the functionality of others. Furthermore, accountability systems can normally adjust to the relative weakness of one layer by adding more strength to another layer. When the institutional structure of policing, for example, is relatively ineffective in holding the enforcer accountable, a tighter judicial overview at the legal layer balances the effect. However, when an entire layer is completely disabled or easily circumvented, the system may fail to regain its balance.

The Dynamic Equilibrium of Accountability

Accountability is a relational concept, gaining its meaning through interactions and reciprocal rights. The answerability of an entity is always in relation to the entity to which it should answer. One may be held account-able in relation to one entity but not in relation to another. Moreover, in interactive multiparty relations, accountability is a multidimensional con-cept which reflects the level of accountability appropriate to each entity vis-à-vis the other entities. Changing the measure of accountability which operates on one entity affects the overall equilibrium.

In the law-enforcement context, the accountability of the individual interacts with the accountability of the enforcer. For example, many cur-rent suggestions relate to an accountable user, who will be required to sus-tain a consistent identity over time. This measure, although it holds the user more accountable, tends to erode the enforcer's accountability. Where that enforcer was previously required to be answerable for the reasons it invoked to unveil the user's identity, now it can potentially chase the user without undergoing inquiry itself.

Further, in a multiparty environment, the accountability of additional parties interacts with both the user's and the enforcer's accountability. For example, if a website owner is allowed to collect data on its users and enjoys the discretion as to whether or not to share the information with the government, governmental accountability is affected vis-à-vis the user. The government can acquire data on users without undergoing judicial review of its information collection practices, without justifying the need and proportionality of its acts, and without facing the user's objections. On the other hand, when a third party enables the user to evade accountability (as, for example, anonymization services do), it affects the accountability dynamic in the reverse manner. In an environ-ment where third parties both are omnipresent and technologically required, they become a dominant factor in the dynamic accountability equilibrium.

A common phenomenon in the online environment is accountability arbitrage. Rational parties often conceive of accountability as an operating cost, which they try to minimize if possible. Thus, when the government can either collect information about a citizen directly and face the burden of proving its justification in a judicial process or alternatively query a commercial database which has already collected the same information in a commercial context, the latter scenario is more likely. Accountability arbitrage enables an entity which is subject to a certain accountability standard to reduce its level of accountability.

We should think of accountability not as a binary condition, but as a continuum. We should set the level of accountability at the point along this continuum which best serves our values. In this continuum, the levels of police accountability, users' accountability, and third parties' accountability represent normative choices about the balance between liberty and security in society.

Do Unaccountable Users Require Unaccountable Policing?

The lack of user accountability online is commonly used as a justification for eroding policing accountability. Because users escape accountability by being untraceable and by acting outside local jurisdictions' accountability rules, it is argued that we need to give the government more leeway in handling these new types of unaccountable criminals and relax the accountability requirements which we impose on policing. The logic is simple: to properly react to the diminishing level of users' accountability, we need to allow reduced governmental accountability.

I claim that this approach is mistaken.

The solution to the diminishing level of users' accountability will arise from creative thoughts about how to reconstruct user accountability in a manner that coexists with governmental accountability. Yes, we should design for user accountability, yet we need also to be aware of imposing too much of an accountability burden on the user. I argue that instead of justifying one erosion in accountability by another and lowering accountability standards altogether, we ought to redesign accountability for both the user and the law enforcer by mutually raising the bar.

I agree with the factual claim that user accountability is being eroded online. Features of that environment enable the user to remain untraceable, as the core Internet was not designed with security in mind. I believe that we can establish a system of user accountability which is based on potential traceability and message attribution within the existing Internet protocol and without changing the architecture of the information environment.

Any system of user accountability system must take into account five functional goals:

- Identification of the user
- Traceability of messages
- Integrity of messages
- Readability of messages
- Retention of evidence for judicial proceedings.

Elsewhere, I have proposed the "traceable anonymity" model, which offers to create an appropriate balance. Based on an existing public-key encryption infrastructure, this model lays out the institutional and architectural foundations of a user accountability system. The aim is to maintain the users' ability to use the Internet anonymously and without being recorded, but at the same time enable law enforcement agencies worldwide, subject to a judicial decision, to trace the identity of a user who misuses his or her anonymity to commit a crime. Any electronic message is signed with a digital signature using a unique private key that is issued to the user after an identification process by a private and regulated certificate authority. A digital certificate that is attached to the message does not reveal personally identifying information but ensures that an identification process was conducted. If the user misuses his anonymity to commit a crime, the court (local or international) may order, with attendant due process protections, the certificate authority to disclose the user's identity. The revealed information links the identified user to the specific crime, but to no other activity, and the digitally signed message serves as evidence of the criminal act. This system would be technologically scalable to the international level and can be used as an efficient mechanism to enable transnational law enforcement efforts. At the same time, the system could accommodate cultural differences and restrain coercive unilateral abuse of the system by regulating the conditions under which a certifying authority follows a foreign order to reveal the user's identity.

The technological and institutional details of this model are beyond the scope of this essay, yet the idea is simple: traceable anonymity ties the accountability of the user to the accountability of the police. It increases the users' accountability from the current level by making users potentially traceable, yet prevents the government from unveiling users' information unless it justifies the need before an independent judicial body. Even then it cannot trace or attribute other actions by the user. The certifying authority serves to help the identification process, but cannot access its own database without judicial order, as the court holds half the key to the database. This also prevents a tyrannical regime from accessing the database unilaterally.

In conclusion, we should not justify the lack of policing accountability as a response to the decrease in users' accountability. Instead we ought to construct an appropriate policing accountability system.

IV. Designing for Accountable Online Policing

Now that we have examined the nature of policing accountability and its interaction with the accountability of other parties, we can lay out guidelines for designing a policing structure that serves both efficiency and liberty. The following concepts should serve as foundations for the design of an accountability system:

Optimal Equilibrium

We should stop the race to the bottom of diminishing accountability for all relevant parties: individuals, law enforcement, and third parties. Instead we should aim to raise the multidimensional equilibrium of accountability. When we design such a system, we should think of the full matrix of accountability and consider dynamically the effect that changes in the accountability mechanisms restraining one party will have on the accountability of other parties.

Liberal Accountability Values

Accountability requirements should correspond with our liberal democratic values. These values require different levels of accountability for different parties. Based on these values, the individual ought to be held accountable only to the minimal level necessary to enable a viable security model; any increase in the level of individual accountability should have to withstand harsh scrutiny. At the same time, policing should be held accountable at the highest optimal level possible in order to control policing power while simultaneously enabling efficient operation.

Medium Sensitivity

When we design accountability mechanisms, we need to be sensitive to their effects on the overall medium. A structure of accountability which affects the architecture also affects the political structure of the information ecosystem. The design of an accountability structure for the communication network influences peoples' relative power to shape public discourse and affects the nature of such discourse. It dictates who controls the flow of information in society, who has the ability to squelch other voices, whose voices will be amplified, and whose voices will be silenced. The design also determines the ability of the government to control the flow of information and to block certain information or certain speakers.[15] An accountability structure for a communication network must consider these political implications of its implementation.

Liability limitations for service providers illustrate such considerations in action. In order to enjoy the benefits of a robust, unmonitored, and open environment, foresighted legislators will refrain from imposing liability on service providers for third parties' content.

Circumvention Analysis

At the design stage, we should simulate possible circumvention of the accountability mechanisms under consideration and, if required, establish mechanisms to monitor or prevent such circumvention.

Functional Equivalency

We need to treat functionally equivalent systems alike with respect to accountability, imposing comparable accountability standards on comparable policing actions to prevent the accountability arbitrage.

Layers of Accountability

We need to consider the functionality of all layers of accountability—legal, institutional, technological, and social—working in tandem. We must design these layers to supplement each other rather than contradict each other. We need to explore opportunities for synergetic effects across layers. Simultaneously, we should evaluate the trade-offs involved in using one layer rather than another.

Continuum of Accountability

When possible, we should create flexible accountability measures that can be adjusted to changing circumstances. This flexibility will enable us to keep accountability mechanisms in operation even when special needs, such as urgent terror investigations, require a reduced level of accountability. A good design offers a continuum of modes of operation, rather than a binary model that only allows one to enable or disable an accountability measure.

Having established a set of guidelines for design, we should think through the new accountability mechanisms in greater detail. New technologies can lead to improved and innovative legal and institutional mechanisms of accountability. The development of new technology opens a window of opportunity to design accountability mechanisms that fit the new environment.

Technological measures can support the establishment of new institutions for the supervision of policing. Technological developments can either strengthen or weaken institutions within society. New developments can enable standard-setting, internal, interorganization, and external supervisory bodies to hold policing accountable. The policing accountability deficit can be corrected if we design technological policing tools to facilitate supervision.

Imagine the following features embedded in database and casefile tools used by law enforcers:

- A tamper-proof log audits the time and date of collection of any piece of information that enters the digital investigation folder.
- Another log audits the access to digital evidence made by the investigator and the queries run on the investigation databases.
- All traffic data to and from the enforcer is retained and visualized to demonstrate the enforcement networks of operation and the sources of information obtained.
- Email and telephone calls made by the investigator are recorded and stored on digital media and can be analyzed with natural language search tools.
- Pattern analysis tools look for suspicious access to information or abnormal investigation processes.

This scenario may sound familiar: it is no different from practices in many corporations which monitor their employees' work to assure compliance with work procedures and to protect the corporations from fraud, abuse, and potential liability. Claims departments in insurance companies, for example, employ such tools to monitor the work of their claims investigators. Employing similar technologies will empower the institutions needed to supervise the policing operation. The main obstacles to efficient supervision have always been resources and information. Technology reduces the costs dramatically and enables remote supervision of all aspects of the policing operation.

Current technology is flexible enough to facilitate the establishment of various institutions to fulfill a variety of supervisory functions. It can produce accounts which are specifically tailored to each supervisory institution and can measure and review different parts of the policing operation. We can imagine supervisory bodies getting selective access to the different layers of accounts and producing distinctive reports based on their position, needs, and authority. Such review can respect existing classifications and can allow access to investigation information without revealing personally identifying information. It enables the supervision of the work of individual officers to prevent the abuse of power. It can enable aggregate analysis of the policing operation to identify patterns of crime and enforcement, such as racial profiling and actual enforcement prioritization.

Technological features can also support the construction of legal procedures that are better equipped to hold policing accountable.

Toward an Accountable Search and Seizure Law

Technology enables us to redesign search and seizure law to hold the government to a higher standard of accountability without compromising the efficacy of investigations.[16] Currently, in an *ex parte* procedure the court issues search warrants which give wide authorization to law enforcement to search designated premises for all documents and devices for incriminating evidence. Why? Because *ex ante* the court has no information on which to base a decision as to how to limit the search to certain files or to predict where the information might be located. Standard warrants therefore fail to genuinely meet particularization and minimization requirements. This procedure is justified by some scholars as a necessary evil, as suspects can save files with misleading names, hide them in unexpected folders, or scramble their content to appear innocent.

In practice, law enforcers hardly ever conduct searches on-site. The officers on-site copy the hard drives and other information found on storage devices and hand the copies to experts for a deferred but thorough search. The initial warrant enables law enforcement to conduct such a thorough search with minimal interference and with no audited process. Only when the search reveals new evidence which seems to exceed the original crime covered by the warrant do the police return to court to obtain an additional warrant. At this stage, when the incriminating evidence is known to the police, the court procedure is a mere rubber stamp.

These searches are conducted with a troubling procedure that potentially strips computer users of all their privacy expectations for even the preliminary investigation of a petty crime. With physical searches, the suspect's presence at the scene enables a two-sided story of the process to deter the government from abusing the warrant, but no such mechanisms operate with digital searches. The supervising court must rely on law enforcement's version of how the search was conducted, which is susceptible to *ex post* "manufacture." This process is analogous to reverse engineering: the enforcer is already familiar with the evidence and reverses the process of production to enable an alternative production path which will not face the same legality concerns. Since retrieval tools can easily track a file once its content and format are known, it requires no special effort after the evidence is known to "manufacture" a legal process of acquisition.

Can search and seizure law become more accountable? Definitely, by changing the sequence to seizure followed by search and by introducing new authorization procedures and auditing requirements. The court can authorize the seizure of the relevant information first. In a simple and cheap copying process, a copy of the information is secured by law enforcement and detached from the suspect's control. At this stage, we can structure various alternative procedures for search authorization which assure better accountability: the court can appoint an expert as an officer of the court to examine the seized data before the police observe it. The expert's input can support the court's decision as to whether or not there are grounds to issue a warrant. Alternatively, we could enable an adversary process in which the owner of the information, other users of the computer, or the suspect can raise objections to the search or to its scope. After all, when the surprise element which was essential to physical searches is no longer required (as the evidence is now safe with law enforcement), why not enable a fair process that truly respects one's right against intrusive invasions?

Alternatively, we can allow law enforcement to conduct searches on the seized information without further procedure but require the use of a tamper-proof and copy-protected copy of the seized information with an audit log. Audited searches will enable the court (and the defendant, in the event of prosecution) to review the actual practice of the search and to question the acts of investigators.

Furthermore, in the current system we have no meaningful judicial review of the legal execution of wiretap orders and search warrants if law enforcement decides not to file for prosecution. Law enforcement can exceed its authorization while facing no accountability by refraining from prosecution. This result conflicts with a core principle of the legal system: that court orders are accompanied with a mechanism to supervise their execution. Normally the existence of an opponent or other interested party suffices to ensure supervision, and in their absence the court in many legal systems is authorized to appoint an officer of the court to supervise the execution of the order. To ensure accountability in the execution of wiretap orders and search warrants, we can design a process which requires law enforcement to report back to the court after execution. We can further employ the technologies described above to supply the court with objective information about the search's execution. Such a process becomes essential as more searches are conducted remotely and without notification, while formerly exceptional "sneak and peek" searches gradually become the norm.

Finally, we should further increase policing accountability by targeting the partnership between the government and private parties and regulating private enforcement. Courts should redraft agency rules to cover the practical partnership practices and the delegations of power which allow law enforcement to utilize private parties. These doctrines should regain their original rationales and question whether private parties are de facto government employees. Currently, the doctrine is applied far too narrowly; recently, in the *Jarrett* case,[17] it failed to regulate even the extreme case of intentional encouragement of a hacker to hack illegally for policing purposes.

We also need to amend the regulation of the current partnership between police and third parties, which replaces liability and openness with immunity and secrecy. The Freedom of Information Act should open for review information which is handed to the government. The trade secrets interests exception should be preserved (albeit only when necessary) by anonyimization of data. This legal regime should be supported with civil liability for negligent handling of information that causes harm to the individual.

Additionally, we should question the third-party's-consent doctrine, which practically treats all information observable by third parties as information whose subject assumes the risk of disclosure to the government. In an environment in which third parties are omnipresent and their

presence is technologically required, the individual does not have a meaningful choice whether to share the information with third parties or not.
Legal doctrine must reflect this reality.

Conclusion

The new information environment empowers us, but simultaneously
introduces unexpected vulnerabilities. To address these vulnerabilities, law
enforcement is rethinking its model of operation. The emerging model of
law enforcement is relatively efficient in addressing the new challenges, but
creates an unchecked policing power. It is now time to introduce accountability into the policing model.

In *Inherit the Wind*, Henry Drummond declares:

> Progress has never been a bargain. You've got to pay for it. Sometimes I
> think there's a man behind a counter who says, "All right, you can have a
> telephone, but you'll have to give up privacy and the charm of distance."[18]

In this essay I respond to Drummond's skeptic. I aim to prove that
progress can be a "bargain." We can have progress with civil liberties. We
can enjoy the benefits of information technologies without paying a price.
We can benefit from a secure online environment that is policed by
accountable law enforcement. A window of opportunity is currently opening for designing the technology, the institutions, and the legal framework
that will work in concert to enhance accountability.

NOTES

1. *See* Neal Kumar Katyal, *Criminal Law in Cyberspace*, 149 U. PENN. L. REV.
1003 (2001).

2. *See* Scott Charney, *The Internet, Law Enforcement, and Security*, 662 PLI/PAT
937 (2001).

3. *See* K. A. Taipale, "Data Mining and Domestic Security: Connecting the
Dots to Make Sense of Data," 5 COLUM. SCI. & TECH. L. REV. (2003). For technical
background, *see* Jesus Mena, Investigative Data Mining and Crime Detection
(Elsevier Science, 2003).

4. *See* Joel R. Reidenberg, *States and Internet Enforcement*, 1 U. OTTAWA L. &
TECH. J. (2004); Neal Kumar Katyal, *Digital Architecture as Crime Control*, 112

YALE L. J. 2261 (2003). For a general discussion on the nature of regulatory forces online, *see* LAWRENCE LESSIG, CODE AND OTHER LAWS OF CYBERSPACE (1999).

5. Michael Birnhack & Niva Elkin-Koren, *The Invisible Handshake: The Reemergence of the State in the Digital Environment*, 8 VA. J.L. & TECH 6 (2003).

6. *See* Reidenberg, *supra* note 4; K. A. Taipale, *Internet and Computer Crime: System Architecture as Crime Control* (Feb, 2003), *at* http://www.taipale.com/papers/CrimeControl.pdf; Katyal, *supra* note 1.

7. *See*, for example, the Assurance of Discontinuance, in lieu of commencing statutory proceedings which was accepted by the attorney general of New York State in the case of PayPal, Inc. The agreement with PayPal relates to clearing gambling transactions. *See* http://www.dag.state.ny.us/Internet/litigation/paypal.pdf (in particular articles 20–21 to the agreement).

8. The general act which regulates such requirements is the Communication Assistance for Law Enforcement Act (CALEA) (HR 4922). *See* Center for Democracy & Technology, CALEA Background (http:///www.cdt.org/digi_tele/background.shtml).

9. *See* Clive Walker & Yaman Adkeniz, "Anti-Terrorism Laws and Data Retention: War Is Over?" Northern Ireland Legal Quarterly 54 (2), Summer Edition, 159 (2003).

10. *See* 18 Pennsylvania Statutes § 7330 (2002). The Center for Democracy & Technology currently questions the validity of the statute in court. *See* CDT & ACLU Memorandum in the case: Center for Democracy & Technology vs. Michael Fisher, Attorney General of the Commonwealth of Pennsylvania (E.D. Pennsylvania, No 03-5051).

11. *See* Richard Jones, *Digital Rule: Punishment, Control and Technology*, Punishment and Society, vol. 2 (1): 5–22.

12. *See* James Boyle, *Foucault in Cyberspace: Surveillance, Sovereignty, and Hardwired Censors*, 66 U. CIN. L. REV. 177 (1997).

13. *See* Amitai Etzioni, *Implications of Select New Technologies for Individual Rights and Public Safety*, 15 HARVARD J.L. & TECH 257 (2002).

14. For a general discussion on the tendency to increase the secrecy of enforcement tools, *see* Marc Rotenberg, *Privacy and Secrecy after September 11*, 86 MINN. L. REV. 1115 (2002).

15. On the political economy of the information ecosystem, *see* Yochai Benkler, *Siren Songs and Amish Children: Autonomy, Information, and Law* 76 N.Y.U. L. REV. 23 (2001).

16. *See* NIMROD KOZLOVSKI, THE COMPUTER AND THE LEGAL PROCEEDINGS—ELECTRONIC EVIDENCE AND COURT PROCEDURE 50–109 (2000) (Hebrew).

17. *U.S. v. Jarrett*, 338 F.3d 339 (4th Cir. 2003).

18. INHERIT THE WIND (MGM 1960).

Counterstrike

Curtis E. A. Karnow

The network's the battlefield now.[1]

I.

The Internet is a vehicle for a variety of threats, and the usual physical means of defense usually do not work. Physical locks and walls do not bar attacks. Tracking evildoers with fingerprints, eyewitness accounts, or blood samples and DNA tracing is obviously ineffective. Digital attackers often have the technological edge and seem always to be just ahead of law enforcement and technical defenses such as spam filters, firewalls, and antipiracy technologies.

Against this background, there has been a growing interest in "self-help" mechanisms to counter Internet-mediated threats.

A Summary of Self-Help Initiatives

For example, content providers such as record labels and movie studios have favored proposed federal legislation that would allow them to disable copyright infringers' computers. Representative Howard Berman introduced a bill described as the "license to hack" bill. Normally, it is not legal to enter a network without authorization, or to view, edit, or delete files on someone else's computer without authorization. Normally, people go to jail for such acts; they are illegal under both state and federal laws. But Berman drafted his bill in response to the broad illegal dissemination of copyrighted materials such as music and film across so-called "peer-to-peer" or P2P networks—networks that share content among thousands (or more) of users without a central computer tracking the distribution— and without, therefore, any efficient way to stop the copyright infringements at a central location. The Berman proposal would have rendered copyright owners immune from liability for hacking into these P2P file trading networks—as long as they did so only in order to stop the dissemination of their copyrighted material. The bill, in other words, would have provided immunity from criminal prosecution and civil liability, for what otherwise would have been an illegal entry into a computer, if that target computer was used for illegal P2P file trading.

In another example, software licensors have backed legislation introduced in many states that would permit the remote disabling of software in use by the licensee when the license terms are breached. For example, if a company licenses software for a certain term, say a year, and tries to use it past that term, or is licensed to use it for ten users but then tries to have twenty users log in, then this law as drafted would allow the software maker to reach into the company's system and turn off the software.

More broadly, Internet security professionals are debating both the propriety and the legality of striking back at computers which attack the Internet through the introduction of worms, viruses, Trojan horses, and other forms of "malware." These small packets of code, when released in the world, replicate at remarkable speeds, infecting thousands and millions of computers within minutes. Often, "innocent" computers are infected and then themselves become the vectors of further infection. Malware disrupts communications, bringing networks to their knees as the computers cope with the computational load of rapidly replicating and spreading code: data can be lost and other programs modified in unpredictable ways.

Increasing Vulnerability on the Internet

Users and system administrators are frustrated that the usual means of enforcing rights do not work on the Internet. National laws and civil jurisdiction usually stop at borders, but attacks are global; those responsible for infringements and network attacks are legion and anonymous. The Internet's massive, instantaneous distribution of software tools and data permits very large numbers of unsophisticated users access to highly efficient decryption tools, and to very powerful data attack weapons. Small children in Hanoi, Prague, and Fairbanks can collapse central web servers in Silicon Valley and Alexandria, Virginia, and freely distribute the latest films and pop tunes. The irony is that as more of the global economy is mediated by the Internet—that is, as we increasingly rely on the Internet—the technologies are becoming more complex and more vulnerable to attack from more people. A single person can do enormous damage to these intimately networked systems: eighteen-year-old Sven Jaschan, author of the Netsky and Sasser viruses, was responsible for 70 percent of the worldwide virus infections in 2004.[2]

Even a cursory look at the figures suggest an almost exponential increase in these vulnerabilities. One company in the business of developing virus detection routines detected 7,189 new strains of malware last year, handling more than 25 new viruses a day. While incident statistics published by CERT are ambiguous (since, as CERT notes, an "incident" may involve one or a hundred sites), the figures are still revealing: reported security incidents increased from 252 in 1990, through 2,412 in 1995, 21,756 in 2000, to 82,094 in 2002, and 137,590 in 2003.[3] An industry research group estimated (perhaps extravagantly) $1.6 trillion in costs to business on account of malware in 2000.[4]

Increased Regulation

One approach to these security assaults is to enact more laws designed to protect private data, to make it illegal to crack data or copyright protection schemes, and to punish those who would attack computer systems. Around the world, these laws are legion; in the United States, they include such statutes as the Digital Copyright Millennium Act (which bars technologies designed to circumvent copyright protection); the Health Insurance Portability and Accountability Act (HIPAA) (which protects personal medical information and requires security safeguards); the Gramm-Leach-Bliley Financial Services Modernization Act of 1999 (which protects the security of customer records held by financial institutions); the Federal Information Security Management Act (which governs federal government computer security programs); the Federal Trade Commission Act (which is used against unfair or deceptive statements on websites about privacy and security); the USA PATRIOT Act (which requires financial institutions to verify the identity of new account holders); the Children's Online Privacy Protection Act (which protects personal information about children); the Sarbanes-Oxley Act (which requires internal controls on financial reporting systems); a plethora of state privacy and security statutes; and so on.

Obstacles to Policing

But simultaneously, the legal system is increasingly incapable of policing the illegal behavior or enforcing the laws on the books. The U.S. court system is ponderous and expensive; one simply cannot go after every malefactor. Practically, it is usually impossible to pursue infringers outside the United States. The Internet and its language of code are global: they are not coterminous with any of the usual means of enforcing laws and values, because the Internet is not coterminous with any country, region, or cultural group. The Internet gathers those who have no contractual relationship, no spoken language in common, and are not bound by a common law. Trade sanctions are too cumbersome to help; nor will nations permit their citizens to be policed directly by authorities across the globe. In my own work, I have tracked down anonymous malefactors to towns in Australia, eastern Europe, and the Bahamas; there, the trail went cold. Only in Australia could we have retained local counsel and perhaps pressed matters with the police; but it was too expensive, all told.

Resorting to domestic police is frustrating. The FBI has understandably rerouted resources to combating terrorism and local authorities do not have the wherewithal to react rapidly to assaults from other parts of the country. By many accounts, conventional law enforcement authorities simply do not have the skills to deal with cyberattacks, and victims such as banks, financial institutions, and others that deal in sensitive data are reluctant to go public and in effect turn over the investigation to the authorities. About 48 percent of companies surveyed in a joint CSI/FBI survey did not report intrusions.[5] Fundamentally, going to law enforcement does not stop an attack, at least in the short term; rather, it starts an investigation which could take months or longer to result in an arrest. That's an eternity in Internet time.

Inadequacy of Defensive Technology

As legal systems become less effective, attention naturally turns to technology: traditionally, defensive technology. A broad range of products help protect networks, keep content encrypted, and so on. Electronic firewalls, intrusion detection systems, authentication devices, and perimeter protection devices are among the services and products available. But two general trends of increasing complexity undermine the efficacy of defensive technologies: increasingly complex systems and increasing connectivity. The complex relationship among multiple layers of hardware and software means that new bugs and avenues to exploitation are being discovered on a daily basis. Larger systems usually include dispersed, networked computers, operated by outsourcers, server farms, other application service providers, and the ultimate end users. Increased connectivity is manifest in both the onslaught of "always on" high-speed Internet clients and in the design of the most popular (Microsoft) software, which favors interoperability and easy data sharing over compartmentalized (and thus more secure) applications. This massive connectivity of machines, many of which are not maintained by users who know anything about security, permits, for example, the well-known distributed denial of service (DDoS) attack. In a DDoS attack, millions of computers ("zombies") can be infected with a worm, which then launches its copies simultaneously against the true target—for example, Amazon, or eBay—shutting the target down.

Together, these factors make it difficult to implement defensive technologies. Relatively few companies have the resources and interest to review and implement every bug fix, and otherwise to keep ahead of the endlessly inventive cracker. "Information technology infrastructures are becoming so complex that no one person can understand them, let alone administer them in a way that is operationally secure," says one computer security expert.[6] "The complexity of modern [operating systems] is so extreme that it precludes any possibility of not having vulnerabilities," says another.[7]

Legal Liability

These vulnerabilities, of course, give rise to legal liabilities for the target of the attack. Target computers often have personal data which are illegally accessed or exposed by the attack. The ultimate victims are often those consumers and businesses whose data resides on the stricken machines. These ultimate victims may sue for the loss of service and for corrupted data. They may be able to state legal claims for breach of contract, privacy incursions, copyright violation, negligence, and so on. A sustained attack can put a victim out of business. One company, SCO, which had provoked the ire of certain folks interested in open source and Linux, had its primary website shut down for over a month. And owners and operators of zombied machines, too, may be sued if the attack can be traced to negligence in the security systems implemented (or rather, not implemented) on the zombies.

Liability for the bad acts of others—indirect, or vicarious liability—is a subject to itself and is well established in the law. Parents are responsible for the acts of their children, companies for the acts of employees, and principals generally for the acts of their agents. A variety of relationships can make one liable for the bad acts of others—for example, for the malicious acts of users, or perhaps for negligence in implementing security technologies which should have blocked the assault.

To rub salt into these wounds, in 2002 California enacted a law, Civil Code § 1798.29, which requires notification by a systems operator to persons whose personal data may have been accessed during a security breach. Because it reaches data pertaining to any Californian, regardless of where the data is held, it affects companies throughout the world. The California law was enacted to prevent identity theft by alerting consumers that their unencrypted personal data may have been compromised. Some have termed this law the "invitation to sue" provision: the required notices may be enough to trigger legal action by users whose data may have been compromised.

II.

Technological Counterstrike Tools

It is against this background that self-help (or "strike back" or "counterstrike") tools have garnered great interest; sharp words have been exchanged on proposals to implement automated counterstrikes. Under these plans, a network that finds itself under attack automatically traces back the source and shuts down, or partially disables, the attacking machine(s). Reminiscent of the Cold War "launch on warning" nuclear deterrent, the premise is that only a computer can react fast enough to detect the attack, trace it to a source, and disable the attacking machine in time to have any chance at all of minimizing the effects of the attack. Recall the vicious speed with which a computer worm can propagate. Slammer/Sapphire "was the fastest computer worm in history. As it began spreading throughout the Internet, it doubled in size every 8.5 seconds. It infected more than 90 percent of vulnerable hosts within 10 minutes." "At its peak, achieved approximately 3 minutes after it was released, Sapphire scanned the net at over 55 million IP addresses per second. It infected at least 75,000 victims and probably considerably more."[8] It would not take much to increase the speed of infection. A "flash worm" can be built which attacks all vulnerable machines within a few seconds.

Software counterstrike tools have been implemented in the past. In response to the Code Red II (CRII) worm attack, someone created a script which reputedly responded to a CRII probe by disabling the offending web server, using a back door installed by the CRII worm in the victim's machine. Other stories abound of other aggressive responses to cyberattacks. The Pentagon reportedly struck back against a group of activists who had flooded the Defense Department's (and other) websites in September 1998. Reportedly, the Pentagon's attack targeted the attacker's browsers and caused their machine to reboot.[9] And Tim Mullen has devised a system named "Enforcer" with reputed strikeback capabilities, although it is unclear whether Enforcer's capabilities extend outside the victim network infrastructure (that is, back to the attacker). The web hosting company Conxion discovered a denial of service attack against one of its clients, and configured its server to send the page requests back—crashing the attacker's machine.[10] More recently, in the summer of 2004, Symbiot Security Inc. announced software known by its acronym iSIMS which can "return fire" against attacking systems.[11] This seems to include tagging data packets released by the attacker so all such packets are recognized by other systems as attacks; or it might reflect an attack back to its source.

Practicalities

It is important to distinguish possibly transitory technical and practical issues from the legal problems: the rationale underlying the commonly accepted belief that it is illegal to strike back is, in fact, not precisely based on a legal analysis. Rather it is usually based on the *practicality* of pinpointing the perpetrator, and the risks of killing the wrong machine or code. As noted below, there is an important relationship between the legal concern and these practicalities, but the two threads need separation.

And there are serious practical issues here. Not all attacks will so plainly reveal a path back to their source as did CRII; tracing an attack to an intermediate attacking machine, let alone the computer owned by the originator in a DDoS attack, may be impossible. And intermediate machines (or zombies in a DDoS attack) may be operated by hospitals, governmental units, and telecommunications entities such as Internet Service Providers that provide connectivity to millions of people. Counterstrikes which are not precisely targeted to the worm or virus could easily create a remedy worse than the disease. Where the offense is spam and its libelous, malicious, or pornographic content, the trace will generally lead to an anonymous account on a server—a server which is legitimately used for other communications as well. Entirely disabling that server is overkill.

There are other considerations. A site which has a reputation for fighting back may become the target of skilled attacks for just that reason, a potential feather in the cap of those seeking greater challenges in the arena of Internet warfare. Some commentators have suggested that a particularly diabolical plot could involve spoofing the source of an attack—for example, making it appear that it comes from the FBI's main site—leading to massive attacks on an innocent site by otherwise equally innocent machines striking back at the perceived threat. But these practical issues might be overcome; they may be no more than temporary technical problems. Perhaps we can assume precision counterstrike weapons; perhaps the recording industry can precisely identify its copyrighted songs, calculate which ones are licensed to which users (or machines), and automatically destroy solely the offending copy. Perhaps data streams can be tagged with the identification number of the originating machine, such that viruses, worms, and other offending code can be accurately tracked back to the source, and disabling mechanisms will target the malware alone. Intel and others proposed roughly similar technology in 1999. Current plans for Microsoft's Next Generation Service Computing Base would support so-called IRM (information rights management) technology. This technology is based on unique identifiers for each client computer, enabling software and content to be licensed to specific machines. The same technology could be used to tag data streams with such a source identifier.

The practical issues may be accommodated by developing technology. Recognizing them for the presently serious issues they are, and setting them aside, allows us to look more carefully at the legal issues.

III.

The fundamental legal issue is this: even the accurate targeting of a perpetrator's machine itself presents serious legal issues. A host of statutes on their face make it flatly illegal to attack or disable computers, including all those connected to the Internet—that is, the very laws which make cyberattacks illegal in the first place. When, then, might a counterstrike be legal?

Self-Defense

The doctrine of self-defense appears to be the best bet here: but does self defense apply on the Internet, and does it justify counterstrike?

Self-defense usually is at stake when a person is threatened with imminent bodily harm. (The focus is on the self-defense of a person, but under some circumstances one may also use self-defense to avoid injury to property.) The test is whether (1) there is an apparent need to use force, (2) the force used was in fact reasonable, and (3) the threatened act was unlawful. There are other factors, but the underlying themes in self-defense are (a) a counterstrike (as it were) which is *proportional* to the harm avoided, (b) a good faith belief (one both subjectively and objectively reasonable) that the counterstrike was necessary in the sense that there were *no adequate alternatives.*

Disabling an evildoer's machine is, I suggest, far less injurious than a DDoS assault; and I suggest that disabling the attacker's machine (although not necessarily destroying his data) is proportional to the threatened corruption of a victim's file. This in turn can justify the counterstrike when the threat is malware. And erasing the pirated copy of a film, song, or computer game is proportional to the harm posed by use (and risk of further distribution) of the infringing copy by the pirate.

The more difficult issue when it comes to malware is that of adequate alternatives. The elementary alternatives, of course, are for the victim to use sufficiently effective defenses to keep the attack from succeeding, and failing that, to disconnect from the Internet to avoid the attack. But that last option is itself often the very harm directly sought to be caused by the malware attack; and classically, self-defense doctrine does not require the victim to back away; in most states, one may "stand one's ground" and not retreat, while still being entitled to self-defense if the attack progresses.

So, how should we think about "adequate alternatives" such as perimeter defenses? Is one always required to rely on that defensive alternative and forgo the offensive? The central problems are that first, we cannot generalize over a wide range of incidents, and second, the subjective perspective—the viewpoint of the information technology professional whose systems are threatened—and the objective perspective of the judge, jury, or prosecutor may diverge wildly.

There is a wide range of security incidents, ranging from inadvertent innocuous incursions by badly written computer scripts to intentional attempts to flood a system with communication requests and shut it down, to deliberate penetrations to obtain or corrupt highly sensitive data. The unauthorized entry may be accomplished because the most elementary security precaution was not taken, or, on the other end of the spectrum, because the perpetrator has devised a brilliant and entirely unexpected method to exploit a hitherto unknown problem in an operating system or browser. A judge or jury could find that "adequate alternatives" existed for a simple, predictable attack, but for not the sophisticated, unanticipated one. This is a difficult problem, both because standards in this area are difficult to come by, and also because the competence of systems administrators and the funding provided to them by upper management are often low. The February 2003 Sapphire worm attack is a good example: although presumably put on notice by prior CRII and Nimda attacks, systems administrators failed to implement simple patches which would have blocked the spread of the similar Sapphire attack:

> In the largest such incident since the Code Red and Nimda worms bored into servers in 2001, the Sapphire worm—also known as Slammer and SQL-Exp—infected more than 120,000 computers and caused chaos within many corporate networks. Some Internet service providers in Asia were overwhelmed.[12]

Microsoft had released the relevant patch six months before the Sapphire attack, but even its own computers were affected by Sapphire. It may be that, as suggested above, systems are too complex and mutate too quickly to guard against every point of failure; and it's true that almost no one can be expected to promptly implement, test, and integrate every patch for every piece of software used in a large, complex system. Indeed, crackers can now examine a patch, locate a new vulnerability, create and release a new exploit all within twenty-four hours of the patch's release.

But in retrospect, at least, any given failure will often appear to have been easily prevented. And then there is this concern: if the counterstrike tool is good enough to identify the attack and pinpoint the cracker's machine, how could it not be good enough to block the attack? In brief, it can be a dicey thing to establish both a good faith and objectively reasonable belief that there were no adequate alternatives to a counterstrike. The plethora of defensive products and services, good practice guidelines (even if more frequently observed in the breach than otherwise), and reliable 20/20 hindsight conspire to make self-defense a tricky maneuver. To be sure, it is not an impossible task: expert testimony, for example, might help. But because the consequences of guessing wrongly here are so onerous—including conviction for a federal felony—the absence of directly relevant case authority should give pause; a long pause.

IV.

Nuisance

There is another legal doctrine, though, that might hold more promise; and it is the venerable doctrine of nuisance. In its amicus brief to the Court of Appeal in *Intel v. Hamidi*, the Electronic Frontier Foundation developed the conceit that an alleged spammer's assault on Intel's internal email system should be thought of not as a trespass on Intel's property, but as a nuisance. Nuisances can be almost anything that interferes with one's enjoyment of one's property. Classic public nuisances include a malodorous factory, diseased plants, fire hazards, and houses of ill-repute. Public nuisances affect the community. Private nuisances are those that affect only a single person, or one's own property; usually they are real property problems such as tree branches and fences which interfere with the use of land.

The remarkable aspect of nuisance law is that it expressly contemplates self-help. A person affected by a private nuisance, or a person who is especially affected by a public nuisance, may use self-help and "abate" (stop) the nuisance—and then sue the malefactor for the costs of the abatement. Abatement includes "removing . . . or . . . destroying the thing which constitutes the nuisance" as long as there is no "breach of the peace" or "unnecessary injury."[13] For example, one can break down doors, smash locks, or tear down a fence if it is reasonably necessary to abate the nuisance (and if the other elements discussed below are met).

"Breach of the peace" is an elastic notion, usually connoting actual or threatened violence or disturbance, sometimes bad language, public nudity, demonstrations peaceful and otherwise; and so on. I read the abatement statutes in their traditional context, where one might enter the property of another to turn off water, put out a fire, or remove smelly detritus. Forswearing a "breach of the peace" suggests such entry without causing a noticeable fuss or threatening force. Assuming an accurate counterstrike, the "no breach of the peace" condition should not interfere with the use of nuisance doctrine to justify the counterattack. In short, nuisance law endorses a reasonable amount of collateral damage.

Thus, the legal investigation ultimately boils down to whether a cyberattack really qualifies as a nuisance. It fits the open-ended statutory definition; of course, much does. Nuisance "has meant all things to all men, and has been applied indiscriminately to everything from an alarming advertisement to a cockroach baked in a pie."[14] But of the three evils originally discussed above—the infliction of malware, copyright infringement, and the unlicensed use of software—only malware appears close to the notion of a nuisance. The other two boil down to the same harm—copyright infringement—but while infringement can be analogized to theft, it doesn't interfere with the copyright holder's ability to use the property involved. Unless nuisance is to swallow every harm, it's a stretch to call infringement even a private nuisance. Indeed, it is the cyberattacks of malware, not infringement, that those advocating counterstrike have in mind. Fundamentally, a nuisance is, among other things, an unreasonable invasion of the victim's interests where there is no reasonable basis for the action, including those actions arising "from a malicious desire to do harm for its own sake."[15] A software worm or virus probably fits the bill.

It is not, of course, clear how a court would apply the old doctrine of nuisance to the Internet. We do know that the even more venerable doctrine of trespass to chattels has been so applied. Can the same act of corrupting computer code, or data intrusion, be both a trespass and a nuisance? The Court of Appeals in *Intel* obscured the issue. The legal debate there came down to a bizarre squabble over whether the electromagnetic signals which constitute the intrusion are "tangible" and do "physical" damage to the property, like "particulate matter" such as dirt (in which case we have a trespass), or whether, on the other hand, they are like the "intangible" encroachments of light, noise, and odors which interfere with the property—in which case we have a nuisance. The squabble is pointless because a computer-based attack is all those things. Just as light (a photon) is both a wave and a particle, so too might a computer virus, winging its electromagnetic path into a network, be either an intangible nuisance or a tangible trespass, as a series of cases have stated.

If legislatures sympathized with the plight of victims of spam, or malware, and with the frustration of using the legal process to address the injury, they could statutorily define selected acts as nuisances (as they have with other acts and conditions), and avoid the suspense. In the meantime, Internet-mediated attacks, at least such as viruses and worms, fit comfortably within the definition of a nuisance and so may authorize and justify counterstrike as "self-help." This includes the doctrine's endorsement of a reasonable amount of collateral damage, such as the temporary disruption of attacking zombies during a DDoS assault.

There is at least one last twist to this view of a cyberattack as a nuisance, permitting (at least legally) self-help or counterstrike. The issue is one only a lawyer could love. It has to do with the efficacy of using the defense of self-help—which is a privilege of *state* law—in an action brought under *federal* law. The issue is the extent to which state privileges and defenses will stave off, for example, a federal criminal prosecution under the Computer Fraud and Abuse Act for unauthorized access to computer files. Normally, of course, federal law only applies to federal claims, and federal law trumps state law. But there are exceptions. Sometimes, even in federal question cases, state law supplies the so-called "rule of decision," such as in copyright cases where a "contract" must be determined, or where the court must decide if peace officers are "authorized" to serve process. This is not a simple issue, because each pertinent federal statute would need to be reviewed to determine if it appeared to be conditioned on, or contemplated, some state-defined notion of privileged access to self-help. But in the Computer Fraud and Abuse Act, for example (the most likely candidate statute for a federal prosecution of a counterstrike attack), it is not a stretch to suggest that the key notion of "unauthorized" access to a computer could be defined under state law—with "self-help" providing the "authorization."

V.

Even under nuisance law, not every counterstrike—or "self-help" effort—is automatically immune from prosecution. It has to be reasonable and proportional to the nuisance, which was an issue I discussed in connection with a similar requirement under self-defense. And as always, applying the light of ancient doctrine to novel technologies will produce both illumination and shadow; courts will fudge on the analysis and struggle for precedent, sometimes testing out the wrong one. Just as no one wants to roll out version 1, no one wants to be the test case in court. It is, as a surgeon might say about a particularly nasty and complex multiorgan transplant, *an interesting case*; not something the patient likes to hear.

NOTES

1. M. A. Davidson, *Cybersecurity Cat and Mouse Game*, BNA PRIVACY & SECURITY LAW RPT., *at* S-15 (July 2004).

2. M. Kotadia, *Bulk of Year's PC Infections Pinned to One Man*, C|NET NEWS.COM (July 28, 2004).

3. CERT, *Cert/CC Statistics 1988–2004, at* http://www.cert.org/stats/cert_stats.html.

4. Doug Bedell, *Southern California Virus Hunter Stalks His Prey*, DALLAS MORNING NEWS (Nov. 4, 2001).

5. *CSI/FBI Computer Crime and Security Survey* at 13 & Fig. 20 (2004), *available at* http://www.gocsi.com/forms/fbi/pdf.jhtml.

6. J. McHugh et al., *Defending Yourself: The Role of Intrusion Detection Systems*, IEEE SOFTWARE 42 (Sept./Oct. 2000).

7. Stephen Northcutt, COMPUTER WORLD (Sept. 3, 2001), *at* 44.

8. David Moore et al., *The Spread of the Sapphire/Slammer Worm, at* http://www.caida.org/outreach/papers/2003/sapphire/index.xml.

9. Niall McKay, *Pentagon Deflects Web Assault*, WIRED NEWS (Sept. 10, 1998); Adam L. Penenberg, *When Art Meets Cyberwar*, FORBES.COM (Sept. 14, 1998), *at* http://www.forbes.com/1998/12/14/penenberg_1214.html.

10. Pia Landergren, *Hacker Vigilantes Strike Back*, CNN.COM (June 20, 2001), *available at* http://www.cnn.com/2001/TECH/internet/06/20/hacker.vigilantes.idg/.

11. Matthew Fordahl, *Information Warfare*, THE EXAMINER (SAN FRANCISCO), *at* 17 (June 21, 2004), *at* http://www.forbes.com/1998/12/14/penenberg_1214.html.

12. Robert Lemos, *Worm Exposes Apathy, Microsoft Flaws*, C|NET NEWS.COM (Jan. 26 2003), *at* http://news.com.com/2100-1001-982135.html.

13. Cal. Civil Code §§ 3495, 3502.

14. W. PAGE KEETON ET AL, PROSSER AND KEETON ON THE LAW OF TORTS § 86 (5th ed. 1984).

15. W. PROSSER, TORTS 574 (4th ed. 1971).

Part IV

New Tools for Law Enforcement
Design, Technology, Control, Data Mining, and Surveillance

Why Can't We All Get Along?

How Technology, Security, and Privacy
Can Coexist in the Digital Age

Kim A. Taipale

The public debate that pits security and privacy as dichotomous rivals to be traded one for another in a zero-sum game is based on a general misunderstanding and apprehension of technology on the one hand, and a mythology of privacy that conflates secrecy with autonomy on the other. Further, political strategies premised on outlawing particular technologies or techniques or that seek to constrain technology through laws alone are doomed ultimately to failure and will result in little security and brittle privacy protection.

Security and privacy are not a balancing act but rather dual obligations of a liberal democracy[1] that present a difficult problem for policy makers. Reconciling these divergent needs requires that policy and technology be developed concurrently and designed from the outset to work together. In a technologically mediated information society, civil liberties can only be protected by employing value-sensitive technology development strategies[2] in conjunction with policy implementations, not by opposing technological developments or seeking to control the use of particular technologies or techniques after the fact through law alone. Development strategies that take privacy concerns into account during design and development can build in technical features that enable existing legal control mechanisms for the protection of civil liberties and due process to function.[3]

Code is not law, but code can bound what law, norms, and market forces can achieve.[4] Technology itself is neither the problem nor the solution; rather it presents certain opportunities and potentials that enable or constrain public policy choice. Technical features alone cannot eliminate privacy concerns, but by incorporating such features into technological systems familiar due process mechanisms are enabled.

This chapter examines how identification, data aggregation and analysis, and collection technologies intersect with privacy and security, and suggests certain technical features to help ameliorate concerns. It also proposes that strategies premised on separating *knowledge of behavior* from *knowledge of identity* based on the *anonymization* of data and the *pseudonymization* of identity can help protect individual autonomy while still meeting security needs.

While I focus on the intersection of technology and domestic security in the context of the "war on terrorism,"[5] the analysis presented herein is applicable to law enforcement more generally—subject, however, to certain caveats. In particular, the lesser the crime targeted, the greater the hurdle for any new technology or wider use that implicates those concerns.

It is beyond the scope of this chapter to attempt to delineate precisely where the line between preemptive and reactive strategies is to be drawn. Post hoc analyses of 9/11 have revealed that much relevant information existed but government agencies were unable to "connect the dots."[6] It would be an unusual polity that now demanded accountability from its representatives for being unable to connect the dots to prevent terrorist acts yet denied them the available tools to do so, particularly if there were to be another catastrophic event. Therefore, I start with the assumption that there exists a political consensus for proactive investigative strategies intended to prevent future acts of terrorism[7] and that we need to enlist advanced information technology to help counter this threat.[8]

At the same time, however, we must recognize that information technology can be intrusive on certain privacy interests that protect individual freedom and political autonomy, and are core to our political liberties.[9] Further, there is no technological silver bullet that will provide absolute security (nor is there any technical solution that will absolutely protect privacy). Technology alone is not a solution to either problem; but neither are simple laws prohibiting the use of a technology or technique sufficient in themselves. Instead, some complex socially constructed system combining organizational structures, rules and procedures, and technologies must be crafted.[10]

Franken-Tech: The Fear of Technology

The public debate on complex policy issues is often dominated by *information entrepreneurs* (including activists and the media) who attempt to engender information cascades to further their own particular agenda.[11] The result is often an unnecessary level of social anxiety and a misallocation of resources to resolve issues in situations where manageable risks are inflated or misunderstood.

The wide proliferation of information privacy horror stories (in particular, the prevalence of identity theft, spam, and hacker stories in the media); the general mistrust of government agencies to handle personal information appropriately; a general apprehension about technology[12] and how it works; and the natural anxiety relating to disclosure of personal information—all spurred on by the *privacy lobby*—has created a public anxiety about electronic privacy out of proportion to the actual privacy risks and has obscured discussion of the very real threat posed by failure to improve security. This anxiety is not unlike the concerns exhibited about the use of credit cards online in the late 1990s when even the long-term success of e-commerce was questioned based on the unwillingness of consumers to use credit cards online—a fear wholly out of proportion to the actual risks.

While some might argue that the government has used the fear of terrorism to push policies without adequate public debate, so too others could argue that the privacy lobby has used fear of electronic privacy intrusion—wholly disproportionate to its actual risk to civil liberty—to oppose technological developments and further their own agenda.[13]

A Fetish for Secrecy

A significant problem in determining policy here is that privacy means different things to different people.[14] It is beyond the scope of this chapter to definitely define privacy or reconcile competing views.[15] However, much of the public debate seems to take place within an unexamined mythology of privacy that conflates privacy with absolute secrecy on the one hand and the maintenance of absolute secrecy with liberty on the other. But this deified notion of privacy based on absolute secrecy and concealment[16] confounds two simpler ideas: knowing what someone does (behavior) and knowing who someone is (identity), and is based on a presumed privacy entitlement for electronic data that exceeds that demanded by real-world experience.

This perception of a privacy entitlement arose not by accident or necessity but from the intentional action of the privacy lobby, who have an interest in promoting online privacy.[17] But it is not my intention to minimize the privacy interests at stake here. Quite the contrary, I argue that we should insist on building in technical constraints to ensure their protection.

We face one of two inevitable futures—one in which technologies are developed with privacy-protecting functions built into the design or one in which we rely solely on legal mechanisms and sanctions to control the use of technologies that have been developed without regard to such protections. In my view, it is the fetish for absolute secrecy promulgated by the privacy lobby that precludes or delays the development of appropriate technologies to improve security while also protecting civil liberties, and leaves us with little security and brittle privacy protection. Privacy is important for the protection of individual political and personal autonomy, not a characteristic of data for its own sake.[18] Thus, a fetish for absolute secrecy of innocuous data (or voluntarily produced data) that results in an alternative intrusion—say, a physical search at the airport (or other physical consequences to the individual, including perhaps death if security isn't improved)—is suspect and should be questioned.[19]

Additionally, the brittle nature of privacy protection based solely on law needs to be considered. If technologies are developed without privacy-protecting features built in but outlawed for certain uses, those laws can be changed in the future in response to a new terrorist attack and the then existing technologies will not be capable of supporting implementation policies that provide any privacy protection at all.

Privacy Interests at Stake

There can be no doubt that vital privacy interests are at stake. We must preserve the general culture of individual freedom that is the basis on which our country was founded and which is incorporated in our Constitution and Bill of Rights.[20] Nevertheless, rights incur responsibilities.[21] Security and liberty are dual obligations and we cannot slight one for the other.[22] The Fourth Amendment implicitly recognizes this duality because the "prohibition on unreasonable searches is not accorded more weight than the permission to conduct reasonable searches."[23] In past crises, particularly when they have threatened national security, many have been willing to sacrifice civil liberties in the short term in order to meet the particular emergency.[24] In many cases, we as a nation later came to regret those actions as having gone too far. In meeting the current challenge of international terrorism we are confronted with two additional complexities.

First, the "war on terrorism" may be one with no definable end. Thus we need to develop doctrine and procedures that serve to protect important values from the outset and that can be maintained indefinitely. Second, we face a threat from actors who move among the general population and take advantage of our open society to mask their own organization and activities. The task therefore is not to defend against outsiders but to identify and investigate potentially malicious actors from within the population without compromising the freedom and autonomy of the vast majority of innocent people. Therefore, neither demonizing a minority nor encouraging suspicion of everyone is a viable or acceptable outcome. However, neither is undermining legitimate security needs by deifying absolute secrecy as the only means of protecting individual autonomy.

The particular privacy concerns with advanced information systems are primarily three: first, the *chilling effect* that information access and data sharing by government might have on innocent behavior; second, the *slippery slope* that may result when powerful tools are used for increasingly petty needs; and third, the potential for *abuse or misuse*.

The Chilling Effect

The chilling effect primarily involves the concern that potential lawful behavior, particularly constitutionally protected activity, would be inhibited due to the potential for a kind of post hoc surveillance ("dataveillance") that may result from the increased sharing of information among currently discrete sources.[25] An awareness that government may analyze activity is likely to cause people to alter their behavior. The risk is that protected rights of expression, protest, association, and political participation may be affected by encouraging conformity, discouraging dissent, or otherwise altering participation in political life.

Maintaining individual privacy, however, is not synonymous with being able to commit or plan terrorist acts in secret without being discovered. Thus, chilling effects-based arguments against measures to protect against catastrophic terrorist acts ought to be required to show privacy impacts on legitimate innocent activity, not just exhibit a fetish for absolute secrecy premised on vague referrals to potentially inhibited acts. The Supreme Court requires that chilling effects-based challenges show both actual harm and a significant effect on protected activities not outweighed by legitimate government interest.[26]

Thus, chilling effects arguments involving the use of technology require determining *confidence intervals*—that is, the acceptable error rate—for a particular application in a particular use (its *reasonableness*). Confidence intervals for policy purposes in domestic security can be viewed as a function of two competing relationships—the number of false positives (innocents identified) adjusted by the severity of the consequences to the individual on the one hand and the number of false negatives (terrorists not identified) adjusted by the consequences to security on the other (including costs associated with misallocation of resources to investigate false positives).

If the consequences of a false positive are relatively low, for example, a bag search at the airport, and the consequences of a false negative are high, for example, the plane crashes into the Pentagon, the acceptable confidence interval for policy purposes might reasonably bias toward false positives and the reduction of false negatives. If, on the other hand, the consequences to the individual from a false positive are severe, for example incarceration, and the consequences of false negatives are slight, for example, a parking ticket scofflaw slips through, then the confidence interval should bias toward reducing false positives at the risk of increasing false negatives.

This is not to suggest that there is some perfect correlation to be calculated among relative risks, only that when it comes to setting policy, recognizing that appropriate controls for a particular use will depend on the totality of the circumstance—including (as discussed below) the scope and method of inquiry, the sensitivity of data, and the security interest or threat—and cannot be rigidly proscribed or even anticipated. Thus, a perfect system design would incorporate flexibility in both its policy and technical controls to allow for changes in circumstances at the point of use, and its reasonableness would be judged on its use in such circumstances.

The Slippery Slope

The slippery slope argument[27] is that measures that might be adopted now for legitimate national security concerns might eventually be used in the ordinary course of law enforcement to investigate and apprehend lesser lawbreakers, resulting in extraordinary procedures becoming the norm—in this case leading to a permanent surveillance society. There will always be an insatiable need for more security as well as a bureaucratic imperative for additional control. There is also the practical consequence of making tools available—they will be used. When these three factors—the need for more security, the imperial bureaucratic drive, and the practical availability of tools—are combined, the threat of the slippery slope is potentially significant.

Structural implementation options can help ameliorate these concerns. For example, the data analysis (intelligence) function can be separated from the law enforcement function, or a separate agency with a narrow charter to process intelligence for domestic security, no independent law enforcement powers, and subject to strict oversight could be created. While these organizational structures do not eliminate concern, they can help. Further, technical architectures to counter the slippery slope also exist. A distributed architecture with local responsibility and accountability for data and access, together with strong credential and audit functions to track usage, can provide protection from a centralized expansion of power.

Abuse and Misuse

Information systems are also open to abuse or misuse. There are many examples ranging from individual IRS agents looking up their neighbor's tax returns and law enforcement officials sharing information with criminal suspects, to such institutionalized abuse as the FBI COINTELPRO. The substance of these concerns (that is, whether to trust the government) need not be resolved. Instead organizational structures, procedures, and technical systems that function together to limit the potential for abuse need to be designed.

The same technologies that give rise to privacy concerns also provide part of the solution—that is, these systems can be turned on themselves to "watch the watchers."[28] Immutable logging, together with strong credentialing, can make "abuse difficult to achieve and easy to uncover" through secure access control and tamper-resistant evidence of where the data goes and who has had access to it.[29] Automated monitoring of system usage and logs (together with appropriate organizational structures) can provide significant checks on both abuse and misuse. Thus, determining where log files are to be kept and under whose authority is not just a technical question but also one with substantive policy implications.

The Technologies

Both the security and privacy effects from any information system are derived from the security and privacy features and design of the overall system in which they are to be used and are not inherent in the technologies themselves.[30]

Technologies of Identification

Identification systems serve to *authenticate* data attribution—that is, they provide confidence that a particular piece of data (an attribute) or collection of data (an identity) correlates with a specified entity (an individual or other object).[31] Authentication generally serves as the first step in one or both of two kinds of security applications—*authorization* and/or *accountability*. Authorization is the process of deciding what an identified individual is or is not permitted to do within a system (including entering into it). Accountability is the process of associating a consequence to an individual for behavior within the system. Both authorization and accountability serve to ensure that rules governing behavior within a system are obeyed.

In any *identification system*, generally three forms of authentication can occur:

- *Entity authentication* is the attribution of an *identifier* (a name, number, or symbol) to a *specific entity* (individual, place, or thing),
- *Identity authentication* is the attribution of an *identifier* to an *identity* (a collection of data related to an entity), and
- *Attribute authentication* is the attribution of an *attribute* (a property or descriptive element) to a *specific entity*.

Individuals may have multiple *identifiers*, even within the same system, and may have one or more *aliases* for each identifier.

Individuals may also have multiple *identities*—that is, discrete sets of related data that pertain to a particular *role*. And multiple identities for the same individual may or may not share *attributes*.

Entity resolution is the process whereby different identifiers or identities are resolved (attributed) to the same individual, usually through the analysis of shared attributes.[32] Some form of entity resolution (or other data normalization) is generally required for automated analysis, including those based on anonymization and pseudonymization.

Identity verification can be achieved through tokens (something you have), passwords (something you know), or a data match (something you are). The highest level of confidence combines all three, for example, a token (ID card), a password (PIN), and a data match (for example, a biometric identifier). Confidence in identification systems depends on the integrity of the process of *enrollment* (issuance) or *verification* (checking). Even technologies with very low error rates for matching can be compromised if the enrollment process is corrupted or if the measurement process is fooled.

After an identity is authenticated it is used for some security purpose—either by authorizing the individual to do or not do something, or by tracking identifying data in some fashion to provide for accountability. Thus, any identification system is only as good as the criteria against which the authenticated identity is compared for authorization, or the deterrent effectiveness of the sanctions for accountability.

Identification-based security is always somewhat vulnerable because of the *trusted systems* problem.[33] Even "secure" systems need to be penetrated—under authorized circumstances—by *trusted* people.[34] Unfortunately, there is no inherent way to prove trust—the best that any identification system can do is confirm not-yet-proven-untrustworthy status (e.g., not being on a watch list). Therefore, identification-based security needs to be part of a larger security system—one consisting of multiple layers, forming a defense-in-depth—that recognizes, and compensates for, this problem. For example, identification-based access systems should be supplemented with random security checks or monitoring within the system to guard against false negatives and the like.

Another general problem is balancing security with *functionality*. Authentication and authorization impose friction on a system and reduce degrees of freedom, and thus can interfere with its usefulness. Security systems that impose too high a cost on functionality risk undermining the very system for which protection is sought. To the extent that any security system imposes privacy or other costs on users out of proportion to the perceived threat, it risks undermining the confidence and support that is required from users for systems to function.

Identification systems can either enhance or intrude upon privacy depending on their use and context. They can enhance privacy when they are used to secure data or protect identity, for example, by ensuring that an individual is the authorized user of a particular resource. They can also provide convenience, for example, by enabling personalized services. On the other hand, identification systems can be intrusive of privacy and their use can be self-proliferating. Proliferation occurs when the prevalence of a security paradigm premised on fully mediated access becomes the norm. For example, once ID checks are common for boarding airplanes or entering government buildings, they become acceptable (or required) for lesser uses—for example, boarding trains or buses, or entering stores.

Additionally, identification itself tends to increase the collection of data, for example, by creating additional transaction records at the time and place of authentication, and may also expose data to additional disclosure at multiple points during the operation of the system or subsequently. Availability of these transaction records may also allow for linkages, profiling, and the ability to create digital dossiers that would otherwise not be possible.

The use of access control strategies may also impact individual autonomy, for example, freedom of speech (by denying access to information or communication systems), freedom to travel or peaceably assemble (by denying access to particular modes of transport), and freedom to petition the government (by denying access to government buildings or other resources).

Certain privacy impacts cannot be eliminated as they are inherent in the act of authentication, which requires the disclosure of some "identifying" information to function. However, they can be minimized through appropriate system design. Pseudonymization strategies described below can be used to protect identity privacy while still meeting security needs.

Technologies of Data Aggregation and Analysis

Recent reports have highlighted the fact that the amount of available data to be analyzed for domestic security purposes exceeds the capacity to analyze it and have recommended the increased use of data aggregation (information sharing) and automated analysis (data mining) technologies to improve security.[35] However, data aggregation and automated analysis are not substitutes for human analytic decision making, but tools that can help manage vast data volumes and potentially identify relationships or patterns in data that may remain hidden to traditional analysis. If successful, these technologies can help allocate available security resources to more likely targets.

Data itself becomes more meaningful through *aggregation* and *sharing*. First, data may be meaningless in any particular location but becomes increasingly useful as people perceive it to be useful within their local context. Second, data may become more valuable in proximity to other data when previously unknown relationships may become evident.

Data aggregation or sharing is intended to overcome the "stovepipe" nature of existing datasets by making information available regardless of where it is located or how it is structured. A threshold systems design issue that has technical, security, and privacy implications is whether to aggregate data in a centralized data warehouse or to access information in distributed databases. An architecture based on distributed data sources can provide additional privacy protection by providing intervention points for imposing rules-based processing and additional organizational checks and balances against abuse by maintaining local control over data. *Automated data analysis* (including data mining) is intended to turn low-level data, usually too voluminous to understand, into higher forms (information or knowledge) that might be more compact (summary), more abstract (descriptive model), or more useful (predictive model).[36]

Domestic security requirements for data mining differ from commercial data mining applications in significant ways. Commercial data mining is generally applied against large transaction databases in order to classify people according to transaction characteristics and extract patterns of widespread applicability. The problem in counterterrorism is to focus on a smaller number of subjects within a large background population and identify links and relationships from a far wider variety of activities.

In general, commercial users want to identify patterns among unrelated subjects based on their transactions in order to make predictions about other unrelated subjects doing the same. Intelligence analysts generally want to identify patterns that evidence organizations or activities among related subjects in order to expose additional related subjects or activities. Automated analysis can help identify and catalog various data and relationships that may remain unnoticed using traditional means and develop descriptive or predictive models to help identify additional people, objects, or activities that may merit further attention.

Compounding the problem is the fact that relevant data (information relating to terrorists) is hidden within vast amounts of irrelevant data and appears innocuous when viewed in isolation. Individual data items—even if identified as relevant—are essentially meaningless unless viewed in relation to other data points. It is the network or pattern itself that must be identified, analyzed, and acted upon.

There are three distinct applications for automated analysis:

- first, subject-based link analysis to learn more about particular data subjects, their relationships, associations, and actions;
- second, pattern analysis to develop a descriptive or predictive model based on discovered patterns; and,
- third, pattern matching, using a descriptive or predictive model to identify other related people or things.

Spectacular terrorist events are generally too infrequent for automated analysis to extract useful predictive patterns from general data sources in the absence of other intelligence. The focus of these techniques in counterterrorism, therefore, is more often to automate the process of looking for connections, relationships, and patterns to known or suspected terrorists; to identify lower-level, frequently repeated events (for example, illegal immigration, money transfers, front businesses, and recruiting activity); or to identify communication patterns evidencing covert organization that together may warrant further attention. The use of these advanced information technologies can cast suspicion by revealing or recognizing relationships between individually innocuous data, and thus raise legitimate privacy concerns. However, much of the public debate is overshadowed by simplifications and misunderstandings about how and to what effect these technologies may be employed, and a misinterpretation of the legal and policy framework for their control.

The significant privacy issues to be considered are primarily those that arise from the aggregation of data on the one hand, and those that arise from the automated analysis of data on the other—the former might be called the *database* problem and the latter the *mining* problem. The database problem is implicated in subject-based inquiries that aggregate data or access distributed databases to find more information about a particular subject. To the extent that maintaining certain government inefficiencies helps protect individual rights from centralized power, the primary privacy question involved in aggregation is one of increased government efficiency and the demise of "practical obscurity."[37] The mining problem is implicated in the use of pattern matching, in which models are run against data to identify unknown individuals. To some, pattern matching raises inherent privacy issues relating to nonparticularized suspicion under the Fourth Amendment. I disagree.

For a particular method to be categorically suspect, its probative value—the confidence interval for its particular use—must first be determined. Thus, for example, racial or ethnic profiling for law enforcement purposes may be unreasonable because race is determined to not be a reliable predictor of criminality and thus cannot be the sole basis for a reasonable suspicion.[38]

However, to assert that automated pattern analysis based on behavior or data profiles is *inherently* unreasonable or suspect without determining its efficacy in a particular use seems analytically unsound. The Supreme Court has specifically held that the determination of whether particular criteria are sufficient to meet the reasonable suspicion standard does not turn on the *probabilistic* nature of the criteria but on their *probative* weight:

> The process [of determining reasonable suspicion] does not deal with hard certainties, but with probabilities. Long before the law of probabilities was articulated as such, practical people formulated certain common-sense conclusions about human behavior; jurors as factfinders are permitted to do the same—and so are law enforcement officers.[39]

The fact that patterns of relevant indicia of suspicion may be generated by automated analysis (data mined) or matched through automated means (computerized matching) should not change the analysis. The reasonableness of suspicion should be judged on the probative value of the method in the particular circumstances of its use, not on its probabilistic nature or whether it is technically mediated. The point is not that there is no privacy issue involved but that the issue is the traditional one—what reasonable expectations of privacy should apply to the data being analyzed or observed?—not a categorical dismissal of technique based on assertions of "nonparticularized suspicion." Automated pattern analysis is the electronic equivalent of observing suspicious behavior in public. The appropriate question is whether the probative weight of any particular set of indicia is reasonable, and what data should be available for analysis. There are legitimate privacy concerns relating to the use of any preemptive policing techniques, but there is no presumptive Fourth Amendment non-particularized suspicion problem *inherent in the technology or technique,* even in the case of automated pattern matching.

The policy issue to be determined regarding automated analysis and pattern matching is what efficacy or confidence interval should be required for any particular use in any particular circumstance, and how does that efficacy relate to what data these methods should be used on? Pattern-based queries are reasonable or unreasonable only in the context of their probative value in an intended application—not because they are automated or not. Determining reasonableness in the circumstances of their use—whether prior to employ (authorization), during their general use (oversight), or after their use in a particular case (judicial review)—requires analyzing the *calculus of reasonableness* described below.

Technologies of Collection

Technologies of *collection* include the identification, aggregation, and analysis technologies discussed above (to the extent that they add new data to systems), as well as surveillance or search technologies often referred to as *sense-enhancing* technologies.[40] Sense-enhancing technologies are simply those technologies used to enhance the human ability to observe or recognize physical characteristics or activities. Generally, these technologies can be further classified as those that *amplify* the existing human senses, and those that *extend* these senses by making previously undetectable phenomena observable. Examples of technologies that amplify human senses include such "low-tech" devices as binoculars, telescopes, and cameras as well as "no-tech" devices such as drug-sniffing dogs. But they also include "high-tech" devices, such as sensors that can hear through walls. Examples of technologies that extend the senses include various devices that measure wavelengths not usually detectable, such as infrared or ultraviolet sensors, radar, and even radio receivers. Additionally, sense-enhancing technologies could be categorized as those that provide a new perspective from which to observe, for example, aircraft overflight or satellite remote sensing, and those that interpose the human senses within mediated information flows, for example, the classic wiretap intercepting electronic representations of human speech from the telephone system.

Privacy issues involving sense-enhancing technologies generally tend to revolve around the appropriateness of the place and manner of their use. In general, the courts have struggled to determine whether the use by government of any particular new technology is a *search* under the Fourth Amendment, and, if so, whether it was *reasonable*.

Historically, the Supreme Court based its analysis on the existence (or absence) of a physical trespass or handling of property in deciding whether a challenged government action amounted to a search requiring a warrant under the Fourth Amendment.[41] However, in *Katz v. United States*,[42] the Supreme Court opined that the Fourth Amendment "protects people, not places" and adopted the two-part *reasonable expectation of privacy* test, which requires finding both an actual *subjective* expectation of privacy and a reasonable *objective* one.[43]

This two-part test has been criticized on several grounds. First, by basing its objective analysis on whether a technology is in *general use*[44] or not the Court has ensured that "the more commonplace that ubiquitous surveillance becomes, the less the Fourth Amendment will be able to protect the average citizen."[45] Second, by holding that there can be no reasonable subjective expectation of privacy for information shared with a third party[46] the Court has based its current conception of Fourth Amendment protected privacy primarily on the maintenance of *secrecy* of information: "The Court's new conception of privacy is one of total secrecy. If any information is exposed to the public . . . then the Court has refused to recognize a reasonable expectation of privacy."[47]

This secrecy-based third-party analysis has been criticized as inappropriate for the information age in which vast amounts of personal information are maintained by third parties in private sector databases, and the very nature of the medium requires that data be shared with, maintained by, or exposed to such third parties. Earlier, I argued that the privacy lobby has a fetish for secrecy of data over the autonomy of the individual. Here then is the source of this fetish: by rooting its conception of privacy narrowly in total secrecy based on concealment, the Supreme Court has constructed an artificial all-or-nothing standard at odds with the implicit balancing of interests required by the Fourth Amendment's demand for reasonableness. This limited conception of privacy as total secrecy is not in keeping with the architecture of power that the Fourth Amendment was meant to provide.[48] A new conception of privacy based on protecting the autonomy of the individual rather than secrecy of information has been proposed.[49]

Reconceptualizing privacy to favor protection of autonomy (over secrecy of data for its own sake) could both extend and restrict the domain of privacy. Nevertheless, the salient point for policy purposes is that a more nuanced view of privacy—for example, one based on protecting individual autonomy, not data secrecy for its own sake—provides opportunities to build technical information systems designed to protect core privacy interests while still improving security. Autonomy can be protected by separating knowledge (or observation) of behavior from knowledge (or discovery) of identity—in effect, using a form of procedurally protected anonymity to protect privacy. Thus, strategies based on protecting what I have called the *privacy divide* (that is, the point where data attribution occurs) by building in procedural interventions through anonymization or pseudonymization can help achieve improved security while also protecting these core privacy interests.

The Privacy Divide

Reconciling competing interests in the privacy-security debate requires determining under what circumstances (and following what procedures) identity is to be associated with behavior or behavior with identity. The privacy divide is the point where attribution of behavior and identity occurs. The key to developing new information technologies and systems that can both improve security and protect privacy is to design systems that allow for procedural intervention and control at that point.

The question for both policy and systems development is when and under what circumstances certain data attribution is to occur—simply put, when is an individual to be associated with data representing their behavior or, conversely, when is behavior (whether observed by physical surveillance or within data) to be attributed to a specific individual?

Controlling the Privacy Divide: The Privacy Appliance as Metaphor

Conceptualizing and designing the appropriate mechanisms to exert control over the privacy divide is the key issue for protecting privacy in networked information systems. The policy challenge is to determine the rules and procedures governing the divide, and the technical challenge is to build in technical features to execute or enforce those rules and to manage accountability. The overall architecture must include organizational, procedural, and technical features in a framework that integrates these control requirements within business process needs.

The notion of a *privacy appliance*—that is, a technical systems component sitting between the point of access and the data itself to enforce policy rules and provide accountability—has been suggested.[50] Here I consider the privacy appliance as a metaphor, that is, as an analytic device representing the need for policy intervention in technical systems to enforce rules, rather than as a particular technical device or application.

From a policy perspective, it is not necessary a priori to decide if the privacy appliance should be a specific piece of hardware, for example, a firewall, or an application, say an analytic filter, as its actual form of technical implementation is secondary to understanding what business needs are to be supported. The point for policy makers is to understand that intervention can happen at many different points in the technical architecture, and can be subject to varying methods of control.[51] For the policy maker, the privacy appliance represents the technical object to enforce policy in systems. Thus who controls them (for example, the party using the data, the party supplying the data, or a trusted or untrusted third party) and how (through direct technical control, automated monitoring, or control of audit logs) and subject to what general oversight and review (for example, executive, legislative, or judicial) are the pertinent policy questions.

For the technologist, understanding the policy needs forms the basis for determining technical requirements. Together, policy needs and system design form an enterprise architecture in which the information management, data, systems, and technology architecture all support the overall business process needs[52]—in this case, enabling certain security processes while still protecting privacy interests.

Technical design strategies that emphasize *anonymization* of data for analysis and *pseudonymization* of identity for identification and surveillance systems can provide intervention points where due process procedures can function. Together with strong user authentication and audit controls, these strategies can mediate between distributed data sources (including collection sensors) and the analyst (at any organizational level). Such procedures are dependant on organizational, structural, and technical design features functioning together to meet articulated policy needs.

Anonymization of Data

An anonymous record is one in which the data cannot be associated with a particular individual, either from the data itself or by combining the transaction with other data.[53] Here traditional encryption strategies need to be distinguished from truly anonymous procedures such as *one-way hashing*. With traditional encryption strategies data is encrypted but can be decrypted with the use of a key. An analogy would be handing over data in a locked box. Theoretically, encrypted data is not truly anonymous as the underlying data can be accessed assuming that it is combined with the key.

By using one-way hashes the original data cannot be reconstructed from the hash. Hashing is a process of passing data through a one-way algorithm that returns a digital signature in place of the original data. This digital signature is unique to the underlying data but cannot be turned back into the original data—much like a sausage can be identified as pork but "cannot be turned back into a pig."[54] One-way hash technologies allow for anonymous data processing to occur in a shared environment since the only thing exchanged is the hash. If a match occurs, the processing party still needs to come back to the original data holder to access the underlying data. This allows organizational and procedural structures to be imposed between data matching and disclosure of the underlying data.

Theoretically, hashing is vulnerable to what is known as a "dictionary attack" in which an attacker compiles a list of all potential inputs and computes a hash function for each, then compares the hashed output from the target data set against the attacker's own list of hashes computed from all possible inputs to determine if there is a match. To counter the dictionary attack, *salt* is used. Salt is a random string that is concatenated to the original data before it is operated on by the hash function. In order to match the hashed outputs you need to share the salt key. Salt keys can be encoded in hardware or software, can be used to control the domain across which sharing occurs, and can even be used to control data expiration. By controlling the sharing of salt, the kind of processing that the data is subject to can be controlled.

Many security needs for data analysis, including list and pattern matching, can be accomplished within an anonymized data framework. Automated data analysis, including some forms of data mining, may also be possible.

A simple example of anonymous list matching follows. Suppose a primary dataset contains traveler data and a second dataset contains suspected terrorists. Before the data is analyzed, both datasets are subject to the same one-way hash algorithm. Now, identifiers for "Joseph K." in the first dataset are represented by encrypted digital hashes that do not reveal the original data but can still be exchanged or matched against the corresponding data in the second set, since the matching name or other identifiers in that database would have a matching hash (digital signature). Should a match occur, the government would be required to follow the appropriate procedures prior to being granted access to the raw data corresponding to the match held by the original owner who maintains exclusive control of the actual data throughout.

As noted above, by controlling the sharing of *salt keys* additional policy restrictions can be enforced. Not only can hashed data not be turned back into the original data, but it cannot be matched or used for any other purpose without a matching salt key. Thus, control of salt variables allows searches to be restricted to certain datasets or domains.

Pseudonymization of Identity

A pseudonymous record or transaction is one that cannot—in the ordinary course of events—be associated with a particular individual.[55] Pseudonymity is a form of "traceable anonymity" and requires legal, organizational, or technical procedures so that the association (or attribution) can only occur under specified and controlled circumstances. Pseudonymity is also referred to as *identity escrow*.[56] A pseudonym can be either *transient* or *persistent*. Persistent pseudonyms develop their own reputational attributes and can be tracked over time or across systems.

Pseudonymity allows for the disclosure of only the particular attribute relevant (and appropriate) for the particular transaction in which an exchange of data is required. For example, in the use of credit cards, the merchant does not actually need the purchaser's name to complete the transaction, as only the authorization (that the issuer will pay the amount of the purchase) is relevant to the transaction. (Whether the cardholder is the authorized user is an authentication issue unrelated to the transaction specifically and also does not require revealing a name.)

Technical means exist to prove authorization without revealing actual identity by using *third-party certification* in which a trusted third party certifies an authorization. The holder of the certificate (digital or otherwise) then presents the certificate to the second party (who may still authenticate that the individual is the authorized user). However, the original party does not have to reveal additional identifiers (or identity) in order for the second party to grant the level of authorization certified by the third party. (There are also methods for certifying untraceable authorizations, for example, digital cash.) Technical means also exist to provide accountability without disclosing identity at the point of verification. Identity escrow is a form of third-party certification, in which the trusted third party certifies that the party knows the "true" identity of the user.

For example, a pseudonymous driver's license based on smart card technology (a smart card is any pocket-sized device that contains a processor or microchip that can interact with a reader) could be designed only to authenticate that the driver is authorized to drive (for example, by producing a digital certificate from the DMV certifying the holder's authorized status) without disclosing a common identifier during a traffic stop. The police officer could still run a data match against, for example, a wanted felon or terrorist watch list (also without revealing a name or common identifier) by reading a hashed identifier keyed (through shared salt) to the felony or watch list database hashing algorithm. If there were an initial data match then additional procedures may or may not be called for. However, without a match, the purpose of the traffic stop could be accomplished without disclosing identity. The same card could be designed to only exchange, for example, age information with a bartender's card reader, or health information with a medical worker, and so on.

An important policy consideration in any such system is determining whether such pseudonymous encounters are themselves logged—that is, do they generate their own transaction records? If so, do such queries become part of the data record subject to whatever policy controls are envisioned? As noted earlier, the issue of logs, and who controls them, has policy implications—both for privacy and for oversight.

In the above example, in addition to whether there should be a government database logging the transaction (and who should control it), there is also the question of whether the card itself should be designed to record the encounter. Arguments in favor would emphasize the empowerment to individuals from an immutable record in their possession of their encounter with law enforcement and a specific record of what queries were run. Arguments against this might include the fact that the card record itself becomes a vulnerability point for privacy—that is, recovery of transaction data from the card itself could be used against the individual at a later date.

Pseudonymity gives policy makers an additional method to control disclosure of identity. For example, in *Hiibel v. Nevada*,[57] the issue was whether a suspect could be compelled to give his name during a *Terry* stop.[58] Among the arguments put forward against disclosure of one's name was that in today's database world, disclosing one's name is the key to unlocking the digital dossier and may lead to "an extensive fishing trip across government databases."[59] One of the arguments in favor of disclosure is the legitimate interest to determine whether the individual is wanted or dangerous. "Obtaining a suspect's name in the course of a *Terry* stop serves important government interests. Knowledge of identity may inform an officer that a suspect is wanted for another offense, or has a record of violence or mental disorder."[60]

Information systems based on pseudonymity, including the use of smart ID cards, could provide another alternative to meet these same needs. As noted in the above example, there are technical methods for an individual to be matched against a watch list (or any other list) without revealing explicit identifying data. Thus, development of a national ID card based on segmented data and pseudonymous identities could improve privacy over existing methods and still meet security needs.[61]

Toward a Calculus of Reasonableness

Assuming that anonymization and pseudonymization strategies are employed to separate identity from behavior (or data), and control over data attribution is enforced through privacy appliances, the policy issue still remains: when and under what circumstances might particular methods of inquiry reasonably be used on specific datasets, and when and under what circumstances might data attribution (or deanonymization) reasonably occur?

It is my general thesis that procedural mechanisms relate to the concept of *reasonableness* (both in Fourth Amendment terms and as that term is more generally understood) through a complex policy calculus involving multiple independent and dependent variables that must be understood individually but considered together and in context. Thus, guiding principles, not rigid standards to be determined a priori for every conceivable use, condition, or context must be derived within which specific administrative procedures, legislative oversight, and judicial intervention and review can be fashioned.

Due Process

Due process is the means for insuring fairness in a system[62] and is essentially a function of four factors: the reasonableness of the *predicate* for action, the *practicality* of alternatives, the *severity and consequences* of the intrusion, and the procedures for *error control*.[63]

Determining the appropriateness of the *predicate* requires understanding error rates and assessing related confidence intervals—that is, it requires determining the probative weight of the indicia of suspicion. Confidence interval for policy purposes is simply the acceptable error rate for a given application. For example, the confidence interval for a screening application can be viewed as a function of two competing relationships, namely, the number of false positives (innocents identified) adjusted by the severity of the consequences to the individual and the number of false negatives (terrorists not identified) adjusted by the consequences to security (and by the potential misallocation of resources from false positives). Determining acceptable confidence intervals for any particular application requires assessing the probative value of the predicate procedures—for example, determining whether the observed behavior (or data analysis) reasonably justifies the consequences of the action or not.

The Supreme Court has also explicitly recognized that the requirement for individualized suspicion is not absolute and, where the government interest serves a need beyond routine law enforcement, the *practicality* of requiring a warrant or individualized suspicion is also a relevant factor to be considered:

> [O]ur cases establish that where a Fourth Amendment intrusion serves special governmental needs, beyond the normal need for law enforcement, it is necessary to balance the individual's privacy expectations against the Government's interests to determine whether it is *impractical* to require a warrant or some level of individualized suspicion in the particular context.[64]

The Court has used the same special needs reasoning in upholding the use of sobriety checkpoints, roving border checkpoints, airport searches, and random drug testing of student athletes. Likewise, policy makers should consider the practicality (or impracticality) of requiring specific procedures or individualized predicates when employing information processing systems for particular uses in counterterrorism.

Another important factor to be considered is the severity of the intrusion and its *consequences.* Thus, where there is an important state interest, and the intrusion minimal and the consequences slight—for example, a brief stop and referral to a secondary inspection or minimal questioning—the courts are likely to find no Fourth Amendment violation.[65] In upholding roving traffic checkpoints to enforce immigration laws, the Court stated:

> Against this valid public interest we must weigh the interference with individual liberty that results when an officer stops an automobile and questions its occupants. The intrusion is modest.[66]

Thus, a legitimate inquiry for policy makers is to determine the severity and consequence of a particular intrusion in light of the state interest. Where there is a significant state interest (for example, preempting terrorist attacks), minimal initial intrusion (for example, an automated review of data), and limited consequences (for example, a routine investigative follow-up that may only include cross-checking against additional data), the courts are likely to uphold the use of advanced information systems to screen data.

The final factor to be considered here in assessing due process is *error detection and correction.* Thus, an important policy and system design consideration is to recognize the inevitable potential for error and to build in robust error compensating mechanisms and procedures. However, error—including falsely identifying suspects (false positives)—is not unique to information systems. To the extent possible, therefore, error detection and error correction mechanisms for automated systems should embrace existing due process procedures, including procedures for administrative and, where appropriate, judicial review.

However, additional complications arise when one considers systems and uses in which the subject may never become aware of the intrusion or the consequences of the query. For example, in access control situations where permission for access is denied, individuals are usually on notice that their autonomy has been affected and corrective procedures can be triggered. More difficult is the situation where the data subject never becomes aware of the query or its consequence.

Also unresolved is whether *derived data* (for example, the query itself, links, or other information generated by the analysis itself) or *metadata* (data about the data, for example, data labels) becomes part of the record and whether it is also (or should be) subject to applicable laws—including error correcting procedures—that the underlying data may be subject to.[67]

Privacy and Security Information Needs

Foreign intelligence, counterintelligence, and law enforcement information is and should be available for appropriate domestic security purposes. The significant policy challenge lies in determining when and under what circumstances domestic intelligence access should be allowed to routinely collected government data or to commercially available (or other third-party) data.[68]

Unlike intelligence or law enforcement data, government-held data collected in the normal course of providing government services is generally subject to restriction for other uses or data matching by the Privacy Act of 1974. However, the Privacy Act has broad exceptions for data matching and interagency sharing for national security and law enforcement purposes. Thus, for practical purposes there may be no restrictions on secondary uses for domestic security applications. A threshold question is whether there should be any additional procedural protections or guidelines for secondary uses of routinely collected data that subsequently comes within the national security and law enforcement exceptions. A more difficult question, however, involves deciding whether the government should have access to, and use of, privately held third-party data, particularly data from commercial data sources, and if so, under what circumstances and what constraints.

That the government should, and will ultimately have access to this data in some form seems foregone. As already noted, it would be an unusual polity that demanded accountability from its representatives to prevent terrorist acts, yet denied them access to available tools or data. Thus, it is the procedures under which such access should be allowed that need to be defined. Here, developing clear goals and concomitant policy guidelines, requiring that the nexus between particular types of information and its use and value for counterterrorism be clearly identified or articulated, and mandating strict oversight and review procedures, are needed to ensure that appropriate government access to potentially useful information is possible while still protecting civil liberties.

Among the policy tools for dealing with access questions is the use of *categorization* to designate certain information sources or types subject to (or exempt from) particular procedures.[69] However, these procedures may require predetermining what information is relevant or subject to special handling, which is not always possible in counterterrorism analysis. Thus, it might ultimately be more practical to control the proposed *use* of data directly through a system based not on categorizing data itself by type but on managing and tracking authorized purpose for use at the time of access, subject to strict technical controls.

Any policy based solely on procedures for predesignating information as relevant for counterterrorism or to be managed under special rules needs to recognize three problems: first, it may be difficult to identify certain information as relevant except in the context of an ongoing investigation or in response to a particular threat; second, designations based on place, method of collection, or nationality of the subject may be outmoded in the context of a worldwide, distributed, networked database and communications infrastructure; and third, classifying data into categories that do not relate to the purpose of the original data collection may not be possible after the fact. In any case, if categorization strategies are to be used, they require that some technical means for data labeling be incorporated into the systems design.

Specific statutes already exist to protect particular classes of information deemed sensitive. These statutes generally require that use of these types of information conform to particular procedures. For example, access to census data, medical records, educational records, tax returns, cable television records, and video rental records, among others, is subject to each one's own statutory protection, usually requiring an elevated level of predicate, for example, a warrant or court order based on probable cause instead of a subpoena based on mere suspicion. Although some of these designations and procedures may need review in the context of domestic security, the general approach of dealing with particularly sensitive personal data by providing additional procedural protections in certain circumstances is workable and could be applied to identification, data aggregation and analysis, and collection systems, assuming that certain technical features, in particular for data labeling, are developed to allow data categorization to be maintained when data is shared or exchanged.

Policy decisions to a priori designate higher standards for sensitive information (or declaring certain information off-limits for certain uses) involve the same policy considerations and problems governing predesignating information or sources as relevant for counterterrorism analysis. Additionally, there may be a trade-off between the sensitivity of information and its relevance for counterterrorism that must be taken into account when such designations are made. If it turns out that certain information deemed sensitive by its nature, for example, financial records, is also quite specifically useful for counterterrorism (for example, following the money trail), policies (and technical features to support those policies) need to be developed, taking both needs into account. Again, strategies based on directly authorizing a particular use at the time and under the circumstances of access, monitored through strict technical controls, may need to be considered rather than continuing to rely solely on predetermined categorization of data sensitivity or predetermined usefulness.

Some are concerned that the use of automated data analysis techniques to allocate intelligence and law enforcement resources is not *particular* enough to protect due process or meet Fourth Amendment requirements. However, as already discussed, there is no absolute constitutional requirement for individualized suspicion and no presumptive constitutional problem with pattern matching.[70] Nevertheless, for the purpose of determining policy, it may be appropriate to address these concerns and recognize that different procedures may be appropriate for different query methods, depending, for example, on whether they are subject-, link- or pattern-based. Subject- and link-based queries generally raise the same issues as outlined above in the general discussion of scope—that is, what data can be accessed and under what circumstances. For some, however, pattern matching also raises additional concerns relating to individualized suspicion.

The policy question is whether there should be additional technical or procedural protections to be applied for pattern-based queries, based on the perception that these methods are potentially more intrusive or problematic. Some have recommended that additional procedures be applied to processes using pattern analysis derived from data mining, including specific preapprovals and stricter oversight.[71] Technical features to support such procedures would be required design features. For example, procedures requiring additional administrative (or judicial) approvals for specific disclosures (for example, of identity) would require technical controls to enforce selective revelation of information.

There is no magic policy formulation that perfectly balances the complex interactions between these many variables. What is called for instead is an analytic framework together with guiding principles—following what have I have called a *calculus of reasonableness*—that can inform the debate as these issues come up in varying contexts as new technologies develop and challenge existing doctrine or precepts in previously unforeseen circumstances. Thus, the ability to decide whether to apply rules (*what* you can do), procedures (*how* you can do something), or guidelines (constraints or *limits* within which you act to accomplish some goal) requires understanding these complexities and recognizing the inchoate nature of any solution, given the rapid pace of technological development and the evolving nature of the threat.

Threat Environment and Reasonableness

Reasonableness may also vary depending on the *threat level* and the particular security need. System bias toward more false positives and fewer false negatives may be reasonable under certain high-threat conditions or in applications requiring high security. In other circumstances, system bias toward fewer false positives and more false negatives may be more appropriate.

Policy considerations are also domain-dependent. For example, decision heuristics used during the development of traditional defense systems are generally inappropriate for domestic security applications. In designing military defenses, the bias is to eliminate any false negatives by accepting additional false positives. On the battlefield, it is better to have a low threshold for triggering a response than to risk not being prepared. However, in the context of a civilian population, false positives or false alarms may be as destructive of certain values (including security) as are false negatives by undermining trust in the system or creating intolerable burdens. Too many false positives and the resulting misallocation of resources will undermine both popular and political support for security measures as well as impact security itself.

Thus, because of the dynamic nature of the threat and security requirements, no system (technical or procedural) should be contemplated that is either constantly at ease or constantly at general quarters. Flexible systems and policy guidelines that can adapt proportionally to perceived threats faster and more efficiently are required. It also seems premature to burden either policy development or technical research and development with a requirement to determine a priori what policy rules will apply in every conceivable use case. Technical development processes are not generally amenable to predictable development paths where ongoing research is in its early stages. An iterative process using value-sensitive design procedures can help guide technical and policy development to achieve both required outcomes—security and privacy. However, achieving this requires joint participation, not knee-jerk opposition.

Nevertheless, guiding policy principles can be developed even without knowing all the potential technologically enabled opportunities or constraints based on a deeper understanding of these process needs. Policy develops rules of general applicability while judicial review examines cases of specific application; systems design must accommodate both.

Conclusion

The development and use by government of advanced identification, aggregation and analysis, and collection technologies in domestic security applications raise legitimate privacy concerns. Nevertheless, such development and eventual use is inevitable and strategies premised on opposition to research or banning certain uses or deployments through law alone are destined to fail, and in any case provide little security and brittle privacy protection. Protecting civil liberties requires that value-sensitive development strategies be used to design technical features and systems that enable familiar due process mechanisms to function.

The mythology of privacy and fear of technology should not keep us from opportunities to improve both security and privacy. Reconciling competing requirements for security and privacy requires an informed debate in which the nature of the problem is understood in the context of the interests at stake, the technologies at hand for resolution, and the existing resource constraints. Key to resolving these issues is designing a policy and information architecture that can function together to achieve both outcomes.

NOTES

The author would like to thank the Yale Information Society Project and the organizers of the Yale Cybercrime conference 2004. A longer version of this chapter appears in 7 Yale J. L. & Tech. 123; 9 Intl. J. Comm. L. & Pol'y 8 (Dec. 2004).

1. Thomas Powers, *Can We Be Secure and Free?* 151 PUBLIC INTEREST 3, 5 (Spring 2003).

2. BATYA FRIEDMAN, HUMAN VALUES AND THE DESIGN OF COMPUTER TECHNOLOGY (1997).

3. K. A. Taipale, *Data Mining and Domestic Security: Connecting the Dots to Make Sense of Data*, 5 COLUM. SCI. & TECH. L. REV. 2 (2003); *see also* Paul Rosenzweig, *Proposal for Implementing the Terrorism Information Awareness System*, 2 GEO. J. L. & PUB. POL'Y 169 (2004); ISAT 2002 Study, *Security with Privacy*, Dec. 13, 2002.

4. LAWRENCE LESSIG, CODE AND OTHER LAWS OF CYBERSPACE 3–8 (1999).

5. I use the phrase "war on terrorism" throughout this chapter because it is the prevailing metaphor. *But cf.* Terry Jones, *Why Grammar Is the First Casualty of War*, London Daily Telegraph, Dec. 1, 2001 ("How do you wage war on an abstract noun?"). *And see* GEORGE LAKOFF & MARK JOHNSON, METAPHORS WE LIVE BY 3–6 (2003) (discussing how metaphors not only affect how we communicate but actually structure our perceptions and understandings from the outset).

6. *See* National Commission on Terrorist Attacks upon the United States, *Final Report* (July 2004); Joint Inquiry into the Intelligence Community Activities before and after the Terrorist Attacks of September 11, 2001 House Permanent Select Comm. on Intelligence & Senate Select Comm. on Intelligence, H. Rep. No. 107-792, S. Rep. No. 107-351 (2002).

7. *See* U.S. Department of Justice, *Fact Sheet: Shifting from Prosecution to Prevention, Redesigning the Justice Department to Prevent Future Acts of Terrorism* (2002).

8. Markle Foundation, *Creating a Trusted Network for Homeland Security: Second Report of the Markle Foundation Task Force* (2003); Markle Foundation, *Protecting America's Freedom in the Information Age: A Report of the Markle Foundation Task Force* (2002); Committee on Science and Technology for Countering Terrorism, National Research Council, *Making the Nation Safer: The Role of Science and Technology in Countering Terrorism* (2002).

9. *See* ALAN WESTIN, PRIVACY AND FREEDOM (1967).

10. *See generally* JOHN AUSTIN, THE PROVIDENCE OF JURISPRUDENCE DETERMINED (1832) ("positive law" as social construction); and THE SOCIAL CONSTRUCTION OF TECHNOLOGICAL SYSTEMS (Wiebe E. Bijker et al. eds. 1994).

11. I do not mean to imply that these actors are not justified in their concerns, only that their particular focus comes to dominate the information flow and their rhetoric sets the terms of the debate. On information cascades generally, *see* Timur Kuran and Cass R. Sunstein, *Availability Cascades and Risk Regulation*, 51 STAN. L. REV. 683, 684 (1999); *see also* CASS R. SUNSTEIN, RISK AND REASON (2002); Cass R. Sunstein, *Terrorism and Probability Neglect*, 26 JOURNAL OF RISK AND UNCERTAINTY 121 (2003), reprinted in THE RISKS OF TERRORISM (W. Kip Viscusi ed. 2003).

12. *See generally* Lewis Mumford, Myth of the Machine: Technics and Human Development (1963, 1934); Jacques Ellul, The Technological Society (1964); Neil Postman, Technopoly: The Surrender of Culture to Technology (1993); Technology, Pessimism, and Postmodernism (Yaron Ezrahi et al. eds. 1994).

13. *See, e.g.*, Heather Mac Donald, *What We Don't Know Can Hurt Us*, 14 City Journal (Spring 2004).

14. *See* Robert C. Post, *Three Concepts of Privacy*, 89 Geo. L.J. 2087, 2087 (2001); Judith Jarvis Thomson, *The Right to Privacy*, 4 Phil. & Pub. Aff. 295–314 (1975).

15. *See* Taipale, *supra* note 3, at 49–58 (for an overview of competing views).

16. Daniel J. Solove, *Digital Dossiers and the Dissipation of Fourth Amendment Privacy*, 75 S. Cal. L. Rev. 1083, 1086 (critiquing the Supreme Court's conceptualization of privacy premised on "a form of total secrecy" and safeguarding only "intimate information that individuals carefully conceal").

17. Steven Hetcher, *Norm Proselytizers Create a Privacy Entitlement in Cyberspace*, 16 Berkeley Tech. L. Rev. 877 (2001).

18. Mark Alfino & G. Randolph Mayes, *Reconstructing the Right to Privacy*, 29 Soc. Theory & Practice 1–18 (2003).

19. Paul Rosenzweig, *Civil Liberties and the Response to Terrorism*, 42 Duq. L. Rev. 663, 715 (2004).

20. *See generally* Alexander Hamilton et al., The Federalist (Benjamin Wright ed., 1961); *see also* The War on Our Freedoms: Civil Liberties in an Age of Terrorism (Richard C. Leone & Greg Anrig, Jr. eds., 2003); Edward Corwin, The Constitution and What It Means Today (1978).

21. *See* Amitai Etzioni, The Spirit of Community: Rights, Responsibilities and the Communitarian Agenda (1993).

22. Powers, *supra* note 1, at 21.

23. Amitai Etzioni, The Limits of Privacy 206 n.77 (1999).

24. Geoffrey Stone, *Civil Liberties in Wartime*, 28 J. S. Ct. Hist. 215 (2003); *see also* William H. Rehnquist, All the Laws but One (1998).

25. *See* Roger Clark, *Information Technology and Dataveillance*, 31 Comm. of the ACM 498–512 (1988).

26. *See* Laird v. Tatum, 408 U.S. 1, 11 (1972) (actual harm or effect); Younger v. Harris, 401 U.S. 37, 51 (1971) (weigh government interest against harm).

27. *See generally* Eugene Volokh, *The Mechanisms of the Slippery Slope*, 116 Harv. L. Rev. 1026 (2003).

28. David Brin, The Transparent Society (1998).

29. Rosenzweig, *supra* note 3, at 196–197; James X. Dempsey and Paul Rosenzweig, *Technologies That Can Protect Privacy as Information Is Shared to Combat Terrorism* (Heritage Foundation, 2004).

30. Throughout this chapter I use the term *system* broadly to mean any bounded system—that is, national borders, air transportation, a particular physi-

cal location, or a computer network—within which one wants to provide *security*, meaning any effort to ensure that "users" of a system comport to the rules of behavior in that system.

31. Much of the discussion of identification in this section follows that set out in NATIONAL RESEARCH COUNCIL, WHO GOES THERE? (2003).

32. Jeff Jonas, Presentation at the Center for Strategic and International Studies, *Data-Mining in the Private Sector* (July 23, 2003).

33. *See* K. A. Taipale, *The Trusted Systems Problem: Security Envelopes, Statistical Threat Analysis, and the Presumption of Innocence*, IEEE Intelligent Systems, Vol. 20, No. 5, pp. 80–83 (Sept.-Oct. 2005).

34. BRUCE SCHNEIER, BEYOND FEAR 181 (2003).

35. *See* references in notes 6 and 8 *supra*; for a detailed discussion of data aggregation and data mining for domestic security, *see* Taipale, *supra* note 3; Mary DeRosa, *Data Mining and Data Analysis for Counterterrorism*, Center for Strategic and International Studies (March 2004).

36. *See* Usama Fayyad et al., *From Data Mining to Knowledge Discovery in Databases*, 17 AI MAGAZINE 37, 38 (Fall 1996); David Jensen, *Data Mining in Networks*, presentation to the Roundtable on Social and Behavior Sciences and Terrorism of the National Research Council, Division of Behavioral and Social Sciences and Education, Committee on Law and Justice (Dec. 1, 2002).

37. U.S. Dept. of Justice v. Reporters Committee, 489 U.S. 749, 780 (1989).

38. *See* United States v. Brignoni-Ponce, 422 U.S. 873, 886 (1975). The Court has never ruled explicitly on whether race can be a *relevant* factor for reasonable suspicion under the Fourth Amendment. *See id.*, at 885–887 (implying that race could be a relevant, but not sole, factor). *See also* Whren v. United States, 517 U.S. 806, 813 (1996); MICHELLE MALKIN, IN DEFENSE OF INTERNMENT: THE CASE FOR RACIAL PROFILING IN WORLD WAR II AND THE WAR ON TERROR (2004).

39. United States v. Cortez, 449 U.S. 411, 418 (1981); *and see* United States v. Sokolow, 490 U.S. 1, 9–10 (1989) (upholding the use of drug courier profiles).

40. *See* David. E. Steinberg, *Making Sense of Sense-Enhanced Searches*, 74 MINN. L. REV. 563 (1990).

41. Olmstead v. United States, 277 U.S. 438, 464 (1928) (*overruled by* Katz).

42. Katz v. United States, 389 U.S. 347 (1967).

43. *Id.*, at 361 (J. Harlan, concurring).

44. Kyllo v. United State, 533 U.S. 27, 40 (2001) ("not in general public use").

45. Michael Froomkin, *The Death of Privacy?*, 52 STAN. L. REV. 1461, 1523 (2000).

46. United States v. Miller, 425 U.S. 435, 441–443 (1976) (financial records); Smith v. Maryland, 442 U.S. 735, 743 (1979) (pen register).

47. Solove, *supra* note 16, at 1133.

48. *Id.*, at 1117–1138.

49. Alfino and Mayes, *supra* note 18; Julie Cohen, *Examined Lives: Informational Privacy and the Subject as Object*, 52 STAN. L. REV. 1373, 1377, 1425 (2000).

50. Adm. John Poindexter, Presentation at DARPAtech 2002 (Aug. 2, 2002).

51. *See* K. A. Taipale, *Designing Technical Systems to Support Policy: Enterprise Architecture, Policy Appliances, and Civil Liberties, in* EMERGENT INFORMATION TECHNOLOGIES AND ENABLING POLICIES FOR COUNTER TERRORISM (Robert Popp and John Yen, eds., Wiley-IEEE Press, 2006) (describing the use of *policy appliance* to enforce rules in technical systems).

52. *See generally* HOWARD SMITH & PETER FINGAR, IT DOESN'T MATTER, BUSINESS PROCESSES DO (2003).

53. Roger Clarke, *Identified, Anonymous and Pseudonymous Transactions: The Spectrum of Choice*, presented at User Identification & Privacy Protection Conference, Stockholm (June 14–15, 1999).

54. Jeff Jonas, SRD, quoted in Steve Mollman, *Betting on Private Data Search*, WIRED NEWS, Mar. 5, 2003.

55. Clarke, *supra* note 53.

56. *See, e.g.*, Joe Kilian and Erez Petran, *Identity Escrow*, in Advances in Cryptology—CRYPTO '98: 18th Annual International Cryptology Conference, Santa Barbara, California, USA, August 1998. Proceedings (H. Krawczyk, ed.).

57. Hiibel v. Nevada, 542 U.S. 177 (2004).

58. Terry v. Ohio, 392 U.S. 1 (1968) (police can detain a suspect for a reasonable period without probable cause to suspect a crime).

59. *See* Brief of Amicus Curiae of the Electronic Privacy Information Center (EPIC) and Legal Scholars and Technical Experts at 6, Hiibel v. Nevada, No. 03-5554 (S. Ct. June 21, 2004).

60. Hiibel, *supra* note 57, at 186.

61. *See generally* Michael Froomkin, *The Uneasy Case for National ID Cards*, Yale Information Society Project Cybercrime 2004 conference paper (2004); *but cf.* Richard Sobel, *The Demeaning of Identity and Personhood in National Identification Systems*, 15 HARV. J. LAW & TECH. 319 (2002).

62. *See generally* RONALD DWORKIN, LAW'S EMPIRE (1988).

63. Related policy considerations in determining reasonableness are the interaction and effect of authorization and oversight mechanisms (either executive or legislative) and judicial review in the context of a particular use.

64. Treasury Employees v. Von Raab, 489 U.S. 656, 665–666 (1989). Emphasis added.

65. United States v. Martinez-Fuerte, 428 U.S. 543, 558–561 (1976).

66. United States v. Brignoni-Ponce, 422 U.S. 873, 879–880 (1975).

67. *See, e.g.*, the Fair Credit Reporting Act (FCRA), 15 U.S.C. § 1681 et seq., in which queries to credit reporting agencies themselves become part of the underlying credit report and subject to the requirements of the Act.

68. *See generally* Solove, *supra* note 16; Second Markle Report, *supra* note 8, at 30–37.

69. For example, under Homeland Security Presidential Directive/HSPD-6, 39 Weekly Comp. Pres. Doc. 1234–1235 (Sept. 16, 2003), certain information is classified as "Terrorist Information" to be handled under specific procedures, and under NSA/CSS United States Signal Intelligence Directive 18 ("USSID 18") (July 27, 1993) certain information about U.S. persons gathered during foreign intelligence SIGINT collection is subject to extraordinary procedures ("minimization").

70. See discussion in section on Due Process above.

71. *See* Safeguarding Privacy in the Fight against Terrorism, The Report of the [Department of Defense] Technology and Privacy Advisory Committee (TAPAC) (March 2004); Rosenzweig, *supra* note 3; Daniel Gallington, *Better Information Sharing and More Privacy in the War on Terrorism—A New Category of Information Is Needed* (Potomac Inst. for Pol'y Studies, July 29, 2003).

9

CALEA: Does One Size Still Fit All?

Emily Hancock

Few would disagree with the argument that lawfully authorized surveillance is vitally important to combating crime and ensuring national security. Just over ten years ago, Congress gave law enforcement authorities a tool to help ensure their ability to conduct surveillance, while also maintaining the privacy of communications in a world of rapidly advancing technology. The Communications Assistance for Law Enforcement Act (CALEA)[1] was enacted in October 1994 as a measure that Congress intended would "preserve the government's ability [pursuant to lawful authority] to intercept communications involving advanced technologies such as digital or wireless transmission modes, or features and services such as call forwarding, speed dialing, and conference calling, while protecting the privacy of communications and without impeding the introduction of new technologies, features, and services."[2]

Before CALEA, in the days when AT&T maintained its monopoly status, virtually all communications were carried over circuit-switched wireline telephony networks. With one company in control, law enforcement had a predictable, understandable mechanism for conducting surveillance on communications. But deregulation brought increased competition, with industry innovators tripping over each other to introduce new technologies to the market. And as competitors rather than regulated monopolists, they couldn't simply add the cost of designing wiretap capabilities to their rate-base. As a result, law enforcement in the early 1990s (and even today) faced challenges because of insufficient technical expertise and funds to adapt to the new technologies. Law enforcement also had to compete with the other demands placed on carriers by their customers—demands for reliable and inexpensive service with all the available bells and whistles.

So while technology was making electronic surveillance easier in many ways, law enforcement also claimed that new technology was "impeding or preventing law enforcement from conducting court-authorized electronic surveillance."[3] As a result, the Federal Bureau of Investigation (FBI) asked Congress to pass a law that would ensure its ability to "ensure a failsafe way for law enforcement to conduct court-authorized wiretapping on the recently deployed and emerging technology."[4]

CALEA—the legislative solution that emerged victorious after years of wrangling and debate—required covered entities to provide law enforcement with standardized tools to carry out lawfully authorized intercepts of call content and call-identifying information. The final draft of the legislation "embodied a simple but novel principle: Telecommunications carriers were obliged not merely to aid law enforcement in using existing equipment to carry out authorized wiretaps but also to ensure that law enforcement could obtain access."[5]

But Congress kept CALEA's focus narrow and attempted to strike a balance among three competing interests: law enforcement needs, privacy, and technological innovation.[6] Only already-regulated "telecommunications carriers"[7] were subject to its requirements. In addition, Congress incorporated provisions designed "to protect privacy in the face of increasingly powerful and personally revealing technologies . . . [and] to avoid impeding the development of new communication services and technologies."[8] Recognizing that CALEA's requirements posed the risk of stifling innovation, Congress laid out limited enforcement rules in the law in order to protect industry's ability to innovate without a permission slip from government.

Now, more than ten years after CALEA's passage, the technology of telephony has changed dramatically. Instead of universal reliance on the ubiquitous circuit-switched analog telephony system, individuals can choose from a wide variety of data and voice communications systems that use different technological applications and platforms—broadband Internet, wireless handheld devices, Voice over Internet Protocol (VoIP), and voice-enabled Instant Messaging, to name a few. All these new services operate differently from the traditional telephone network that CALEA was designed to address. For example, VoIP allows individuals to transmit voice over the Internet in packet form—and to separate voice from call-signaling information. Some VoIP calls may be routed through the old-fashioned circuit-switched network, while others may bypass it. And there are even different types of VoIP architectures. In one model, call content passes through a VoIP provider's network, which lets the provider control call quality and routing, among other things. In another model, a provider merely supplies users with the necessary software, and then individuals can send call content directly to one another without the provider's involvement—much like peer-to-peer music sharing.

However, many of these new communications technologies created new challenges for law enforcement. The Internet has a multilayered, open architecture and supports a multitude of diverse applications. As a result, law enforcement authorities—especially local authorities—have at times struggled to keep pace with technology, and they do not always succeed in understanding where the focus of interception should be, which provider to contact in order to conduct the interception, and what call-identifying information can be gleaned as a result of the interception. Which leads us to the current wrangling over CALEA. Arguing that carriers "have deployed new technologies without regard to law enforcement's ability to execute court-ordered electronic surveillance,"[9] the Department of Justice (DOJ), FBI, and Drug Enforcement Administration (DEA) asked the Federal Communications Commission (FCC) to expand CALEA. They argued that CALEA was outdated and that in order for the authorities to be effective in combating crime and terrorism, CALEA should be extended to apply to Internet communications and some types of VoIP.[10]

Many industry members, privacy advocates, and others vigorously disagreed with law enforcement's position. In the end, however—and after considering the issue for more than a year—the FCC sided with law enforcement, finding that CALEA "applies to facilities-based broadband Internet access providers and providers of interconnected [VoIP] service."[11] In the era of ever-changing technology, it is apparent that while CALEA strikes a balance between the interests of law enforcement on the one hand and the interest of privacy and innovation on the other, this balance is tenuous. In the eyes of many, the FCC upset this balance by extending CALEA to cover services that should have been exempt.[12] Nevertheless, communications technologies will continue to evolve in innovative ways, which means the "how far does CALEA reach" question is likely to be raised again and again.

But in examining whether to preserve CALEA as it now exists or to expand its reach even further—whether that expansion takes place at the regulatory level or in the form of new legislation—parties on both sides of the debate should continue to ask, "At what cost?" What harm is being done to public safety and national security if law enforcement does not have full access to all types of communications? And, if CALEA were applied to new technologies in a way that allows law enforcement to set the terms or pace of technical change in the telecommunications industry, what will be the cost to U.S. innovation? Even though the FCC decided this latest round in favor of extending CALEA to most types of broadband Internet access providers and VoIP providers, these questions will continue to hang in the balance as new communications technologies are introduced.

CALEA—What Does It Do?

As enacted, CALEA does a reasonably good job of straddling the fine line between aiding law enforcement's investigative needs while protecting privacy and innovation. CALEA requires telecommunications carriers to isolate and to enable the government to intercept communications and "call-identifying information that is reasonably available to the carrier."[13] But it also requires carriers to facilitate "communications interceptions and access to call-identifying unobtrusively and with a minimum of interference with any subscriber's telecommunications service" and to do so in a way that protects "the privacy and security of communications and call-identifying information not authorized to be intercepted."[14]

In order to protect innovation, CALEA explicitly states that the intercept capability requirements of section 103(a) of the statute do not apply to "information services," which, in 1994, was shorthand for Internet communications.[15] Instead, CALEA's requirements only apply to "telecommunications carriers"[16]—providers of "the components of the public switched network where law enforcement agencies have always served most of their surveillance orders."[17] Basically, "telecommunications carriers" provide telephony services while "information services" are "current and future advanced software and software-based electronic messaging services, including email, text, voice and video services" and other Internet applications.[18] And not only did Congress exclude "information services" from CALEA's requirements, but Congress constructed CALEA so that applying the law's definition of "telecommunications carrier" to new technologies would require a public interest finding and substantial market penetration as a replacement for local telephone exchange service.[19]

Congress sought to further protect innovation by putting the development of compliance standards in the hands of industry. For example, law enforcement cannot require service providers to adopt—or prohibit a service provider from adopting—any "specific design of equipment, facilities, services, features, or system configurations.[20] Determining compliance standards is up to industry.[21] And law enforcement cannot penalize carriers for noncompliance. That responsibility rests only with the courts in situations where alternative technologies were not reasonably available to law enforcement and where compliance by a carrier was reasonably achievable.[22]

Similarly, Congress did not guarantee that all future communications would be tappable. CALEA explicitly states that telecommunications carriers are not "responsible for decrypting, or ensuring the government's ability to decrypt, any communication encrypted by a subscriber or customer, unless the encryption was provided by the carrier."[23] By not limiting the ability of subscribers to use encryption, CALEA left in place an important privacy protection.

Thus, Congress drafted CALEA with a narrow scope. It preserved the status quo as intended so that "technological developments did not erode law enforcement access to call content and identifying information," but it also left room for law enforcement to be able to take advantage of technological developments.[24] However, that balancing act has left room for law enforcement to argue that CALEA as written "leaves organized criminals, terrorists, and spies with a wide range of uncovered, thus untappable, alternative means of communicating with one another."[25]

DOJ accepted that compromise only grudgingly, and it began to question the wisdom of the deal it accepted in 1994. According to DOJ, "In investigating terrorism, espionage, and other serious crimes, electronic surveillance is not only one of the most effective tools government has, but often it is the *only* effective tool."[26] Yet "[t]here have been occasions where, because of technological gaps with respect to certain services, telecommunications carriers were unable to provide, or where unable to provide in usable form, the content of communications or related information as required by court orders."[27] Given these concerns, it is not surprising that law enforcement would begin to challenge CALEA's narrow scope and the balance it strikes between aiding law enforcement and preserving the freedom to innovate. After all, any statute that seeks to achieve such a balance among competing interests is likely to succeed in making all stakeholders only marginally satisfied.

Changing CALEA to Address Twenty-First-Century Technology?

With the argument that critical communications are escaping interception because law enforcement cannot access certain communication technologies as a backdrop, the DOJ, FBI, and DEA in March 2004 petitioned the FCC to extend CALEA's requirements to broadband Internet access services and some kinds of VoIP services.[28] Law enforcement also sought greater FCC regulatory and enforcement power over communications service providers, including greater government input in and authority over the industry standards process.[29] The FCC opened a rulemaking,[30] and the debate about the future of communications surveillance began.

The problem with regulating to give law enforcement access to new technology, however, is the cliff effect. Most technology is unregulated, but all technological change has an effect on law enforcement. Fast computers make strong encryption easily available; electronic databases of personal information increase the risk of rapid, widespread identity theft; prepaid calling cards and mobile phones are a wiretapper's worst nightmare; fast cars extend the reach of all criminals. Are we going to regulate all these technologies or, worse, insist that they solve any law enforcement problems they may cause before letting them reach the market? Probably not. At some point, law enforcement's right to regulate new technology has to reach a stopping point. From law enforcement's point of view, that is the cliff edge—the point where regulation ends and the free market begins. In 1994, CALEA set the edge of the cliff at rate-regulated telecommunications carriers. Ten years later, law enforcement believed it reached the edge of the cliff and petitioned the FCC to throw in some landfill to extend CALEA to cover communications systems that were exempted when the law was enacted.

Law enforcement encountered substantial resistance, though, from the industries that expect to be buried under all that fill—broadband access service providers and VoIP providers. Critics of law enforcement's efforts argued that CALEA was drafted to be a narrowly focused statute aimed at "addressing the advent of digital technology *within the [public-switched network]*—which is the only place where law enforcement was facing problems in 1994."[31] Many parties also argued that law enforcement did not provide sufficient evidence to justify CALEA's expansion and, moreover, that law enforcement was asking the FCC "to go beyond its statutory authority" by subjecting information services to CALEA.[32] Parties opposed to law enforcement's request argued that if the FCC granted law enforcement's petition, the decision "would have a harmful impact on innovation because such action would give to Law Enforcement the right to pre-approve new technologies and services."[33]

Despite these arguments, the FCC in 2004 tentatively adopted many of law enforcement's requests for expanding the reach of CALEA. Not only did the FCC agree with the suggestion to expand CALEA to cover broadband Internet access providers and certain types of VoIP providers (as "substantial replacements" to the PSTN), but the FCC also suggested that it could create broad regulations, including enforcement mechanisms, at the agency level to ensure that providers are complying with CALEA.[34] Critics of law enforcement's proposal as adopted by the FCC argued that the proposal and the FCC were seeking to overturn key aspects of the carefully balanced statute.

These arguments were to no avail. In a decision released September 23, 2005, the FCC adopted many of its tentative conclusions and voted to interpret CALEA as covering facilities-based broadband Internet access providers and providers of interconnected VoIP services.[35] The FCC's conclusion rested on what many critics considered a tortured statutory interpretation. The FCC found that even though, in other proceedings, it had deemed services such as broadband Internet access and VoIP to be "information services" not subject to regulation as "telecommunication carriers" under the Communications Act, CALEA's definition of "telecommunications carrier" was more inclusive.[36]

A discussion of the FCC's analysis is beyond the scope of this chapter. Briefly, though, CALEA's definition of "telecommunications carrier" includes entities: "providing wire or electronic communication switching or transmission service to the extent that the Commission finds that such service is a replacement for a substantial portion of the local telephone exchange service and that it is in the public interest to deem such a person or entity to be a telecommunications carrier for purposes of [CALEA]."[37] Relying on the language and legislative history of this "substantial replacement provision," the FCC stuck with its tentative conclusion that broadband Internet access services and interconnected VoIP services were substantial replacements for the public telephone network and therefore should be covered under CALEA. In June 2006, this reasoning was upheld by the U.S. Court of Appeals for the D.C. Circuit.[38]

About eight months after it released its decision to extend coverage of CALEA, the FCC released a second Report and Order resolving some remaining open issues. In that Order, the FCC adopted its tentative conclusion that it should give itself the ability to bring enforcement actions against carriers that fail to comply with CALEA, and established parameters for the situations in which providers could petition the FCC for relief from CALEA obligations, among other things.[39]

The FCC also stuck to its original tentative conclusion and found "that it would be inconsistent with the legislative history of CALEA and inappropriate as a matter of policy for the Commission to identify future services and entities that may be subject to CALEA."[40] The FCC sided with industry and against law enforcement in finding that the FCC should not require providers to get a ruling on whether new technologies or services would be subject to CALEA before providers began deploying such technologies or services.[41] Instead, the FCC said, requiring providers to obtain advance rulings about "CALEA's applicability to a new service in advance of that service's introduction to the marketplace . . . would have a chilling effect on innovation."[42]

CALEA Today—Where Are We Headed?

The FCC's most recent pronouncements on CALEA raise several important concerns about the future. CALEA's one-size-fits-all approach has already been adapted once to the new world of communications technology diversity—will future adaptations occur in the same way? Or will we see legislative efforts supplant the FCC's rulemaking role? In either case, how will lines be drawn in the future to determine which new services, if any, will be covered? The FCC has given itself increased regulatory and enforcement powers—to what end? What impact will this have on innovation and communications privacy? And have the FCC's actions in 2005 and 2006 meant that providers are or will be in danger of losing the autonomy and independence that CALEA originally gave them to develop compliance solutions free from undue government influence or approval?

1. Subjecting New Services to CALEA
(a.k.a. How to Draw a Line, FCC Style)

When the FCC first issued its Notice, it tentatively concluded that information services should be covered sometimes—when they are a substantial replacement for telecommunications carriers.[43] But in proposing to apply CALEA obligations to certain "information services"—broadband access and VoIP services—that were not previously subject to Commission regulation, the Notice did not draw a clear line between where it believed CALEA coverage ended and unregulated "information services" began.[44] The FCC attempted to clarify this line in its First Report and Order. The FCC's initial mushy bottom-line approach seemed to give the FCC the discretion to reach out and regulate a little bit more when it chooses—leaving providers to wonder whether they are regulated or not.

The question of whether and how to draw a line between certain types of broadband access providers and certain types of VoIP providers did not have a glaringly obvious answer—especially for VoIP. Broadband providers can, with relative ease, be divided into two rough categories—facilities-based providers of the underlying broadband access networks, and providers of applications that ride over the network. And this in fact was the division the FCC suggested in its Notice[45] and kept in its First Report and Order. The FCC ultimately concluded that facilities-based providers[46] of any type of broadband Internet access service are subject to CALEA. According to the FCC, this category includes—but is not limited to—"wireline, cable modem, satellite, wireless, fixed wireless, and broadband access via powerline" where such broadband access service is offered on a common carrier basis.[47]

Determining which—if any—VoIP providers should be subject to CALEA was more difficult for the FCC given the myriad VoIP services currently in existence. Plus, in 2004 as now, while the provision of basic broadband Internet access is a relatively well-developed business model, VoIP providers are still in experimental stages.

VoIP works by using a complex and developing suite of protocols to transmit voice content over the Internet or other IP networks. Generally, the IP networks transmit packets in a consistent manner regardless of their content—much of the "intelligence" that processes the content is located in hardware or software at the network edge. This content-independent network architecture is different than that of circuit-mode telephone networks, which are designed and optimized specifically for transmitting voice calls. Meanwhile, because VoIP relies on one set of protocols for call signaling and another for call content, such call-signaling information and call content can be handled differently, over different network paths.[48]

Within this architecture, there are different VoIP business models. Some models involve active call management by the provider, including connecting users with the public, circuit-switched network in order to complete calls. Other models, such as Skype, allow users to download software and make and complete calls and the provider is not involved in call connection. These latter models act much like P2P networks—they are highly decentralized, and extremely difficult to regulate and control. In its Notice, the FCC said it only intended to expand CALEA to "managed or mediated" VoIP services that connect calls to the circuit-switched network because only those VoIP services could be considered "substantial replacements" for basic telephony service.[49] In its First Report and Order, however, the FCC concluded that CALEA applies to providers of "interconnected VoIP services," which are defined as VoIP services that "(1) enable real-time, two-way voice communications; (2) require a broadband connection from the user's location; (3) require IP-compatible customer premises equipment; and (4) permit users to receive calls from *and* terminate calls to the PSTN."[50] The FCC was arguably required to adopt this limit, since trying to regulate the software provider would simply have led to the development of open-source versions of VoIP software—eliminating the last commercial entity that could conceivably be regulated.

Even with this limitation, any regulation of VoIP services poses a number of threats for innovation. Not only is there a risk that providers may attempt to design their services so as to avoid falling within a type of VoIP application that has been designated a "substantial replacement" and therefore subject to CALEA, but providers in the United States very likely will find themselves at a competitive disadvantage compared to their foreign counterparts. VoIP services for U.S. residents could easily be run from outside the United States. This means that non-U.S. providers would be outside the reach of CALEA VoIP regulation and therefore would not be required to invest the time and expense in developing CALEA compliance solutions. These non-U.S. competitors likely would be able to offer VoIP service more cheaply than their counterparts in the United States, and they would not face a risk that could be possible for U.S. providers—that a CALEA compliance solution might degrade the quality of the communication. Thus, CALEA will impede the ability of U.S. VoIP providers to compete, while not meeting the objective law enforcement was hoping to achieve.

2. More Power to the FCC? Or Not?

In its CALEA Notice, the FCC proposed to turn CALEA into a new FCC regulatory program, something that was not thought necessary when

CALEA was enacted or in the ten years since. The FCC proposed that it should have a role in enforcing manufacturers' and providers' CALEA compliance, even though the language of the statute clearly places enforcement in the hands of lawsuits to be brought by the Justice Department. But the FCC, citing its general enforcement authority under the Communications Act, tentatively concluded that it should promulgate CALEA rules that can be enforced against all entities deemed subject to CALEA.[51]

In its Second Report and Order, the FCC decided that its tentative conclusion—a conclusion supported by the Department of Justice[52]—was correct. The FCC concluded that the Communications Act gives the Commission authority to "prescribe such rules as are necessary to implement the requirements of [CALEA]" and that nothing in CALEA would limit the Commission's general enforcement authority.[53] As written, CALEA directed that if a court issuing a surveillance order deemed that a telecommunications carrier failed to comply with CALEA as required, then the court could direct the carrier to comply and could also impose civil penalties.[54] The FCC found that these provisions do not limit the FCC's "authority to promulgate and enforce CALEA rules against manufacturers and support service providers."[55]

The FCC has yet to issue further regulations pursuant to CALEA, but in its Second Report and Order, it reminded carriers that FCC rules "already include various CALEA requirements that we may enforce."[56] Two such requirements are system security and records management requirements for carriers subject to CALEA. The FCC also stated that it would codify CALEA's statutory requirement that carriers are to comply with the assistance capability requirements in section 103 of CALEA,[57] and it therefore clarified "that all carriers subject to CALEA are to comply, at a minimum, with the assistance capability requirements of section 103."[58]

The FCC only very recently concluded that it has regulatory and enforcement authority under CALEA, so the effects of this conclusion remain to be seen. But if the FCC takes a heavy-handed approach to regulation and enforcement, this could move CALEA away from being a statute that historically has regulated through performance standards and instead transform CALEA into a top-down regulatory scheme. It also could extend the FCC's authority into computer and Internet communications—and even hardware design. These are industries that have grown strong without FCC regulation, and the effect of bringing them into the FCC's fold is unknown.

At bottom, it is important that any enforcement framework allow for flexibility. Often, there is no simple answer to the question of how CALEA should be implemented. Instead, decisions in this area require a sophisticated balancing of the costs and benefits of various approaches. The CALEA framework is driven by industry standards and consultation between industry and law enforcement. This negotiation-based approach is well-suited to the complex environment of CALEA compliance.

Now that the FCC has asserted its enforcement authority, it remains to be seen whether this action will transform CALEA into a top-down regulatory scheme or whether such regulations will be able to exist in harmony with the already complex CALEA-compliance process.

3. Timing Is Everything . . .

In its current form, CALEA sets a performance standard for companies. It requires companies subject to CALEA to make every call isolatable and deliverable to law enforcement. CALEA doesn't care how providers accomplish that feat. CALEA also says that telecommunications carriers will not be challenged about how they make their calls isolatable and deliverable to law enforcement unless and until a law enforcement agency comes to the carrier and complains.[59] That gave carriers time to find CALEA-compliant solutions. Under the terms of the FCC's Second Report and Order, however, facilities-based broadband Internet access service providers and VoIP providers newly subject to CALEA now must achieve compliance by May 14, 2007.[60] The FCC found that a uniform compliance date "will avoid any skewering effect on competition and will prevent migration of criminal activity onto networks with delayed compliance dates."[61]

Throughout the CALEA rulemaking process, some providers expressed concern that after the FCC set a compliance date, the FCC would go on to require providers to negotiate with the FBI or get the blessing of the FBI even before launching a new technology in order to determine how the new technology would meet CALEA requirements from the day of the launch.[62] Ultimately, however, the FCC decided against this approach, finding that providers should not be required to "obtain advance clearance from the government before deploying a technology or service."[63] Yet the FCC also created an "optional expedited declaratory ruling procedure" in the event that a service provider sought a ruling on whether its new service was required to be CALEA-compliant. These "telecommunications carriers and manufacturers, as well as [law enforcement], may petition the Commission for a declaratory ruling as to CALEA obligations with regard to new equipment, facilities and services."[64] While the FCC's ruling makes clear that its predeployment declaratory ruling process is optional, the Department of Justice and FBI demonstrated throughout the course of the rulemaking proceeding their desire for the FCC to adopt procedures for determining whether products and services would be subject to CALEA prior to deployment. Only time will tell whether pressure will be brought to bear on providers to obtain such CALEA-compliance rulings before deploying new products or services. For example, if it were to threaten fines or cease-and-desist orders against noncompliant companies, the FCC could arrive at a regime that has the effect of forcing innovators to get permission from the FCC and Justice Department before deploying any new technology that falls into the wide gray zone created by the FCC's vaguely defined regulations described above. An inventor who must get a government permission slip before trying out his invention is not likely to be first to market. While American innovators are still cooling their heels in Quantico, waiting to explain a new technology to the FBI Lab, their competitors in Singapore, China, Japan, and Europe will be manufacturing already. The U.S. market could end up a laggard, getting technologies after they've been sufficiently proven in the rest of the world to justify the engineering and lobbying costs needed to get an assurance of CALEA compliance.

4. Preserving Innovation Is Mission Critical

Industry advocates argue that the CALEA of the future should not set aside Congress's original insight, namely, that industry knows more than the government about how to design new telecommunications equipment.[65] Even the DOJ and FBI acknowledged this in their joint comments on the FCC's Notice.[66] Industry-led standards development efforts are critical to the cost-effective and successful implementation of CALEA, and Congress recognized this when it enacted CALEA. For example, when Congress had to make a choice between innovation and law enforcement control over CALEA compliance, Congress choose innovation, with its eyes wide open.[67] Congress knew that the FBI wanted authority to oversee and even dictate the technical details of equipment manufacturers' CALEA-compliant solutions. But Congress rejected that approach and instead enacted CALEA with a provision that prohibited law enforcement from requiring "any specific design of equipment, facilities, services, features, or system configurations."[68] At the same time, in Section 107(a) of CALEA, Congress explicitly noted the special role it gave to industry in creating standards to meet CALEA obligations. Section 107(a) "establishes a mechanism for implementation of the [CALEA] capability requirements that defers, in the first instance, to industry standards organizations."[69]

Further, a leading role for industry in CALEA standards-setting is essential to further Congress's goal to "not impede the development of new communications services and technologies."[70] Industry is by far best situated to design CALEA compliance standards in a complex, rapidly changing technology environment. An industry-led standards process permits U.S. companies to press forward with technological innovation, which has been one of the key drivers of the U.S. economy in recent decades. At the same time, an industry-led standards process affords industry-appropriate, lawfully authorized electronic surveillance capabilities for evolving communications technologies.

Conclusion

Privacy advocates, civil libertarians, and law enforcement authorities alike agree that ensuring lawful law enforcement access to communications is an important goal—as important as preventing highway deaths or ensuring clean air or workplace safety. But if the last twenty-five years of regulatory history have demonstrated anything, it is that an assertion that a new regulation will serve an important social goal cannot be merely accepted without scrutiny or question. No matter how important the goals they serve, some regulations make sense and some don't. Some go beyond statutory mandates. Some impose burdens that are nowhere near being cost-effective, stifling new industries and sending jobs overseas.

Of course, maintaining the ability of law enforcement access to investigate crime is a good thing, at least when done within the law. But preventing highway deaths is also a good thing, and there's no doubt that there would be fewer fatal accidents if the speed limit on interstate highways was lowered to thirty miles an hour. The speed limit has not been reduced so drastically, though, because the costs of such a regulation simply are not worth the added benefit. The same is true for wiretaps—except that today, there's a real risk that increased regulation could impose the wiretap equivalent of a 30 MPH speed limit on some of the nation's most innovative and competitive new communications industries.

The risks of overregulating and stifling innovation were well recognized ten years ago when Congress drafted CALEA. CALEA was the result of a compromise that gave law enforcement a very carefully limited role in influencing the course of future technologies. Congress rejected the idea that the federal government should design or even have a veto over the design of new technologies. Instead, it set forth a very limited performance standard for wiretap access that would apply to a limited portion of the telecommunications industry.

When it was enacted, CALEA struck a delicate, tenuous balance using a narrow focus. Now, with new technologies, greater threats to national security, and an increased reliance on interception techniques as a crime-fighting tool, law enforcement and the FCC have broadened CALEA's focus. What remains to be seen in this world of CALEA's expanded reach is whether CALEA can hold steady in its balancing act of giving law enforcement the surveillance assistance it needs while protecting privacy and preserving innovation.

NOTES

With thanks to my former colleague Stewart Baker, who first got me involved in CALEA and whose work on CALEA heavily influenced this article. Thanks also to EB and JH for their assistance in finalizing this piece. The opinions or statements expressed herein should not be taken as a position or endorsement of Yahoo! Inc. or its subsidiaries and may not reflect the opinions of their affiliates, joint ventures, or partners.

1. Pub. L. No. 103-414, 108 Stat. 4279 (1994) (codified as amended at 47 U.S.C. §§ 1001–1010 (1994 and Supp. 1996) and in scattered sections of 18 U.S.C. and 47 U.S.C.).

2. H.R. Rep. No. 103-827, 103d Cong., 2d sess., at 9 (1994) (hereinafter "House Report").

3. Digital Telephony and Law Enforcement Access to Advanced Telecommunications Technologies and Services: Joint Hearings on H.R. 4922 and S. 2375 before the Subcomm. on Technology and the Law of the Senate Comm. on the Judiciary and the Subcomm. on Civil and Constitutional Rights of the House Comm. on the Judiciary, 103d Cong. at 5–6 (1994) (hereinafter "Digital Telephony Hearing") (statement of Louis J. Freeh, Director, FBI).

4. Digital Telephony Hearing, at 6 (statement of Louis J. Freeh, Director, FBI).

5. Lillian R. BeVier, *The Communications Assistance for Law Enforcement Act of 1994: A Surprising Sequel to the Break Up of AT&T*, 51 Stanford. Rev. 1049, 1072 (1999).

6. James X. Dempsey, *Communications Privacy in the Digital Age: Revitalizing the Federal Wiretap Laws to Enhance Privacy*, 8 Alb. L.J. Sci. & Tech. 65, 90 (1997).

7. A "telecommunications carrier" is defined as "a person or entity engaged in the transmission or switching of wire or electronic communications as a common carrier for hire," including wireless carriers, and "a person or entity engaged in providing wire or electronic communication switching or transmission service to the extent that the Commission finds that such service is a replacement for a substantial portion of the local telephone exchange service and that it is in the public interest to deem such a person or entity to be a telecommunications carrier"—except that information service providers are excluded. 47 U.S.C. § 1001(8).

8. House Report, at 13.

9. Hearing on Electronic Surveillance in the Digital Age before the Subcomm. on Telecommunications and the Internet of the Comm. on Energy and Commerce, 108th Cong., 2 (2004) (hereinafter "Electronic Surveillance Hearing") (statement of Laura H. Parsky, Deputy Assistant Attorney General, Criminal Division, Department of Justice).

10. *In re United States Department of Justice, Federal Bureau of Investigation and Drug Enforcement Administration, Joint Petition for Rulemaking to Resolve Various Outstanding Issues concerning the Implementation of the Communications Assistance for Law Enforcement Act*, Joint Petition for Expedited Rulemaking, ET Docket No. 04-295, RM-10865, at 15 (March 10, 2004) (hereinafter "Joint Petition for Rulemaking") (urging the FCC to find that under CALEA's definition of "telecommunications carrier," "CALEA applies to two closely related packet-mode services that are rapidly growing in significance for law enforcement: broadband access service and broadband telephony service.").

11. *In re Communications Assistance for Law Enforcement Act and Broadband Access and Services*, First Report and Order and Further Notice of Proposed Rulemaking, ET Docket No. 04-295, RM-10865, at ¶ 1 (Sept. 23, 2005) (hereinafter "First Report and Order").

12. *See, e.g., In re Communications Assistance for Law Enforcement Act and Broadband Access and Services*, Notice of Proposed Rulemaking and Declaratory Ruling, ET Docket No. 04-295, RM-10865, Joint Comments of Industry and Public Interest (Nov. 8, 2004).

13. 47 U.S.C. §§ 1002(a)(1), (2).

14. *Id.*, at § 1002(a)(4).

15. CALEA states that its Section 103(a) intercept capability requirements do not apply to "(A) information services; or (B) equipment, facilities, or services that support the transport or switching of communications for private networks

or for the sole purpose of interconnecting telecommunications carriers." *Id.*, at § 1002(b)(2). The definition of "information services" includes the "offering of a capability for generating, acquiring, storing, transforming, processing, retrieving, utilizing or making available information via telecommunications," and includes (i) a service that permits a customer to retrieve stored information from, or file information for storage in, information storage facilities; (ii) electronic publishing; and (iii) electronic messaging services. *Id.*, at § 1001(6).

16. CALEA's definition of "telecommunications carriers" excludes providers of "information services" such as electronic mail and online service providers. 47 U.S.C. § 1001(8)(C).

17. House Report, at 18.

18. Hearing on S. 2281, The VoIP Regulatory Freedom Act of 2004 before the Senate Committee on Commerce, Science and Transportation (June 16, 2004) (Statement of James X. Dempsey, Executive Director, Center for Democracy and Technology).

19. 47 U.S.C. § 1001(8)(B)(ii). CALEA also exempts from coverage "equipment, facilities, or services that support the transport or switching of communications for private networks or for the sole purpose of interconnecting telecommunications carriers." *Id.*, at 1002(b)(2)(B).

20. *Id.*, at § 1002(b)(1).

21. *Id.*, at § 1006(a)(2). CALEA ensures that industry is in charge of writing the standards under which providers have a safe harbor and are deemed CALEA-compliant. *Id.* Only if industry failed to develop acceptable standards—and only if law enforcement or a government agency could prove that industry failed to develop acceptable standards—would the FCC be able to step in and develop standards with which industry would be required to comply. *Id.*, at § 1006(b).

22. *Id.*, at §§ 1007, 1008(b).

23. *Id.*, at § 1002(b)(3).

24. Dempsey, *supra* note 6, at 95.

25. BeVier, *supra* note 5, at 1093.

26. Electronic Surveillance Hearing, at 4 (statement of Laura H. Parsky, Deputy Assistant Attorney General, Criminal Division, Department of Justice).

27. *Id.*, at 8.

28. DOJ and FBI argued that even though broadband Internet access services were "information services" under CALEA, they should be regulated under CALEA because they were substantial replacements for telecommunications services. Joint Petition, at 15–22.

29. *See generally* Joint Petition.

30. *In re Communications Assistance for Law Enforcement Act and Broadband Access and Services*, Notice of Proposed Rulemaking and Declaratory Ruling, ET Docket No. 04-295, RM-10865 (Aug. 9, 2004) (hereinafter "CALEA NPRM").

31. *In re Communications Assistance for Law Enforcement Act and Broadband Access and Services*, Notice of Proposed Rulemaking and Declaratory Ruling, ET Docket No. 04-295, RM-10865, Joint Comments of Industry and Public Interest at 16 (Nov. 8, 2004). The public-switched network, or "PSTN," refers to the circuit-switched telephony network.

32. CALEA NPRM, at ¶ 29.

33. *Id.* DOJ's Parsky, however, asserts that "[l]aw enforcement cannot—nor do we seek to—dictate to any carrier how best to design its services or what services it can or cannot offer." Electronic Surveillance Hearing, at 12 (statement of Laura H. Parsky, Deputy Assistant Attorney General, Criminal Division, Department of Justice).

34. CALEA NPRM, at ¶¶ 114–116.

35. First Report and Order, at ¶ 1.

36. First Report and Order, at ¶ 10. On the same day the FCC released the CALEA First Report and Order, it issued a Report and Order in a separate rulemaking proceeding in which it found that the Communications Act's definitions of "telecommunications service" and "information service" are mutually exclusive. *Id.*, at ¶ 15 (citing *In re Appropriate Framework for Broadband Access to the Internet Over Wireline Facilities; Universal Service Obligations of Broadband Providers; Review of Regulatory Requirements for Incumbent LEC Broadband Telecommunications Services; Computer III Further Remand Proceedings*, Report and Order, CC Docket Nos. 02-33, 01-337, 95-20, 98-10 at ¶¶ 12–17 (Sept. 23, 2005) (stating that "wireline broadband Internet access service provided over a provider's own facilities is an 'information service'")).

37. 47 U.S.C. § 1001(8)(B)(ii).

38. American Council on Education v. Federal Communications Commission, No. 05-1404, 2006 U.S. App. LEXIS 14174 (June 9, 2006).

39. *In re Communications Assistance for Law Enforcement Act and Broadband Access and Services*, Second Report and Order and Memorandum Opinion and Order, ET Docket No. 04-295, RM-10865, at ¶¶ 5, 27–56 (May 12, 2006) (hereinafter "Second Report and Order").

40. Second Report and Order, at ¶ 80.

41. Second Report and Order, at ¶ 77.

42. Second Report and Order, at ¶¶ 78, 80.

43. CALEA NPRM, at ¶ 1.

44. *See, e.g., In re Communications Assistance for Law Enforcement Act and Broadband Access and Services*, Notice of Proposed Rulemaking and Declaratory Ruling, ET Docket No. 04-295, RM-10865, Comments of the United States Internet Service Provider Association, at 5; Comments of Earthlink, Inc., at 5–7 (Nov. 8, 2004).

45. CALEA NPRM, at ¶ 47.

46. First Report and Order, at ¶ 24 & n. 74 (explaining that "facilities-based" means "entities that 'provide transmission or switching over their own facilities between the end user and the Internet Service Provider (ISP).'").

47. First Report and Order, at ¶ 24. Under the Communications Act, a "common carrier" is an entity that provides, for hire, "interstate or foreign communication by wire or radio" 47 U.S.C. § 153(10) and is generally subject to the provisions in Title II of the Act.

48. *See generally In re Communications Assistance for Law Enforcement Act and Broadband Access and Services*, Notice of Proposed Rulemaking and Declaratory Ruling, ET Docket No. 04-295, RM-10865, Comments of the United States Internet Service Provider Association, at Appendix A.

49. CALEA NPRM, at ¶¶ 56–59.

50. First Report and Order, at ¶ 39.

51. CALEA NPRM, at ¶¶ 114–116.

52. Second Report and Order, at ¶ 65.

53. *Id.*, at ¶ 66 (citing 47 U.S.C. § 229).

54. 18 U.S.C. § 2522.

55. Second Report and Order, at ¶ 66.

56. *Id.*, at ¶ 68.

57. Section 103(a)(1) requires telecommunications carriers to establish the capability of providing to law enforcement call content information pursuant to proper legal authorization, and Section 103(a)(2) requires carriers to establish the capability of providing to law enforcement call-identifying information pursuant to proper legal authorization. 47 U.S.C. § 1002(a)(1), (a)(2).

58. Second Report and Order, at ¶ 68.

59. *Id.*, at § 1006(b).

60. Second Report and Order, at ¶ 15.

61. *Id.*, at ¶ 15.

62. *In re Communications Assistance for Law Enforcement Act and Broadband Access and Services*, Notice of Proposed Rulemaking and Declaratory Ruling, ET Docket No. 04-295, RM-10865, Comments of US ISPA, at 42 (Nov. 8, 2004) (arguing that Section 108 of CALEA, which gives CALEA enforcement authority to the courts alone, "allows innovators to bring their products to market without first negotiating a full CALEA compliance scheme with the FBI. . . . [A]n innovator might decide to market a new product without a complete CALEA solution— trusting that a partial solution, combined with information available to law enforcement from other sources, would be sufficient in the unlikely event that a wiretap is needed in the first months of service. In those circumstances, the defenses to enforcement actions under CALEA are crucial protectors of innovation. The alternative—the prospect of an immediate cease-and-desist order and/or fine before any wiretap order has been served and before the first cus-

tomer has signed up—will discourage all but the most confident innovator from going to market without a fully negotiated CALEA agreement with the FBI.").

63. Second Report and Order, at ¶ 77.

64. *Id.*, at ¶ 80.

65. *See, e.g., In re Communications Assistance for Law Enforcement Act and Broadband Access and Services*, Notice of Proposed Rulemaking and Declaratory Ruling, ET Docket No. 04-295, RM-10865, Comments of the Telecommunications Industry Association, at 9–15 (Nov. 8, 2004); Comments of the United States Internet Service Provider Association, at 30–34 (Nov. 8, 2004); Comments of SBC Communications, at 20–21 (Nov. 8, 2004); Comments of the United States Telecom Association, at 9 (Nov. 8, 2004).

66. *In re Communications Assistance for Law Enforcement Act and Broadband Access and Services*, Notice of Proposed Rulemaking and Declaratory Ruling, ET Docket No. 04-295, RM-10865, Comments of the United States Department of Justice, at 39–44, 54–56 (Nov. 8, 2004).

67. Congress's preference for industry control and innovation is evident from the text of CALEA. *See, e.g.,* 47 U.S.C. § 1002(b) (preventing law enforcement from being able to require or prohibit specific equipment or system designs); *id.*, at § 1006(a) (giving industry the ability to establish standards for CALEA compliance in order to qualify for a safe harbor).

68. 47 U.S.C. § 1002(b)(1).

69. House Report, at 26.

70. *Id.*, at 19.

Part V

New Procedures
E-Prosecution, E-Jurisdiction, and E-Punishment

10

The Council of Europe's Convention on Cybercrime

Susan W. Brenner

On November 23, 2001, the Convention on Cybercrime was opened for signature in Budapest.[1] The Convention was developed to address what is perhaps the distinguishing characteristic of cybercrime: its ability to transcend national boundaries and, in so doing, to elude the grasp of local law enforcement.

Background

The Convention is the culmination of efforts that began decades ago, when it became apparent that computer technology could be used to engage in various types of undesirable activity. Some of this activity took the form of traditional crime; computers were, and are, used to facilitate the commission of such conventional crimes as theft, fraud, extortion, and stalking. Computers can also be used to engage in activities that are "new" in varying degrees, such as hacking into computer systems, damaging data contained in computer systems, and launching denial of service attacks on computer systems. By the 1980s, countries had begun to enact laws that specifically criminalized both "new" activities and the use of computer technology to commit conventional crimes. This was particularly true of Europe and North America; by the 1990s, countries in both regions had adopted laws criminalizing a core set of activities that included gaining unauthorized access to computer systems, damaging data held in such systems, and releasing malware.

And this, it was implicitly assumed, was all that was needed to enable nations to deal with cybercrime; after all, the historical response to emerging varieties of undesirable conduct has been to criminalize it. Criminalizing conduct means local law enforcement can respond to instances of the proscribed behavior; those who engage in the behavior can be apprehended, prosecuted, convicted, and sanctioned, which impedes their ability to reoffend and discourages others from following their unfortunate example. Of course, not all those who offend will be apprehended and prosecuted; the incidence of proscribed behaviors in a society can be kept within manageable bounds if the overall apprehension and conviction rate for crimes is sufficient to persuade most would-be offenders that it is inadvisable to engage in such activities.

This proposition is the foundation of criminal justice systems in every modern nation and was therefore the premise of the cybercrime laws nations adopted in the 1980s and 1990s. These laws were "internal" laws; that is, they assumed that the activities they proscribed would be committed entirely within the territorial boundaries of the nation adopting the laws and would involve a perpetrator and victim who, if they were not citizens of that nation, were situated within it when the cybercrime occurred. Those assumptions have historically held for criminal activity, which has in many ways remained more primitive than its civil counterparts. Commerce long ago began transcending national boundaries and national laws, but crime remained provincial for the most part, at least until recently, because it was predicated on a personal dynamic—a face-to-face encounter between perpetrator and victim. It is, for example, impossible to commit rape if the rapist and the victim are fifty miles apart; and in a nontechnological world it is equally impossible to pick someone's pocket or take his or her property by force if the thief and victim are in different countries.

Cybercrime

Many things become possible in a technological world. While it is still impossible to commit rape remotely, the computer-facilitated commission of most traditional crimes can easily transcend national boundaries. This is also true of the "new" crimes that have emerged from cyberspace; hacking, malware, denial of service attacks, and related endeavors ignore territorial and jurisdictional boundaries. As this aspect of cybercrime became apparent, it became equally apparent that the "internal" laws nations had adopted to deal with cybercrime were insufficient to deal with externally based activity.

Cybercrime is not, of course, the first instance of externally based criminal activity. Countries long ago devised mechanisms for dealing with the formerly rare instances in which criminals or criminal activity transcended national borders: An idiosyncratic network of Mutual Legal Assistance Treaties (MLATs) bound various countries to assist each other in investigating real-world criminal activity, such as the drug trade; if no MLAT was in effect, authorities could "invoke the ancient procedure of sending letters rogatory" to obtain evidence from abroad.[2] And extradition treaties could be used to secure the person of an offender for trial.

While these mechanisms may be an acceptable way of approaching the investigation of real-world crime and/or the apprehension of real-world criminals, they are so unsuitable as to be almost futile with regard to cybercrime and cybercriminals. One problem is that, notwithstanding the national legislation adopted in the 1980s and 1990s, many countries lack cybercrime law. If Country A seeks assistance from Country B because one of its citizens has been the victim of a cybercrime (under the laws of Country A) committed by a citizen of Country B (which lacks cybercrime laws), the latter's failure to criminalize the activity at issue means that (i) no MLAT will be in effect that requires it to assist with the investigation; (ii) letters rogatory are likely to be equally unavailing; and (iii) the offender, if identified, cannot be extradited for prosecution in Country A, where her conduct is illegal. The outcome is the same if Country B has adopted *some* cybercrime laws but has not criminalized the precise activity at issue. The de facto result is that cybercriminals can operate with impunity from Country B as long as they limit themselves to external attacks, that is, as long as they only attack citizens of countries other than Country B.

In this scenario, Country B is a haven for cybercrime, just as certain cities were havens for high-seas pirates centuries ago, when the seas were as "uncivilized" as cyberspace is today. A country's status as cybercrime haven can be advertent or inadvertent, the product of design or neglect. The impetus for a country's achieving haven status is irrelevant; what matters is the effect. Laws designed to prevent citizens of a country from preying upon other citizens of that country are irrelevant when crime becomes an externality; we have no laws, no mechanisms, that are designed to prevent citizens of one country from preying upon the citizens of another country. Since we assume the influence of physical boundaries, we divide threats into internal ("crime") and external ("war") and assign responsibility for each to a separate institution (law enforcement and the military). This approach works satisfactorily for physically based activities but not for cybercrime; what we define as "internal" threats can now come from external, civilian actors. We must, therefore, devise a new approach.

This brings us to the Convention on Cybercrime, which is meant to be the new approach that solves the problems outlined above. It is the culmination of efforts that began over twenty years ago with an Organisation for Economic Co-operation and Development (OECD) study of the possibility of harmonizing national cybercrime laws; the premise was that improving the consistency of national laws could improve law enforcement's ability to respond to cybercrime. The OECD issued a report recommending that countries criminalize a core set of cybercrimes. At around the same time, the Council of Europe began studying the same issue, an effort which eventually led to the Convention on Cybercrime.[3]

The Convention

The Convention represents a traditional approach to the problems cybercrime poses for law enforcement agencies and the societies they protect. It equates cybercrime with crime and therefore treats cybercrime as an internal threat which is to be dealt with by the criminal justice system of a nation whose citizens have suffered "harm" from a particular activity. Instead of focusing on the issue noted above—the fact that cyberspace lets the citizens of one society prey remotely upon citizens of other societies—the Convention incorporates the traditional approach to crime and treats cybercrime as an affront to a specific nation-state. It consequently articulates strategies that are intended to improve nation-states' ability to respond to cybercrime.

This section examines the approach the Convention takes; the Conclusion considers approaches it could have taken.

Crimes

The Convention begins by requiring parties to define certain activities as cybercrimes. This aspect of the Convention (Articles 2–9) is designed to address the "haven" issue discussed in the previous section by ensuring a baseline of consistency on certain core offenses. The goal is unobjectionable, but the methodology is peculiar. Parties to the Convention must criminalize (i) several activities targeting computer systems and data; (ii) computer-facilitated forgery; (iii) computer-facilitated fraud; (iv) the use of computer technology to create, distribute, or possess child pornography; and (v) the use of computer technology to commit intellectual property crimes.[4] The activities targeting computer systems and data consist of gaining unauthorized access to computer systems or data, damaging computer systems or data, and the "misuse of devices."[5]

There is nothing peculiar about calling upon countries to criminalize most of these activities; the exception is the "misuse of devices" offense, which has been criticized both for suppressing free speech and for criminalizing the legitimate activities of computer security professionals. What is peculiar is that this rather limited list of offenses does not seem an effective way to address the "haven" issue; as explained earlier, cybercriminals can exploit the lack of cybercrime laws generally or in specific areas to commit crimes with relative impunity. One of the Convention's goals is to eliminate this opportunity by "harmonising the domestic . . . substantive law elements of offences . . . in the area of cyber-crime."[6] But the Convention only requires parties to criminalize a subset of the illegal activities that can be facilitated by computer technology; it does not, for example, require countries to criminalize the use of computers to commit theft, extortion, stalking, terrorism, or to inflict physical injury upon persons or property.

One might argue that it was not necessary to include these traditional crimes because they are already outlawed by the criminal codes of modern nations, but the Convention does include at least three traditional crimes: forgery, fraud, and child pornography. The rationale for including them was presumably that the use of computer technology raises issues that may elude the conventional definition of these crimes, but that can be equally true of other crimes, such as theft. Neither the Convention nor the accompanying Explanatory Report indicates (i) why only a subset of the cybercrimes we have encountered were included in the Convention, and (ii) why this particular subset was chosen. Except for the misuse of devices, the crimes targeting computer systems and data were obvious choices for a cybercrime Convention; but the same is not true of the other offenses. It is true that computer technology can exponentially enhance one's ability to commit fraud and produce and disseminate child pornography, but this is equally true for other crimes, such as extortion.

There are two other peculiarities in the way the Convention approaches harmonizing substantive cybercrime law. One is that it does not provide model legislation which parties to the Convention would implement; such a document would do a great deal to ensure consistency in the implementation of laws adopted by various nations. Model legislation would also alleviate the burden it will be for some countries to develop implementing legislation. The United States was very influential in drafting the Convention, so it tends to track American law; consequently, implementing the Convention should be a simple matter for this country. That will not be true for other countries.

The final peculiarity in the Convention's substantive law provisions is that most of the "crime" articles allow parties to reserve the right not to impose liability in accordance with all the provisions of an article. Article 9, for example, addresses child pornography and requires, as its default, criminalizing the use of computer technology to produce, disseminate, or possess both "real" and "virtual" child pornography. Countries can elect not to criminalize (i) the use of computer technology to procure and/or possess child pornography, or (ii) any activity involving computer-generated or "virtual" child pornography.[7] While the ability to limit liability imposed pursuant to the Convention gives countries some flexibility, it also undermines, to some extent, the goal of harmonizing national cybercrime laws.

Procedure

The lengthiest and most controversial provisions of the Convention deal with the investigation and prosecution of cybercrimes. Essentially, the Convention requires parties to adopt legislation that is designed to facilitate investigations by (i) expediting the preservation and production of electronic evidence; (ii) applying search and seizure law to computer systems; and (iii) authorizing law enforcement to collect traffic data and content data.[8] Parties must also cooperate in (i) extraditing offenders; (ii) sharing information; and (iii) preserving, accessing, intercepting, and disclosing traffic and content data.[9] And each must designate a 24/7 point of contact who is responsible for ensuring "immediate assistance" in cybercrime "investigations or proceedings."[10]

The goal is to expedite the processes of evidence- and offender-sharing between countries. As noted earlier, investigators have traditionally relied on a patchwork of MLATs or on letters rogatory, which allows a court in one country to request a court in another country's assistance in accomplishing a goal, such as obtaining evidence. Both procedures are very slow, which makes them unsuitable for cybercrime investigations.

For the most part, cybercrime investigations focus on digital evidence, for example, on the content of email messages, the "address" information used to send email messages, logs of computer activity, and data stored on laptop or desktop computers. Countries have developed the procedural law over the last century or so to deal with real, physical evidence such as guns, drugs, paper documents, fingerprints, and the like. Physical evidence can be lost but is not easily destroyed; and it is usually very difficult, if not impossible, to alter physical evidence. Digital evidence is fragile and can easily be destroyed or altered. An Internet Service Provider, for example, may routinely delete logs documenting online activity; but these logs can contain evidence cybercrime investigators need. Investigators therefore need some way to ensure that evidence is preserved and can be made available for their use. Neither the MLAT nor letters rogatory procedures are suitable for this because both operate so slowly. The Convention is designed to improve the processes used to locate, preserve, and share digital evidence across national boundaries; it supplements the provisions of existing MLATs and acts as an MLAT when no treaty is in place.

As noted earlier, the procedural provisions have proven controversial, with much of the controversy focusing on three issues. One derives from Article 14, which defines the scope of these provisions. It requires parties to apply the procedures established in accordance with the Convention not only to crimes defined in accordance with the Convention but also to (i) the investigation of *any* crime "committed by means of a computer system," and (ii) to the collection of electronic evidence for use in prosecuting any *other* crime. Articles 20 and 21 do allow countries to limit the interception of content data and the real-time collection of traffic data to investigations involving "serious offences" under their "domestic law," but aside from this the broad powers conferred under the Convention apply to the investigation of any cybercrime and to the investigation of any crime involving electronic evidence.

The Convention does not explain why its procedural provisions apply more broadly than its substantive provisions, that is, why they apply to non-Convention cybercrimes and to non-cybercrimes. Aside from anything else, this seems to make the Convention's substantive provisions irrelevant. If the procedures required by the Convention can be used to investigate any crime the commission of which involves the use of computer technology or electronic evidence, then of what import are the offense definitions contained in Articles 2 to 11? The same result could presumably have been achieved by simply applying the Convention's procedural provisions (i) to any cybercrime, and (ii) to any non-cybercrime that generates electronic evidence. And there is a potential for abuse: a party to the Convention might find itself obligated to assist another party in the latter's investigation of activity that is not a cybercrime (or not a crime) under its domestic law. Traditionally, extradition treaties have required dual criminality, that is, they have required that the activity at issue be a crime in both the country seeking extradition and the country asked to extradite; and while this has not always been true of MLATs, they generally include provisions stating that a country can deny assistance if the request involves a "political offense."

This issue of dual criminality also arises under another provision. Articles 23 to 35 set out the standards and requirements for international cooperation. Article 25 requires parties to provide "mutual assistance to the widest extent possible for the purpose of investigations or proceedings concerning criminal offences related to computer systems and data, or for the collection of evidence in electronic form of a criminal offence." According to the Explanatory Report, the drafters imposed "an obligation to co-operate as to this broad class of crimes because there is the same need for streamlined mechanisms of international co-operation as to both of these categories."[11] Many, particularly in the United States, criticize the lack of a dual criminality requirement. As one group pointed out,

> the treaty would require U.S law enforcement authorities to cooperate with a foreign police force even when such an agency is investigating an activity that, while constituting a crime in their territory, is perfectly legal in the U.S. No government should be put in the position of undertaking an investigation of a citizen who is acting lawfully.[12]

Those who defend the Convention note that Article 25 allows parties to condition their providing assistance upon the existence of a generic dual criminality. They also note that under Article 27(4), a country can refuse to assist when a request (i) involves what it regards as a political offense, or (ii) is "likely to prejudice its sovereignty, security . . . or other essential interests." This provision apparently would allow the United States to decline to provide assistance when investigations implicated free speech and other constitutional guarantees.

The third issue that has generated substantial controversy is privacy. Article 15 is the only provision of the Convention that addresses privacy and other rights. Article 15 requires parties to ensure that the "implementation and application of the powers and procedures" the Convention prescribes "are subject to conditions and safeguards . . . which shall provide for the adequate protection of human rights and liberties." It references the 1950 Council of Europe Convention for the Protection of Human Rights and Fundamental Freedoms, the 1966 United Nations International Covenant on Civil and Political Rights, and other applicable international human rights instruments. Many find Article 15 to be completely inadequate. The Electronic Privacy Information Center, for example, claims that Article 15 is "quite vague" and that the Convention fails

> to respect fundamental tenets of human rights espoused in previous international Conventions, such as the 1948 Universal Declaration of Human Rights and the 1950 Convention for the Protection of Human Rights and Fundamental Freedoms. The Cybercrime Convention also ignores a multitude of treaties relating to privacy and data protection, including the Council of Europe's 1981 Convention for the Protection of Individuals with regard to the Automatic Processing of Personal Data, and the European Union's 1995 Data Protection Directive.[13]

Others concur. Ironically, perhaps, some attribute what they see as the Convention's neglect of privacy guarantees to the influence of the United States:

> A Convention developed by the Council of Europe should have given a high priority to data protection issues. . . . Such important safeguards . . . were left out to accommodate the US government's interests which do not favour data protection laws as a policy. Unlike in the European Union . . . there is no comprehensive data protection legislation in the USA. States within the CoE region should have avoided pandering to what constitutes the lowest common denominator in the field of data protection.[14]

Privacy advocates criticize the Convention not only for its failure to include general privacy guarantees, but also for some of the powers it confers on law enforcement. Article 18(1)(a), for example, requires parties to take such "legislative or other measures" as are necessary to authorize their "competent authorities" to order someone in their territory "to submit specified computer data in that person's possession or control." And Article 19(4) requires parties to take similar measures "to empower" their "competent authorities to order any person who has knowledge about the functioning of the computer system or measures applied to protect the computer data therein to provide" the information needed to search a computer system or a "computer-data storage medium." Critics of the Convention contend that, when read together, these two provisions authorize law enforcement to force individuals to divulge their encryption keys, which would violate "rights such as privacy of communications" and the privilege against self-incrimination.

Critics of the Convention also cite other specific problems with its procedural provisions, such as a lack of judicial oversight for computer search warrants, data interception orders, and production orders. They also raise another general criticism that goes not to the provisions of the Convention but to the process by which it was created. Many claim that the Convention was drafted in a

> very secretive and undemocratic manner. The Council of Europe's Committee of Experts on Crime in Cyberspace . . . completed nineteen drafts of the Convention before the document was released to the public. Between 1997 and 2000, no draft was released and no public input was solicited. The Convention was drafted by persons and groups primarily concerned with law enforcement, and reflects their concerns almost exclusively, to the detriment of privacy and civil liberties interests.[15]

Those who make these claims contend that because they were given only a limited time in which to review and comment on the Convention, their suggestions were not included in the final draft. U.S. Department of Justice representatives, at any rate, reject the idea that the Convention is the product of secret negotiations.

Conclusion

The Convention on Cybercrime is a complex document that has generated complex reactions from various constituencies. It is difficult, at this point in history, to assess what, if any, impact it will have on the struggle against cybercrime. There are reasons to believe its impact may be minimal.

One is empirical: the so far surprisingly slow pace of ratification. The Convention was opened for signature and ratification on November 23, 2001. Three years later, it had been signed by thirty-eight countries but ratified by only eight: Albania, Croatia, Estonia, Hungary, Lithuania, Romania, Slovenia, and the former Yugoslav Republic of Macedonia. None of the major European countries had ratified it, nor had the United States, Canada, or Japan. In November 2003 President Bush asked the Senate to approve ratification, and a Senate committee held hearings on the Convention in June 2004, but nothing has happened since. In September 2004, the Council of Europe held a conference, the purpose of which was to encourage more countries to sign and ratify the Convention. When asked about the slow pace of ratification a conference speaker attributed it to the complexity of the issues it raises.

The prime movers behind the Convention have ignored it for three years; ratification and implementation are obviously not a high priority for these countries. Their inaction is puzzling and somewhat unsettling. It may be, as the conference speaker suggested, that the Convention is falling prey to its own ambitions—that the nature and extent of the effort required to implement it is discouraging countries from ratifying it. It is difficult, though, to understand why this should be true of the major European countries and of the United States; since they all participated in drafting the Convention, it presumably incorporates principles and practices they found to be acceptable and achievable. Indeed, the Department of Justice has noted that if the United States ratifies the Convention it will not need to adopt implementing legislation; existing law is adequate.

For the Convention to achieve its goal—the harmonization of national substantive and procedural cybercrime law—it must be ratified and implemented by every country in the world. Otherwise, the "haven" scenario goes unaddressed. The lack of expedition with which the United States and the major European countries are approaching the Convention suggests it is unlikely to achieve its goal. If ratification continues at its present glacial pace, it will take many years for the world's remaining, roughly one hundred eighty countries to implement the Convention (if, indeed, all are willing to do so). In the interim, the Convention may prove a useful device for facilitating cooperation among the countries that implement it; it remains to be seen, after all, how well its provisions will work in practice and whether they will survive the challenges that will certainly be brought in some countries. It may be that the Convention ultimately serves only as a first step in a process that will take years to accomplish.

And this brings us to another issue: the approach the Convention takes to cybercrime. As noted earlier, it treats cybercrime like crime, that is, as an internal problem to be handled unilaterally by an offended nation-state. It is true that cybercrime is a form of crime, but it might accurately be characterized as crime-plus. It has the basic characteristics of traditional crime (perpetrator, victim, and the infliction of a socially intolerable harm) but it is not territorially based. Unlike crime, cybercrime can easily transcend national boundaries. The Convention's response to this circumstance is traditional: like an MLAT, it requires countries to assist each other with nationally based investigations and prosecutions. This continues the localized, decentralized system of law enforcement we have had for centuries.

Perhaps we need a new system for cybercrime. Perhaps we cannot adapt our existing approach to deal effectively with cybercrime. Perhaps the otherwise puzzling lack of progress in implementing the Convention attests to the futility of trying to adapt traditional, nationally based law enforcement to nonterritorially based crime. So, maybe we should consider an alternative.

Logically, there are three ways to structure law enforcement's response to cybercrime: one is the Council of Europe's distributed approach, in which the responsibility for reacting to cybercrime is parsed out among nation-states, each of which defines cybercrime, investigates cybercrime, and prosecutes and punishes cybercriminals. As we have seen, the problem with this approach is that it is territorially based but cybercrime is not.

Another approach is to centralize law enforcement in a single agency that is responsible for controlling cybercrime around the world. In its most extreme form, this option would produce a global agency that would be preemptively responsible for outlawing cybercrime, investigating it, prosecuting cybercriminals, and sanctioning them. Conceptually, this approach would be based on the premise that cyberspace has become another jurisdiction, another arena for human activity, and as such, requires its own law enforcement institutions. Implementing this approach would require us to accept what seems to be inevitable, which is not unknown in the law.

Inevitable or not, countries are unlikely to be willing to surrender complete responsibility for cybercrime in the near future, and this brings us to the third approach, which is a compromise between the first two. Here, the prosecution and sanctioning of cybercriminals would remain the responsibility of discrete nation-states, but the processes of investigating cybercrime and apprehending cybercriminals would be delegated to a central agency, a sort of super-Interpol. Unlike Interpol, this agency would not simply coordinate investigations among law enforcement officers from various countries; instead, it would be responsible for conducting the investigations and for delivering evidence and offenders to the offended nation-state. In this scenario, nation-states would presumably bear primary responsibility for defining what is, and is not, a cybercrime; it might be advisable to establish some system for ensuring that their laws were substantially consistent. Aside from expediting the base processes of investigating cybercrime and apprehending cybercriminals, this approach could have the added virtue of improving the overall response to cybercrime. A centralized global agency could track trends in cybercrime, identifying them long before they could become apparent to investigators scattered around the globe, each working within the confines of a separate institutional structure.

Obviously, the last two approaches are speculative. The visceral reactions that crime (and cybercrime) generate guarantee that our approaches to both will continue to be parochial for the foreseeable future. We are sufficiently invested in territorial reality to find it difficult to surrender control over those who offend our sense of morality to an "outside" entity; like the Founding Fathers, we believe crime and punishment are local concerns. The challenge we face is reconciling that belief with the reality that is emerging in cyberspace.

NOTES

1. Council of Europe Convention on Cybercrime (CETS No. 185)—Chart of Signatures and Ratifications, *at* http://conventions.coe.int/Treaty/Commun/ ChercheSig.asp?NT=185&CM=8&DF=10/31/04&CL=ENG.

2. Stefan D. Cassella, *Bulk Cash Smuggling and the Globalization of Crime: Overcoming Constitutional Challenges to Forfeiture Under 31 U.S.C. § 5332*, 22 Berkeley J. Int'l L. 98, 99 n. 2 (2004).

3. *See* Council of Europe, 583 Meeting of the Ministers' Deputies, February 4, 1997, Appendix 13, *at* http://www.cm.coe.int/dec/1997/583/583.a13.html.

4. *See* Articles 2–10, Council of Europe Convention on Cybercrime (CETS No. 185).

5. *See id.*, Articles 2–6.

6. Explanatory Report—Council of Europe Convention on Cybercrime (CETS No. 185), ¶ 16, *at* http://conventions.coe.int/Treaty/en/Reports/Html/185.htm.

7. *See* Article 9(4), Council of Europe Convention on Cybercrime (CETS No. 185).

8. *See id.*, Articles 16–21.

9. *Id.*, Articles 23–34.

10. *Id.*, Article 35.

11. Explanatory Report—Council of Europe Convention on Cybercrime (CETS No. 185), ¶ 253.

12. Electronic Privacy Information Center, Letter to Richard Lugar, Chairman of the Senate Committee on Foreign Relations (June 17, 2004), *at* http://www.epic.org/privacy/intl/senateletter-061704.pdf.

13. *Id.*

14. *Id.*

15. *Id.*

Digital Evidence and the New Criminal Procedure

Orin S. Kerr

The use of computers in criminal activity has popularized a new form of evidence: digital evidence, and should trigger new rules of criminal procedure because computer-related crimes feature new facts that will demand new law. The law of criminal procedure has evolved to regulate the mechanisms common to the investigation of physical crimes, namely, the collection of physical evidence and eyewitness testimony. Existing law is naturally tailored to law enforcement needs and the privacy threats they raise. Digital evidence is collected differently from eyewitness testimony or physical evidence. The new ways of collecting evidence are so different that the rules developed for the old investigations often no longer make sense for the new. Rules that balance privacy and public safety when applied to the facts of physical crime investigations often lead to astonishing results when applied to the methods common in digital evidence investigations. They permit extraordinarily invasive government powers to go unregulated in some contexts, yet allow phantom privacy threats to shut down legitimate investigations in others.

The new dynamics demonstrate the need for procedural doctrines designed specifically to regulate digital evidence collection. The rules should impose some new restrictions on police conduct and repeal other limits with an eye to the new facts and new social practices that are common to the way we use and misuse computers. Further, we should look beyond the judiciary and the Fourth Amendment for many of these new rules. While some changes can and likely will come from the courts, more can come from legislatures and executive agencies that are able to offer new and creative approaches not tied directly to our constitutional traditions.

Some changes already have begun. A number of new rules are beginning to emerge from Congress and the courts. In the last five years, a few courts have started to interpret the Fourth Amendment differently in computer-crime cases. They have quietly rejected traditional rules and substituted new ones. At the legislative level, Congress has enacted computer-specific statutes to address other new threats to privacy. The changes are modest ones so far. Taken together, however, the new constitutional and statutory rules may be seen as the beginning of a new subfield of criminal procedure that regulates the collection of digital evidence.

I. Physical Evidence versus Digital Evidence

Rules of criminal procedure are organic rules, contingent on the facts of the investigations they regulate. Changing facts exert pressure to change existing legal doctrine. To see why digital evidence creates pressure for new rules of criminal procedure, we need to compare the investigative facts of traditional crimes to the investigative facts of crimes involving digital evidence. By comparing these two types of crimes, we can see how the mechanisms of electronic crimes and physical crimes are often distinct. These different mechanisms lead to different evidence, different investigative steps, and, ultimately, the need for different legal rules.

Physical Crimes and Physical Crime Investigations

Imagine that Fred Felony decides to rob a bank. Fred drives to a local branch office, parks his car outside, and goes in. When it's his turn at the teller, Fred slides over a note that reads, "This is a stick up. Give me all your money and no one will get hurt." The teller sees the note and observes the barrel of a pistol protruding from Fred's jacket. The teller nervously hands Fred a bag of money. Fred grabs the bag and runs out of the bank. Once outside, he jumps into his getaway car and speeds away.

Now imagine that a police detective is called to investigate the bank robbery. His goal is to collect evidence of the crime so that he can identify the robber and then help prove the case in court beyond a reasonable doubt. But how? The detective's first strategy will be to collect eyewitness testimony. The detective will ask the teller and other people at the bank to describe what they observed. What did the robber look like? How tall was he? Was his voice unusual? Did anyone see the getaway car? The eyewitness testimony will consist of reports from people about what they observed with their eyes and heard with their ears. By visiting the bank and asking questions, the investigator will become an eyewitness of sorts himself: He will be able to testify about what he saw and heard when he arrived at the bank and investigated the crime.

The detective's second strategy will be to collect physical evidence. This will help connect the crime to a suspect beyond a reasonable doubt. For example, the detective will recover the note that Fred Felony left with the teller and analyze it for fingerprints or distinctive handwriting. Perhaps Fred left behind other physical clues as well. Perhaps he dropped the gun when he rushed out of the bank. Perhaps he lost a button, or dropped a receipt he had been carrying in his pocket. This physical evidence can be presented and explained to the jury to create a powerful tangible connection between the defendant and the crime.

If the eyewitness testimony and physical evidence from the bank do not make the case against Fred, the police may need to look for additional evidence elsewhere. The police may interview other suspects to see if they know who was behind the bank robbery. They may look around town for cars matching the description of the getaway car. If the police have particular suspicions about Fred, they may search his house for evidence such as marked stolen bills or clothes matching those worn by the robber. The goal will be to collect additional eyewitness testimony and physical evidence that can help prove that Fred robbed the bank. If any of these tactics yield additional evidence, the police will add the new evidence to the physical evidence and eyewitness testimony found at the crime scene.

Let's assume the detective gathers sufficient evidence to show that Fred committed the bank robbery. Fred is charged, and the case goes to trial. At trial, prosecutors will assemble the eyewitness testimony and physical evidence to prove that Fred committed the crime. The teller will testify about how Fred Felony approached him and handed him the note. Other eyewitnesses will testify about what they saw and heard during the robbery. Witnesses who are personally familiar with the physical evidence will help shepherd it into evidence so the jury can consider it in the jury room during deliberations. For example, if Fred dropped his gun on the way out of the bank and the detective found it, the detective will take the stand and testify about how and where he found the pistol. The pistol will then be admitted into evidence. If the police executed a search at Fred Felony's home, an agent who participated in the search will testify about what he found. The sequence of witnesses at trial will build the case against Fred Felony and attempt to establish his guilt beyond a reasonable doubt.

Computer Crimes and Computer-Crime Investigations

Now let's switch to an electronic version of this crime. Let's replace the physical visit to the bank and the retrieval of paper money with a virtual "visit" to the bank and the theft of digital funds from a bank computer. The point of the comparison is not to find an exact analog to the physical bank robbery; there are obvious differences between the two. Rather, the goal is to get a sense of how the crime and the evidence changes when we turn from physical crimes to crimes involving digital evidence.

This time, Fred Felony decides to steal money using a computer. Instead of visiting the bank in person, he goes online from his home. Fred logs on to the Internet from an account he holds with a local Internet Service Provider (ISP). Although his ultimate goal is to hack into the bank's computers, Fred first loops his attack through a few intermediary computers to disguise his tracks. He picks computers with poor security and little need to keep detailed records of who used their servers. If anyone tries to trace Fred's misconduct back to him, they will have to go through the intermediaries first. Let's say Fred selects a server run by a private university in California as his first intermediary, and a server operated by a public library in Kansas as the second. From his ISP, he first hacks into the university computer; with access to the university computer established, he then hacks into the library computer. With access to the library computer established, Fred targets the bank's main server. After several tries, Fred eventually guesses the master password correctly and logs on to the bank's server.

With full system privileges on the bank's computer, Fred sets up a new bank account and instructs the computer that the account contains $500,000. He then wires the money from the new account to an untraceable offshore account. The next day, a bank employee notices that an unauthorized account was created and that money is missing. The bank employee calls the police.

Imagine that the case is assigned to the same detective who investigated the physical bank robbery. Once again, his goal is to gather enough evidence to identify the wrongdoer and establish a case in court. But how? The detective will immediately notice that the crime scene looks very different. There are no eyewitnesses at the bank, and there is no physical evidence. No one saw the intrusion occur, and there is no tangible evidence to manipulate. From the standpoint of the human senses, the crime occurred inside closed wires and boxes via the rapid shifting of invisible and silent electrical impulses. Computer technicians and system administrators can look through computer files and try to reconstruct what happened. They can observe what their computer screens show them. But the underlying evidence is no longer eyewitness testimony or physical evidence. It is digital evidence: the zeros and ones of electricity.

How to begin the investigation? The detective's first step will be to ask the system administrator in charge of the bank's computer to gather all the information relating to the theft that may be stored on the computer. In all likelihood, this information will tell him very little. With the physical crime, the chances were good that the crime scene would yield substantial leads. Even if no one could identify Fred in a lineup, his physical presence at the crime scene greatly narrowed the number of suspects. The electronic crime scene looks very different. In most cases, evidence gathered at the victim site will tell the investigator only that someone, located somewhere in the world, hacked into the bank. In most cases, the biggest investigative lead comes in the form of an originating Internet Protocol (IP) address recorded by the bank's servers. An IP address is the Internet equivalent of a telephone number; the bank's server likely kept a log of Fred's connection to the bank computer and recorded its originating IP address as part of that log. To find Fred Felony, the detective must start with the IP address and try to follow the trail of electronic bread crumbs from the bank back to Fred's home computer. He must find and collect the bits and bytes of digital evidence stored around the country (if not around the world), and assemble them in a way that identifies Fred and establishes his guilt beyond a reasonable doubt.

The process of collecting electronic evidence in computer hacking cases can generally be divided into three steps. It begins with the collection of stored evidence from third-party servers, turns next to prospective surveillance, and ends with the forensic investigation of the suspect's computer. These three steps encompass the basic mechanisms of digital evidence collection: collecting digital evidence while in transit, collecting digital evidence stored with friendly third parties, and collecting digital evidence stored with hostile parties such as the target. Each mechanism presents unique facts and requires special considerations.

The first and most basic investigative step is obtaining stored records from the system administrators of the various computer servers used in the attack. Fred connected to four computers to commit his offense: servers operated by his ISP, the university, the library, and the bank. It is possible (although not certain) that each of these servers retained records of Fred's connection. The detective will attempt to assemble these records to trace back the attack from the bank's server through the intermediary computers to the ISP in a step-by-step fashion. This cumbersome procedure is necessary because the packets that carry Internet communications list only their immediate origin and destination points. If Fred launches an attack from his ISP through the university and library servers and then onto the victim bank, the communications received at the bank computer will bear the originating IP address of the library server, not Fred's ISP. The detective must contact the system administrator at the library to determine if they have any records of the connection to the bank at the particular time that the attack occurred. If comprehensive records exist at the library, those records should indicate that the attack against the bank originated at the university. The detective will then repeat the process by contacting the system administrator at the university. If comprehensive records exist at the university, those records will indicate that the attack originated not at the university, but at Fred's ISP. The detective will then contact Fred's ISP. If comprehensive records exist at the ISP, those records should indicate that Fred's account was being used to access the Internet at the time of the attack. The ISP should also have a credit card or billing address for Fred in its records, allowing the detective to focus the investigation on Fred.

Investigations are rarely this simple, however. The trail of evidence usually is interrupted somewhere along the way. Few system administrators keep comprehensive records, and those records that are kept often are deleted after a brief period of time. Hackers routinely target intermediary computers known to keep few or no records so as to frustrate investigators. When the chain of stored records contains a broken link, the detective must shift gears to a second method of evidence collection I have elsewhere called prospective surveillance. Prospective surveillance refers to the use of logging software or hardware to monitor future Internet traffic and create a record of that traffic. The scope of prospective surveillance depends on where the surveillance device is installed and how it is configured. It may encompass invasive wiretapping that intercepts private emails, or may merely point to the most immediate source address of an attack.

The basic idea behind prospective surveillance is that criminal activity may recur or be ongoing, and investigators and victim system administrators can complete the missing links in the chain of evidence by monitoring future activity. Fred may come back to try to set up another account and siphon away more money. If the evidence trail went cold at the bank server itself, the bank could monitor its server for unauthorized efforts to set up an account. If the trail went cold at the university, the police may install a monitoring device at the university server to monitor any communications directed from the server to the bank. If Fred Felony strikes again, prospective surveillance can create a fresh trail of evidence back to Fred's ISP.

This brings us to the third and final stage of electronic evidence collection. Recall that in the case of Fred's physical crime, it was possible that the police would need to execute a search warrant at his home to gather sufficient proof that Fred had committed the robbery. In the digital version of the crime, that step is likely to be essential. Digital evidence taken from servers may show that a particular account was used to steal money from the bank, but will almost never prove that a particular person was controlling the account. Something important is missing: a substitute for biometric eyewitness testimony or physical evidence to connect the existing evidence to a specific person. Without that connection, the government will be unable to prove its case beyond a reasonable doubt.

The key in most cases will be recovering the computer used to launch the attack. If the police can find and analyze Fred's home computer, it will likely yield damning evidence. The records kept by most operating systems can allow forensics experts to reconstruct with surprising detail who did what and when. Even deleted files often can be recovered, as a delete function normally just marks storage space as available for new material and does not actually erase anything. An analysis of the computer may reveal a file containing the bank password used to set up the unauthorized account. It may reveal records from that account, or records taken from some of the intermediary computers. Even if no such documents are found, it may be possible to tell whether the attack was launched from the computer. Such proof can provide persuasive evidence of guilt. While innocent explanations may exist for why the suspect's personal computer was used to launch an attack, connecting the attack to the suspect's private property can go a long way toward eliminating reasonable doubt.

Computer forensics experts have developed a detailed set of procedures that forensic analysts ordinarily follow when they seize and analyze a target's computer. The technical details aren't important here, but the broad outline is. First, the detectives ordinarily seize the computer and bring it back to a government forensic laboratory for analysis. This is considered necessary because the forensic process is very time-consuming; computer experts normally cannot find the evidence on a hard drive in the time that would allow the search to occur on site. Back at the lab, the analyst begins by generating a "bitstream" or "mirror" image of the hard drive. The bitstream copy is an exact duplicate not just of the files, but of every single bit and byte stored on the drive. The analyst then performs his work on the copy rather than the original to ensure that the original will not be damaged or altered by the investigation.

The analyst may try a range of techniques to locate the evidence sought. For example, the examiner may begin by executing string searches for particular extensions, phrases, or textual fragments that relate to the evidence justifying the search. Alternatively, he may open all files with particular characteristics or sample from the files until he finds the evidence linking the suspect to the crime. In Fred's case, for example, an investigator might begin by searching the hard drive for the bank's password, or perhaps for the name of the bank. If that doesn't work, the investigator might begin looking for documents date stamped on the day of Fred's attack, or might just look for any financial documents. Once he understands how Fred stored the data on his hard drive, he may find a great deal of incriminating information. Assuming Fred was not tipped off to the investigation and has not permanently erased the relevant files, the analyst may find the bank's master password, account records, and other evidence linking the computer and its owner to the crime.

Let's assume that these tactics are successful, and that an analysis of Fred's computer reveals evidence of the attack. Fred is charged, and the case goes to trial. The prosecutor will put witnesses on the stand in a way that tracks the course of the investigation. First, a bank employee will testify about the attack and the bank's losses. Next, the system administrators of the intermediary computers will testify about their link in the chain of evidence, and an employee from Fred's ISP will testify about the electronic clues leading back to Fred's account. Finally, government agents will testify. The detective will testify that he recovered the computer inside Fred's home, and the computer forensics expert will testify that Fred's computer contained evidence of the attack together with Fred's personal files. The government's case now proves beyond a reasonable doubt that Fred committed the online bank theft.

II. Digital Evidence and the Failure of Existing Rules

The existing rules of criminal procedure are organic products naturally tailored to the facts of physical crime investigations. Comparing the contours of existing rules of criminal procedure to the investigative steps common to such traditional investigations reveals an obvious match. The contemporary rules of criminal procedure are physical-world rules that reflect the realities of physical-world investigations. They attempt to balance privacy and law enforcement needs in light of the way police collect physical evidence and eyewitness testimony.

Applying existing doctrine to the collection of digital evidence produces some startling results, however. Rules that sensibly regulate the investigation of physical crimes based on physical facts lead to surprising outcomes when applied to the new investigations. At many stages, those outcomes impose few if any limits on government investigations. At a few stages, they impose unnecessary barriers to successful investigations.

Physical Crimes and Rules of Criminal Procedure

The existing rules of criminal procedure are naturally tailored to the facts of physical-world crimes. Consider the Fourth Amendment's prohibition on unreasonable searches and seizures. The rules on unreasonable "searches" regulate the collection of evidence in the form of eyewitness testimony by police officers. The search rules govern where and in what circumstances officers can go to report what their senses observe. By regulating where officers can go, the search rules regulate what officers see and hear; by regulating what they see and hear, the rules limit the scope of evidence they can collect. This function is often obscured by the Court's famous quip in *Katz v. United States* that "the Fourth Amendment protects people, not places."[1] As Justice Harlan noted in his *Katz* concurrence, the question of what protection it provides to people "requires reference to a 'place.'"[2] Under Justice Harlan's formulation, the Fourth Amendment remains heavily tied to places; in William Stuntz's formulation, the law "regulate[s] what police officers can see and hear," focusing on where they can go more than what they do once they get there.[3]

Specifically, the *Katz* "reasonable expectation of privacy" test has been interpreted in a way that effectively demarcates physical spaces that are public from physical spaces that are more private. An officer can enter any space that is not protected by a reasonable expectation of privacy; such an entrance does not count as a "search." This allows officers to roam public streets or other places open to the public without restriction. In contrast, an officer can enter spaces protected by a reasonable expectation of privacy only under special circumstances. The entry into private space such as a home or an office constitutes a search, and is reasonable (and therefore constitutional) only if justified by special circumstances. Those special circumstances might include the presence of a valid search warrant, the consent of someone with common authority over the space, or the existence of exigent circumstances. Once an investigator has legitimately entered a particular space, he is free to testify about whatever he observes without implicating the Fourth Amendment. The police need not "avert their eyes from evidence of criminal activity."[4] Anything the officer sees is in "plain view," anything he smells is in plain smell, and anything he overhears is unprotected under the Fourth Amendment.

While the search rules regulate the collection of eyewitness testimony by police officers, the seizure rules govern the collection of physical evidence. The Supreme Court has defined a "seizure" of property as "meaningful interference with an individual's possessory interests in that property."[5] Under this test, the gathering of physical evidence is a seizure. Fourth Amendment cases explain when such seizures are reasonable, and thus allowable. Very brief seizures undertaken for legitimate law enforcement purposes are usually reasonable, but extended seizures are usually unreasonable unless the police obtain a warrant. Seizures that do not infringe directly on possessory interests are usually reasonable; for example, an investigator can take evidence if its owner consents, or if the evidence has been abandoned.

Constitutional provisions beyond the Fourth Amendment also regulate traditional investigative steps. The Fifth Amendment provides that no person "shall be compelled in any criminal case to be a witness against himself." This right against self-incrimination limits the collection of eyewitness testimony by regulating when investigators can use statements against a defendant. Similarly, the Sixth Amendment guarantees every defendant "compulsory process for obtaining witnesses in his favor," empowering defendants to collect eyewitness testimony of their own. Both sets of rules are focused on balancing the rights of the government and the defendant in traditional investigations into traditional crimes.

We can see how traditional rules of criminal procedure work in practice by revisiting the investigation into Fred's physical bank robbery. The detective is free to examine the outside of the bank: there is no reasonable expectation of privacy in that which is exposed to the public. He can enter the bank during business hours to look around, as well; because the bank is open to the public, entering the bank is not a search. If he wants to look more closely at the bank after hours, however, he needs the consent of a bank employee. Consent will render the search reasonable, and therefore constitutionally permissible. The investigator can also speak with eyewitnesses and record their observations of the crime. If the investigator finds Fred Felony's gun, he can seize it. The seizure is reasonable under the Fourth Amendment so long as the gun's usefulness as evidence is immediately apparent. If he comes across other evidence with no apparent relation to the crime, however, he normally cannot seize it. If the police opt to search Fred's house for evidence, they will need a search warrant to justify the entry into his private space. The Fourth Amendment rules governing search warrants ensure that the search will be narrowly tailored. It must be limited to the particular physical place where the evidence is likely present and the search must be limited to specific items associated with the bank robbery. The detective is then free to testify about whatever he observed during the investigation. Taken together, the existing rules of criminal procedure effectively regulate the collection of physical evidence and eyewitness testimony.

Digital Evidence and Physical-World Rules

The picture changes considerably when we switch from traditional investigations involving eyewitness testimony and physical evidence to investigations requiring the collection of digital evidence. As noted earlier, there are three basic mechanisms of digital evidence collection: the collection of stored evidence from third parties, the collection of stored evidence from the target, and the collection of evidence in transit. Applying existing doctrines to these three mechanisms reveals several difficulties. The traditional rules tend not to translate well to the new facts. Caution is warranted: surprisingly few cases exist that apply traditional doctrine to the collection of digital evidence. Mapping the old rules onto the new facts requires some speculation. At the same time, a comparison of the basic contours of existing law and the dynamics common to digital evidence cases demonstrates the poor fit between them. In many circumstances, the traditional rules fail to provide any real limit on law enforcement practices. In other circumstances, they allow phantom privacy threats to block necessary investigative steps.

1. EVIDENCE FROM THIRD PARTIES AND THE SUBPOENA PROCESS

Consider the first stage of most electronic crime investigations, in which investigators contact system administrators and obtain stored evidence relating to the crime from servers used in the course of the crime. This process raises important privacy concerns suggesting the need for careful legal regulation. Internet users routinely store most if not all of their private information on remote servers, and all that information is available to system administrators. System administrators can read private email, look through stored files, and access account logs that record how individual subscribers used the network. As a result, the power to compel evidence from ISPs can be the power to compel the disclosure of a user's entire online world. Plus, disclosure can occur without notice to the user, and it can involve multiple accounts. The power to compel evidence from ISPs can be the power to disclose the online profile of hundreds or even thousands of users at once, all in total secrecy.

Remarkably, existing Fourth and Fifth Amendment doctrine offers virtually no privacy protection to regulate this process. Investigators can compel system administrators to disclose information stored on their servers using subpoenas. Subpoenas are lightly regulated by the Fourth Amendment. Existing law requires only that the information or property to be compelled must be relevant to an investigation, and that its production must not be overly burdensome to the recipient of the subpoena.[6] The relevance standard covers almost everything, as it includes merely checking to make sure that no crime has been committed.[7] The limits of burdensomeness are similarly toothless in the context of electronic evidence: it is generally simple for an ISP to copy voluminous files and give the copy to investigators. Indeed, there can be an inverse relationship between the amount of evidence investigators seek and the burden it places on the recipient of the subpoena; ISPs often find it easier to hand over information en masse rather than filter painstakingly through files to identify the precise file sought. The person under investigation need not be informed of the subpoena's existence. No Fifth Amendment privilege applies because the recipient of the subpoena is an innocent third party. In light of these realities, applying the traditional Fourth and Fifth Amendment rules to the new network crimes leaves the first stage of network crime investigations almost entirely unregulated.

How could the law allow such an astonishing result? The explanation lies in the shift from the role that third-party evidence collection plays in traditional investigations to the role it plays in digital evidence cases. In the past, third-party evidence collection has played a narrow but important role that implicates privacy in relatively limited ways. The role is narrow because perpetrators of physical crimes generally keep the evidence to themselves rather than give it to third parties. If Fred Felony robs a bank, he is going to keep the loot and store his tools in a secure location. He is not likely to share incriminating evidence with people he doesn't know. In that context, the subpoena power poses a relatively small threat of invasive government overreaching. If a police officer suspects that Fred Felony is the bank robber, he cannot simply issue a subpoena ordering Fred to hand over any evidence or fruits of the crime. As a practical matter, Fred would be unlikely to comply, and issuance of the subpoena would tip him off to the investigation. As a legal matter, Fred would enjoy a Fifth Amendment privilege to decline compliance with the subpoena. Because complying would show knowledge and possession of the loot, the privilege against self-incrimination would render the subpoena a legal nullity.

Subpoenas do serve an important purpose in a specific set of traditional cases: they are essential in document-intensive white-collar crime investigations. As William Stuntz has observed, the weak protections that regulate the subpoena power can be understood at least in part as a contingent product of Fourth Amendment history.[8] In the early case of *Boyd v. United States*, the Supreme Court took the view that an order to compel the disclosure of evidence should be regulated just as carefully as a direct search involving the police knocking down your door.[9] The Court backed off that standard twenty years later in *Hale v. Henkel*, however, when it replaced *Boyd* with the low threshold that a subpoena satisfied the Fourth Amendment so long as it was not "sweeping."[10] Today the law remains roughly similar to that announced a century ago in *Henkel*. Why the change? The regulatory climate of the late nineteenth and early twentieth centuries had seen the rise of white-collar crime investigations, and those investigations demanded easy access to documents that could prove wrongdoing. As Stuntz has explained, "a probable cause standard for subpoenas would end many white-collar criminal investigations before they had begun."[11] The combination of the essential role for subpoenas in a narrow class of document-intensive cases and the generally limited threat to privacy elsewhere has combined to create an environment in which the subpoena process is only very lightly regulated.

A lax subpoena rule makes no sense for computer-network crime investigations, however. Computer users often store much of their information with third-party servers. It's how the Internet works. Applying the traditional rule to the new facts suggests that the entire Internet world of stored Internet communications can be subpoenaed via the intermediaries of ISPs. Neither the Fourth Amendment nor the Fifth Amendment offers much protection. The Fourth Amendment does little because its privacy rules are so weak, and the Fifth Amendment fails because third parties such as ISPs can divulge information without implicating any privilege against self-incrimination of their own. Whereas the subpoena power is fairly narrow in traditional cases, in computer crime cases it is incredibly broad. For investigators, compelling the ISP to disclose information is even preferable to the alternative of searching through the ISP's server directly: officers can simply fax a copy of the subpoena to the ISP's headquarters and await a package or return fax with the relevant documents. No technical expertise or travel to the ISP is required. A reasonable rule developed in response to the realities of physical-world investigations turns into an unreasonable and unbalanced rule when applied to the new facts of digital crime investigations.

2. PROSPECTIVE SURVEILLANCE AND THE PROBLEM OF WIRETAPPING

We encounter similar problems when investigators conduct prospective surveillance by monitoring a stream of Internet traffic. Prospective surveillance can be broad or narrow, depending on what information the investigators seek. The basic investigative step is the same in every case, however: the only difference between broad and narrow surveillance lies in how the filter is configured. This is true because the Internet works by jumbling information together during transmission, and tasking computers that receive the information to reassemble it. The zeros and ones passing through a particular cable at a particular time could be anything—part of a very private message, the front page of NYTimes.com, an image of pornography, a hacker's command to a remote server, or generally meaningless computer-to-computer network traffic. The filter setting determines the information collected, with an open setting resulting in total surveillance and an advanced setting tightly regulating the type and amount of information collected.

Although no court has applied the Fourth Amendment to these precise facts, existing doctrine appears poorly equipped to regulate prospective surveillance. From the standpoint of policy, a sensible rule might permit police officers to collect information that tends to be less private under relatively relaxed rules, but require greater authority such as a search warrant to authorize collection of more private information. The legal threshold would hinge on the filter setting, linking the degree of privacy protection to the invasiveness of the monitoring. If detectives merely want to determine the originating IP address of a particular communication, a low threshold should be imposed; if detectives wish to monitor private emails, the law should impose a high threshold.

Generating such a rule from Fourth Amendment doctrine proves surprisingly difficult. The first problem is that Fourth Amendment rules traditionally focus on the justification for entry into a space, not whether the item to be seized after the space is entered should be deemed public or private. The police need a warrant to enter your home regardless of whether they plan to read your personal diary or just want to see the morning newspaper and break in to read your copy. Similarly, the police do not need a warrant to collect and analyze your private documents left out in a public park. The traditional focus on the entry into the space makes sense for physical investigations. In the physical world, regulation of where an officer goes determines what the officer will see, smell, hear, and feel. The officer's human senses will record observations that the officer can later recall and testify about in court. Regulating entry therefore serves as a functional way of regulating evidence collection. The "reasonable expectation of privacy" test divides public from private, limiting observation to public spaces absent special reasons justifying entrance into private spaces.

This focus makes little sense when applied to prospective surveillance. The entry to the tapped line of Internet traffic occurs regardless of whether the monitoring is extremely narrow or breathtakingly broad. Instead of representing a crossing of the line between public and private, entry is now merely a prerequisite for any evidence collection. It is presently unclear whether or when Internet users have a reasonable expectation of privacy in their Internet communications, and thus whether a wire containing Internet traffic should be deemed private or public space for Fourth Amendment purposes. As I have explained elsewhere, significant arguments exist for both positions.[12] But either way, the resulting legal rule would no longer correlate with the invasiveness of the relevant surveillance practice. If courts view wires of Internet traffic as public spaces in which individuals cannot retain a reasonable expectation of privacy, traditional rules will impose no constitutional limits on prospective surveillance. If courts construe them as private spaces that do support a reasonable expectation of privacy, surveillance designed to target even nonprivate information will nonetheless require strong legal justification. Neither rule matches intuitive notions of how the law should divide public from private.

The basic problem remains even if courts move beyond this difficulty and try to protect private material more directly. Imagine that courts hinge the scope of Fourth Amendment protections on whether the particular information collected seems public or more private. While this sounds plausible in theory, it proves quite difficult to attain in practice. Technology provides the first hurdle. Existing surveillance filters can identify types of traffic, such as the difference between an email and a web page. Filters can identify particular words, or record communications from or to particular Internet addresses. But no filter can make an informed judgment as to whether a particular set of zeros and ones is public or private. The difficulty is not just the technology, but the limits of deduction: communications normally will not indicate who or what sent or received them, or the context in which they were sent or received. Without that information, it is hard to tell whether particular zeros and ones happen to be part of a communication that the Fourth Amendment might protect in an analogous physical setting. The architecture of the physical world solves this problem in traditional cases by demarcating public spaces from private ones. The same goes for traditional wiretapping over phone lines. When tapping a phone line necessarily intercepts a human-to-human call, the phone line is akin to a virtual private booth. Everything on the line is private. In the case of prospective surveillance of Internet communications, however, private and public are mixed together. There is no obvious way to obtain the context needed to draw traditional Fourth Amendment lines.

3. SEARCHING THE TARGET'S COMPUTER AND THE WARRANT RULE

The final stage of computer crime investigations exposes particularly deep problems of fit between traditional rules and the new facts. At this stage, the police seize and then analyze the suspect's personal computer. A warrant is plainly required, both to enter the home and to seize the suspect's property. But how much does the warrant actually limit what the police can do? In traditional cases, the rules governing the warrant process ensure that the search and seizure remain relatively narrow. The warrant must name both the specific place to be searched and the specific evidence to be seized. The seizure must be limited to the evidence described in the warrant—which itself is limited by the scope of probable cause to believe that the evidence is on the premises—as well as other evidence discovered in plain view during the course of the search. These rules help ensure that warrant searches do not devolve into general warrants that authorize general rummaging through a suspect's property.

Applying these rules to digital evidence sets up a series of puzzles, however. Consider the first step of the seizure process, in which investigators take the defendant's computer off-site for forensic testing. Seizure of the entire computer is necessary for practical reasons, but can be difficult to justify based on the traditional rules. In many cases, computer hardware is merely a storage device for evidence rather than evidence itself. The evidence is the electronic file that the police are looking for and that just happens to be stored along with many innocuous files inside the container of the computer hardware. Under traditional rules, then, seizing computer hardware to get a handful of files would appear to be overbroad. It's roughly analogous to seizing an entire house and carting off its contents to mine them for evidence of crime, which the Fourth Amendment prohibits. The problem is that the traditional rule requires a level of surgical precision and expertise that is possible for physical evidence but not digital evidence. When Fred Felony robbed the physical bank, the police could obtain a warrant to search his home for the stolen bills and search the home in a few hours. There was no need to cart off everything in the house and search it weeks or even months later in a laboratory. A rule requiring officers to look for the bills and retrieve only the bills named in the warrant is a sensible rule in such an environment. A computer search is different: it takes much more time, and may require considerable technical expertise. The approach that works for physical evidence does not work well for digital evidence.

Fast forward to the next stage, in which investigators generate a bitstream image of the seized computer. The need for legal regulation is clear. The imaging process allows the government to re-create its own perfect copy of everything on a suspect's computer. After obtaining their own copy, investigators have the technical ability to mine it for clues without limit. They can search through the copy for hours, weeks, or even years. Remarkably, traditional Fourth Amendment rules appear to impose no limits on this process. Under the traditional rules, copying a computer file does not "seize" it, and analysis of the government's copy would appear not to constitute a "search." The problem is the traditional definition of seizure, which remains tied to the physical notion of depriving another of his or her property. A seizure occurs when a government official causes "meaningful interference with an individual's possessory interests in that property."[13] This test serves as a useful guide to limit interference with physical property, but it fails when applied to digital evidence. Detectives no longer need to impose a meaningful interference on a possessory interest to obtain digital evidence. Because police can create a perfect copy of the evidence without depriving the suspect of property, the new facts unhinge the rule from its traditional function of limiting police investigations.

At the final stage of the investigation, investigators look through the copy for evidence of the crime. This raises a threat to privacy that I call the needle-in-a-haystack problem. Because computers can store an extraordinary amount of information, the evidence of crime is akin to a needle hidden in an enormous electronic haystack. If no rules regulate how investigators look through the haystack to find the needle, any justification for a search may justify an invasive look through computer files that represent a small city's worth of private information. Existing Fourth Amendment rules have been developed to prevent this sort of general rummaging in searches for physical property. The place to be searched must be limited to a specific physical location, such as an apartment or an office, and the search must be objectively consistent with a search for the evidence named in the warrant. The rules attempt to ensure that searches pursuant to warrants remain narrowly tailored to the government's interest.

These rules do little to regulate searches for electronic data, however. Digital evidence alters the relationship between the size of the space to be searched and the amount of information stored inside it. In physical space, the particularity requirement limits the scope of a search to a place on the order of a house or apartment. Limiting the space to be searched serves as a key limitation on the scope of the search. That limitation does not hold in the case of a computer search. In late 2004, the hard drive on a typical new home computer stored at least forty gigabytes of information, roughly equivalent to twenty million pages of text or about half the information stored in the books located on one floor of a typical academic library. By the time you read this essay the capacity no doubt will have increased; the storage capacity of new hard drives has tended to double about every two years. Given how much information can be stored in a small computer hard drive, the particularity requirement no longer serves the function in electronic evidence cases that it serves in physical evidence cases. Whatever remaining function it serves diminishes every year. Today, limiting a search to a particular computer is something like limiting a search to a city block; ten years from now, it will be more like limiting a search to the entire city.

To some extent this problem was presaged by physical cases involving many boxes of paper documents. But searches for paper documents have not caused the same order of heartburn that searches for computer files will raise, and have not triggered new rules to address the needle-in-a-haystack problem. *Andresen v. Maryland* illustrates the dynamic.[14] In *Andresen*, police searched through paper files at a lawyer's office for evidence of fraud relating to a real estate transaction. The defendant objected that the warrant was insufficiently particular, but the Supreme Court easily approved the warrant. The Court found it sufficient to address the needle-in-a-haystack problem with only a general aside tucked away in a footnote: "We recognize that there are grave dangers" inherent in document searches, the Court explained. "In searches for papers, it is certain that some innocuous documents will be examined, at least cursorily, in order to determine whether they are, in fact, among those papers authorized to be seized." The Court offered a warning but no legal rule to address this problem, stating only that "responsible officials . . . must take care to assure" that such searches "are conducted in a manner that minimizes unwarranted intrusions upon privacy."[15]

The lost functionality of the particularity requirement in digital evidence searches cannot be restored merely by requiring greater specificity. Existing technology simply gives us no way to know ahead of time where inside a computer a particular file or piece of information may be located. In the physical world, different spatial regions are used for different purposes. This allows the police to make educated guesses as to where evidence may or may not be found, which allows them to generate ways to limit the search. Consider the warrant obtained to search Fred Felony's home in the physical-world bank robbery investigation. The warrant can be limited to Fred's home because he is unlikely to store evidence in the street or in a public park. In the computer context, however, the decision of where within a storage device to place particular information is determined primarily by the particular software installed and the contingent questions of what else happens to be stored on the same storage drive. For the most part, this is impossible to know before the item is seized and analyzed at the government's lab.

Even in the controlled setting of a forensics lab, existing Fourth Amendment rules fail to generate useful guides to investigative conduct. Consider two potential legal limitations on the scope of the forensic analyst's search: first, limits on which regions of a hard drive the analyst can look in for evidence named in the warrant, and second, limits on the analyst's ability to look for evidence of other crimes. The general Fourth Amendment rule is that investigators executing a warrant can look anywhere in the place to be searched where evidence described in the warrant might conceivably be located.[16] In traditional investigations for physical evidence, this rule means that officers cannot look in places smaller than the evidence they wish to seize. If the police have a warrant to recover a handgun, the warrant does not justify opening a personal letter. But electronic evidence can be located anywhere. Files can be mislabeled, hidden, or otherwise stored in a way that the investigator can never rule out a particular part of the hard drive ex ante. As a result, officers can look through the entire digital haystack to find the needle. The traditional rule imposes a substantial limit for physical searches, but not for searches for electronic evidence.

The same occurs with the rules that enforce the scope of the warrant. When evidence beyond the warrant is seized under the plain view exception, defendants routinely move to suppress that evidence on the ground that it was discovered in a search that exceeded the warrant's scope. Existing law calls on judges to ignore the officer's subjective intent to look for items beyond the warrant.[17] The doctrine asks instead whether the search that the officer actually conducted was objectively consistent with the kind of search that might reasonably be conducted for the evidence the warrant describes. If it was, the unrelated evidence can be admitted under the plain view exception; if it was not, the evidence is suppressed. This rule appears plausible in the context of a search for physical evidence. An officer's subjective intent may be difficult to know, but it is generally possible to gauge whether an officer's steps are consistent with searches for particular types of evidence. A search for a stolen television might look different than a search for stolen paper bills. The rule does not impose a real limit on searches for electronic evidence, however. Because electronic evidence can be located anywhere on a hard drive, it is difficult, if not impossible, to say that a particular search was objectively unjustifiable. The physical-world rules do not prevent a general rummaging through electronic evidence.

Finally, existing law imposes no time limits on computer searches and pays little attention to when or whether seized computers must be returned. Neither the Fourth Amendment nor the Federal Rules of Criminal Procedure require the police to begin the forensic examination process in a prompt way. Once the computer has been seized, the police ordinarily can keep it indefinitely. Federal law provides only a very limited mechanism for the return of property seized pursuant to a warrant; the suspect must file a motion seeking a return of property and prove either that the seizure was illegal or that the government no longer has any need to retain the evidence. If no motion is filed, the property need not be returned. Even if a motion is filed and granted, an order to return the computer does not require the police to return or destroy the bitstream copy they have generated. Because the existing rule is focused on the suspect's property interest rather than a privacy interest, the police can keep the copy and continue to search it without apparent limit. Such rules may make sense for physical property but they show a surprising lack of attention to the legitimate interests that users have in their computers and files.

III. Toward New Rules of Criminal Procedure

Our constitutional tradition has tasked judges with implementing the Bill of Rights through specific rules. Those rules evolve in piecemeal fashion over time. In the case of the Fourth Amendment, judicial implementation has generated a complex doctrinal structure that fills several volumes in leading treatises. That doctrine attempts to effectuate the Fourth Amendment's prohibition against "unreasonable searches and seizures" and the history of concern against general warrants through specific rules governing what law enforcement can and cannot do in specific situations.

Digital evidence exposes the contingency of the existing rules. It reveals how the rules generated to implement constitutional limits on evidence collection are premised on the dynamics of physical crimes and traditional forms of physical evidence and eyewitness testimony. When those implementing rules are applied to the facts of digital evidence collection, they no longer remain true to the purpose they were crafted to fulfill. Digital evidence changes the basic assumptions of the physical world that led to the prior rules, pointing to results that no longer reflect the basic goals and purposes of the Fourth Amendment.

In a narrow sense, this is nothing new. Evolution of the Fourth Amendment in response to technology is an old story, dating perhaps as far back as the first automobile exception case in 1925.[18] More recently, the "reasonable expectation of privacy" test from *Katz v. United States* was designed to update the Fourth Amendment to help regulate telephone surveillance, and more broadly to achieve some kind of technology neutrality within search and seizure law. Similarly, courts have seen cases involving paper documents for years. All this is true, but it only tells part of the story. While *Katz* emphasized the need for change, its impact on the law has been surprisingly narrow. *Katz* focused on only the preliminary question of what counts as a "search," and as I have shown elsewhere, has had surprisingly little effect on Fourth Amendment law as a whole.[19] In similar vein, courts have not responded to searches for paper documents by generating new rules to regulate paper searches. While cases involving telephones and paper documents introduced the conceptual shift from physical evidence to rawer forms of data, they are neither so common nor so different from traditional cases as to have triggered major shifts in the law of criminal procedure.

The increasing reliance on computers in almost every facet of American life raises quite different considerations. We are no longer dealing with microphones taped to telephone booths or stacks of papers resting in file cabinets. Today a growing portion of our lives is conducted via the intermediacy of computers. Digital evidence collection and analysis is becoming an increasingly routine and essential part of a broad array of criminal investigations. Our societal reliance on computers combines with the differences between physical evidence and digital evidence to generate a pressing need for a rethinking of the procedural rules that govern digital evidence collection.

Lawrence Lessig has argued that courts should engage in "translation" when they apply the Constitution to the Internet.[20] Translation is an effort to update rules of law in response to changing technologies and social practice. It justifies altering doctrinal rules to ensure that the basic role and function of constitutional commands remain constant across time. For example, Lessig argues that the Fourth Amendment should be understood as a general command to protect privacy. When applying the Fourth Amendment to the Internet, he suggests, judges should adopt rules that protect privacy given the realities of how the Internet works.[21] Lessig's approach offers interesting possibilities, but generates only a partial answer. While translation permits doctrinal evolution in response to changing technologies and social practices, it remains locked into preexisting institutional arrangements. It requires the courts to assume the role they have traditionally assumed and to take the lead in reshaping the rules in light of technological change.

A better approach is to open the possibilities of a new criminal procedure to new institutional arrangements. The courts should retain an important role: where needed changes fit nicely into the traditional scope and purposes of Fourth Amendment rules, courts can retailor existing rules in light of new facts. But this evolutionary approach is only part of a broader response legal institutions can offer. Some of the new challenges raised by digital evidence map cleanly onto traditional Fourth Amendment principles; others may not. When they do not, legislatures and executive agencies can offer new and creative solutions to regulate digital evidence collection. While the judicial branch is limited by stare decisis, the legislative and executive branches can experiment with a wide range of approaches. They can identify and enact new rules in response to the dynamics of new technologies. In addition, legislatures and executive agencies can regulate comprehensive solutions without waiting for cases and controversies to arise. The greater flexibility of legislative and executive branch rule making suggests that we should not look only to the courts, and the judiciary's relative institutional difficulties in the regulation of developing technologies suggests that other branches should play an important role.[22] We should rethink the law and its purposes from first principles, looking beyond constitutional traditions that have functioned effectively in traditional cases but may not prove entirely adequate when applied to digital evidence.

Changes in technology often trigger changes in law. Legal rules evolve in response to changes in the underlying facts. Given our heavy reliance on computers and the specific ways they operate, the use of computers in criminal activity poses significant challenges for traditional rules of criminal procedure. By substituting the gathering of digital evidence for the collection of physical evidence and eyewitness testimony, investigations involving computers replace traditional mechanisms of search and seizure with quite different forms of surveillance and new forms of forensic analysis. The law naturally will change in response. Although some changes will come from the courts in the form of a slow evolution of doctrinal rules, others should follow from a rethinking of the best rules to regulate digital collection and the best institutions to generate and implement those rules. The problem of digital evidence should inspire the creation of a new criminal procedure, a set of rules that both builds upon and expands from traditional solutions to embrace new and creative mechanisms for regulating evidence collection and use.

NOTES

1. 389 U.S. 347, 351 (1967).

2. *Id.*, at 361 (Harlan, J., concurring).

3. *See* William J. Stuntz, Reply, 93 Mich. L. Rev. 1102, 1102 (1995).

4. California v. Greenwood, 486 U.S. 35, 41 (1988).

5. United States v. Jacobsen, 466 U.S. 109, 113 (1984).

6. *See* United States v. Dionisio, 410 U.S. 1, 10 (1973).

7. *See* United States v. Morton Salt Co., 338 U.S. 632, 642–43 (1950).

8. *See* William J. Stuntz, Commentary, O. J. Simpson, Bill Clinton, and the Transsubstantive Fourth Amendment, 114 Harv. L. Rev. 842, 857–59 (2001).

9. 116 U.S. 616, 630 (1886).

10. 201 U.S. 43, 76 (1906).

11. Stuntz, *supra* note 8, at 860.

12. *See* Amicus Curiae Brief of Professor Orin Kerr in Support of the Appellant, *at* 6–8, United States v. Bach, 310 F.3d 1063 (8th Cir. 2002) (No. 02-1238), *available at* 2002 WL 32139374.

13. United States v. Jacobsen, 466 U.S. 109, 113 (1984).

14. 427 U.S. 463 (1976).

15. *Id.*

16. United States v. Ross, 456 U.S. 798, 824 (1982).

17. *See* United States v. Van Dreel, 155 F.3d 902, 905 (7th Cir. 1998) ("[U]nder *Whren*, . . . once probable cause exists, and a valid warrant has been issued, the officer's subjective intent in conducting the search is irrelevant."); United States v. Ewain, 88 F.3d 689, 694 (9th Cir. 1996) ("Using a subjective criterion would be inconsistent with *Horton*, and would make suppression depend too much on how the police tell their story, rather than on what they did.").

18. *See* Carroll v. United States, 267 U.S. 132, 149 (1925) (holding that an automobile can be searched without a warrant if probable cause exists to believe contraband was stored within it). The rule announced in *Carroll* was based, at least in part, on the technological reality of automobiles. A warrant requirement would not be practicable, the Court noted, "because the vehicle can be quickly moved out of the locality or jurisdiction in which the warrant must be sought." *Id.*, at 153. The rule also appeared to factor in the social realities of automobile use in the

Prohibition era. Probable cause was required, the Court suggested, because "[i]t would be intolerable and unreasonable if a prohibition agent were authorized to stop every automobile on the chance of finding liquor and thus subject all persons lawfully using the highways to the inconvenience and indignity of such a search." *Id.*, at 153–54.

19. See Orin S. Kerr, The Fourth Amendment and New Technologies: Constitutional Myths and the Case for Caution, 102 Mich. L. Rev. 801, 807 (2004).

20. *See generally* Lawrence Lessig, Code and Other Laws of Cyberspace (1999).

21. *See* Kerr, *supra* note 19, at 115–16.

22. *See generally id.*

About the Contributors

Jack M. Balkin is Knight Professor of Constitutional Law and the First Amendment at Yale Law School, and the founder and director of Yale's Information Society Project. His work ranges over many fields, from constitutional theory to cultural evolution, from law and cyberspace to law and music. He is the author of many articles on various aspects of legal theory, society, and culture. His books include *Cultural Software: A Theory of Ideology* (Yale Univ. Press, 1998); *The Laws of Change: I Ching and the Philosophy of Life* (Schocken, 2002); *Processes of Constitutional Decision-making* (Aspen, 5th ed., 2006, with Brest, Levinson, Amar, and Siegel); *What Brown v. Board of Education Should Have Said* (NYU Press, 2001), and *What Roe v. Wade Should Have Said* (NYU Press, 2005). He writes political and legal commentary at the weblog Balkinization (http://balkin.blogspot.com).

Susan W. Brenner is NCR Distinguished Professor of Law and Technology at the University of Dayton School of Law, where she teaches courses on Cybercrime, Criminal Law, and Criminal Procedure. She is the author of many articles on cybercrime and her internationally known website, http://www.cybercrimes.net, has been featured on "NBC Nightly News." She is the author of *Federal Grand Jury Practice* (West, 1996) and *Precedent Inflation* (Rutgers Univ. Press, 1990).

Daniel E. Geer, Jr. is Principal, Geer Risk Services and an expert in modern security protocols. He founded and served as president of Geer Zolot, a pioneering security consulting firm specializing in the financial industry, and also served in senior leadership roles for MIT's groundbreaking Project Athena, Digital Equipment Corporation's External Research Program, Open Market, OpenVision Technologies (now Veritas), CertCo, and @stake. Dr. Geer has testifed before Congress on multiple occasions on security issues. His 2003 coauthored paper, "CyberInsecurity: The Cost of Monopoly," alerted the public to the dangers of monoculture produced by Microsoft's dominance in operating systems. Dr. Geer is a past president of USENIX, the advanced computing systems association, and serves as an adviser to the board of the Financial Services Information Sharing & Analysis Center (FS/ISAC) under the auspices of the United States. Dr. Geer holds a Sc.D. in biostatistics from Harvard University's School of Public Health as well as an S.B. in electrical engineering and computer science from MIT. He is the author of *The Web Security Sourcebook: A Complete Guide to Web Security* (Wiley, 1997) (with Avi Rubin and Marcus Ranum).

James Grimmelmann is a Fellow of the Information Society Project at Yale Law School. He received his J.D. in 2005 from Yale Law School, where he was Editor-in-Chief of LawMeme, and a member of the Yale Law Journal. He holds an A.B. in computer science from Harvard College. He has worked as a programmer for Microsoft and as a legal intern for Creative Commons and the Electronic Frontier Foundation. He clerked for Judge Maryanne Trump Barry of the United States Court of Appeals for the Third Circuit. He studies the law of technology with the goal of helping lawyers and computer technologists speak intelligibly to each other. He has written and blogged about intellectual property, virtual worlds, the legal regulation of search engines, electronic commerce, problems of online privacy, and the use of software as a regulator. His paper *Regulation by Software*, 114 Yale L.J. 1719 (2005), was awarded the Michael Egger prize for best student scholarship in volume 114 of the Yale Law Journal.

Emily Hancock is a legal director with Yahoo! Inc., where she manages law enforcement outreach and provides advice regarding compliance with law enforcement requests for all of Yahoo!'s U.S.-based services. In her role as Yahoo!'s liaison to law enforcement agencies, Ms. Hancock also focuses on online child safety initiatives and providing training to law enforcement. Formerly, Ms. Hancock was an attorney in the Washington office of Steptoe & Johnson LLP, where she was a member of the E-Commerce and Technology groups. Her practice there focused on e-commerce, data privacy and security regulatory matters, national security matters related to high-tech transactions, and counseling Internet service providers on compliance and policy matters relating to law enforcement requests for access to voice and Internet communications and compliance with the Communications Assistance for Law Enforcement Act (CALEA).

Beryl A. Howell is Managing Director and General Counsel of the Washington, D.C., office of Stroz Friedberg, LLC, and a Commissioner on the U.S. Sentencing Commission. Her firm provides consulting and technical services in the use of digital forensics in connection with civil, criminal and regulatory litigation, and cybersecurity investigations. Ms. Howell is the former General Counsel of the Senate Committee on the Judiciary, where she worked on Internet and cybersecurity legislation, including the Communications Assistance for Law Enforcement Act (CALEA), the No Electronic Theft Act, and the Homeland Security Act. In 1996, Ms. Howell was inducted into the Freedom of Information Hall of Fame for her work. From 1987 to 1993 she was Assistant U.S. Attorney for the Eastern District of New York and Deputy Chief of the Narcotics Section. She is a graduate of Bryn Mawr College and Columbia University School of Law, where she was a Harlan Fiske Stone Scholar.

Curtis E. A. Karnow is a Superior Court judge in San Francisco. While in private practice he specialized in intellectual property litigation and technology law. From 1978 to 1980, Judge Karnow was an Assistant U.S. Attorney for the Eastern District of Pennsylvania. He is the author of *Future Codes: Essays in Advanced Computer Technology and the Law* (Artech House: London/Boston, 1997), and coauthor of *eBusiness and Insurance* (CCH, 2001), *International eCommerce* (CCH, 2001), and *Network Security: The Complete Reference* (McGraw-Hill, 2004).

Eddan Katz is the Executive Director of the Information Society Project at Yale Law School as well as a Fellow of the ISP. He received his J.D. at Boalt Hall School of Law in Berkeley in 2002, with a Certificate in Law and Technology and honors in Intellectual Property Scholarship. While at Boalt, Mr. Katz was the principal student involved in the creation of the Chilling Effects Clearinghouse project with the Electronic Frontier Foundation (EFF). He received the Sax Prize for Excellence in Clinical Advocacy for his public interest work with the Samuelson Clinic for Law, Technology, and Public Policy spanning over two years.

Orin S. Kerr is an Associate Professor at George Washington University Law School and a nationally recognized expert in computer crime, whose articles have appeared in many different journals including Harvard Law Review, Michigan Law Review, New York University Law Review, Georgetown Law Journal, and Northwestern University Law Review. He is also the author of a forthcoming casebook on computer crime law that will be published by West. From 1998 to 2001, Professor Kerr was an Honors Program trial attorney in the Computer Crime and Intellectual Property Section of the Criminal Division at the U.S. Department of Justice, as well as a Special Assistant U.S. Attorney for the Eastern District of Virginia. Since leaving the government, Professor Kerr has served as a criminal defense attorney on a pro bono basis, and has testified before Congress about the implementation of the USA Patriot Act. Professor Kerr earned engineering degrees from Princeton and Stanford and his law degree from Harvard, and clerked for Judge Leonard I. Garth of the U.S. Court of Appeals for the Third Circuit and Justice Anthony M. Kennedy at the U.S. Supreme Court. He also blogs at The Volokh Conspiracy, at http://volokh.com.

Nimrod Kozlovski is a Fellow of the Information Society Project at Yale Law School. Mr. Kozlovski has been an Adjunct Professor of Law at New York Law School, teaching CyberCrime, CyberTerror, and Digital Law Enforcement, and a lecturer in Cyberlaw and E-commerce at Tel-Aviv University and the Tel-Aviv College of Management. He is an editor of the International Journal of Communications Law and Policy (IJCLP). He received his law degree from Tel-Aviv University and his S.J.D. from Yale Law School. He clerked for Hon. Dr. Michael Chesin of the Israeli Supreme Court. He currently serves as a member of the Israeli governmental e-commerce committee, as an advisor to the legislative committee on e-signatures and the Internet subcommittee, and as a Cyberlaw lecturer in the Israeli Institute for the Training of Judges. He is the author of *The Computer and the Legal Process* (Israeli Bar Association Press, 2000) and numerous articles on the Internet and privacy law, computer search and seizure, and electronic evidence.

Helen Nissenbaum is Associate Professor in the Department of Culture and Communication and the Director of the Information Law Institute, New York University. She specializes in the social, ethical, and political dimensions of information technology. She has served on committees of the National Academy of Sciences, National Science Foundation, UNESCO, AAAS, and the ACM, and on the Board of Trustees of E the People. Before joining NYU, Nissenbaum was a Member of the School of Social Science, Institute for Advanced Study, Associate Director of Princeton University Center for Human Values, and Postdoctoral Fellow at the Center for the Study of Language and Information, Stanford University. She earned a B.A. (Honors) from the University of Witwatersand, Johannesburg, and a Ph.D. in philosophy from Stanford University. She is the author of *Emotion and Focus* (University of Chicago Press, 1985), coeditor (with D. J. Johnson) of *Computers, Ethics and Social Values* (Prentice-Hall, 1995), coeditor (with Monroe Price) of *Academy and the Internet* (Peter Lang Publishing Company, 2003) and one of the founding editors of the journal Ethics and Information Technology (Kluwer Academic Press).

Kim A. Taipale is the founder and executive director of the Center for Advanced Studies in Science and Technology Policy, a private, nonpartisan research and advisory organization focused on information, technology, and national security policy. He is also a senior fellow at the World Policy Institute and an adjunct professor of law at New York Law School. Mr. Taipale is a member of the Markle Task Force on National Security in the Information Age, the Science and Engineering for National Security Advisory Board at The Heritage Foundation, and the LexisNexis Information Policy Forum. He is also a partner in Stilwell Holding LLC, a private investment firm, and serves on the advisory board of Parkview Ventures, a technology-focused merchant bank. Mr. Taipale was previously the director of new media development for Columbia Innovation Enterprise and a senior fellow at the Institute for Learning Technologies at Columbia University. Prior to that, he was an investment banker at Lazard Freres & Co., an executive at The Pullman Company, and a lawyer at Davis Polk & Wardwell. Mr. Taipale received his B.A. and J.D. from New York University and his M.A., Ed.M., and LL.M. from Columbia University.

Lee Tien is a Senior Staff Attorney with the Electronic Frontier Foundation, specializing in free speech law, including intersections with intellectual property law and privacy law. He is the author of several articles on children's sexuality and information technology, anonymity, surveillance, and the First Amendment status of publishing computer software. Lee received his undergraduate degree in psychology from Stanford University, where he was very active in journalism at the *Stanford Daily*. After working as a news reporter at the *Tacoma News Tribune* for a year, he received his J.D. from Boalt Hall Law School and did graduate work in the Program in Jurisprudence and Social Policy at UC-Berkeley.

Shlomit Wagman is a Fellow of the Information Society Project at Yale Law School. She is a member of the Israeli Bar and clerked for the Honorable Chief Justice Aharon Barak, the President of the Israeli Supreme Court. She has also served as an adviser to the Israeli Ministry of Justice on matters of information technology and privacy. She is a graduate of the Honors Joint Degree Program at Hebrew University and holds an LL.M. from Yale Law School. Her current research focuses on legal issues pertaining to software and liability for software malfunction.

Tal Zarsky is a Lecturer at the University of Haifa Faculty of Law where he teaches Contracts, Advanced Property, Cyberlaw, and Telecommunications Law & Policy. He writes on issues of law, privacy, data mining, and technology. Professor Zarsky holds a J.S.D. and an LL.M. from Columbia Law School, and received his B.A/LL.B. degree (summa cum laude) in Law and Psychology from the Hebrew University of Jerusalem. He is a fellow of the Information Society Project at Yale Law School.

Acknowledgments

This book arose out of a conference held at Yale Law School on March 26–28, 2004, entitled Digital Cops in a Networked Environment. The editors would like to thank all of the participants in the conference and everyone involved in its planning and execution, including Deborah Sestito, the Yale Journal of Law and Technology, and the International Journal of Communications Law and Policy. We would also like to thank Katherine McDaniel for her editing assistance.

The editors would also like to acknowledge the following publications of papers originally presented at the 2004 ISP conference, and from which chapters in this book were drawn.

Chapter 3: Lee Tien, "Architectural Regulation and the Evolution of Social Norms," 7 Yale Journal of Law and Technology 1 (2004–2005); International Journal of Communications Law and Policy, IJCLP Web-Doc 1-Cy-2004. Reprinted with permission of the author, YJOLT, and the IJCLP.

Chapter 4: Helen Nissenbaum, "Where Computer Security Meets National Security," Ethics and Information Technology (2005) 7:61–73. Reprinted with permission of the author.

Chapter 5: Beryl A. Howell, "Real-World Problems of Virtual Crime," 7 Yale Journal of Law and Technology 103 (2004–2005); International Journal of Communications Law and Policy, IJCLP Web-Doc 5-Cy-2004. Reprinted with permission of the author, YJOLT, and the IJCLP.

Chapter 7: An earlier version was published as Curtis E. A. Karnow, "Launch on Warning: Aggressive Defense of Computer Systems," 7 Yale Journal of Law and Technology 87 (2004–2005); International Journal of Communications Law and Policy, IJCLP Web-Doc 4-Cy-2004. Reprinted with permission of the author, YJOLT, and the IJCLP.

Chapter 8: An earlier version was published as Kim A. Taipale, "Technology, Security and Privacy: The Fear of Frankenstein, The Myth of Privacy, and the Lessons of King Ludd," 7 Yale Journal of Law and Technology

123 (2004–2005); International Journal of Communications Law and Policy, IJCLP Web-Doc 2-Cy-2004. Reprinted with permission of the author, YJOLT, and the IJCLP.

Chapter 11: An earlier version was published as Orin S. Kerr, "Digital Evidence and the New Criminal Procedure," 105 Columbia L. Rev. 279 (2005). Reprinted with permission of the author and the Columbia Law Review.

Index